Better Day Care for the Young Child

Through a Merged Governmental and Nongovernmental Effort

The Story Of Day Care In New York City
As The Responsibility Of A Department Of Health
1943 – 1963
And Nearly A Decade Later — 1972

by

CORNELIA GOLDSMITH

National Association for the Education of Young Children
Washington, D.C.

Photographs

Frontispiece: Lori Daena Cooke, Tikameon, Salt Point, N.Y.

Page 81: The Edward W. C. Arnold Collection. Lent by the Metropolitan Museum of Art. Photo courtesy Museum of the City of New York.

to

HERTHA and GERDA

CONTENTS

PREFACE

The first comprehensive and official standard-setting and licensing program in the United States that affected all day care groups of young children in one given area was legally established by the Board of Health of New York City in February, 1943. This was during the critical years of World War II. The pattern took shape under the gifted leadership of Dr. Leona Baumgartner, then Director of the Bureau of Child Hygiene.[1]

The setting up of a Day Care Unit in the New York City Department of Health was a "first," both historically and legally. As an old outdated section, number 198 of the Sanitary Code was thoroughly revised, updated and expanded. Its legal authority, granted to the Board of Health by the City Charter, made the regulations mandatory. The revision of Section 198 extended its relevance to include all groups of children under six years of age who regularly received daytime care outside their own homes and away from their parents. The Health Department's concerns would now, for the first time, go far beyond the mere physical aspects of the premises occupied by the children and far beyond the mere assessment of their physical health. At long last the total day-by-day living of the child in his group environment was to be closely looked at and evaluated. This had never been attempted before. There were no precedents to follow. Preliminary innovative thinking and farsighted planning had already been achieved by a small, dedicated group of knowledgeable individuals representing a variety of related professions and a nonprofessional. This "Spearhead Group" of

---

1. Later called the Bureau of Child Health.

community leaders originated the concept of a Day Care Unit in the Department of Health and continued to serve as its advisory board. This board was comprised of two educators, two social workers, a pediatrician and a lay member. All were representatives of recognized groups concerned with the day care of young children. They were:

Leona Baumgartner, M.D., Pediatrician

Edna Geisler, Social Worker

Adele Levy, Philanthropist

Helen Harris, Social Worker

Amy Hostler, Educator

Alice V. Keliher, Educator

The Unit began with a full-time multiprofessional staff of three consultants (the fourth, a pediatric consultant was on call) and three field workers:

Cornelia Goldsmith, Unit Head and Educational Consultant

Yetta Bokhaut, Health Consultant and Public Health Nurse Supervisor

Hila Thompson, Social Work Consultant

Dorothy Dillon
Grace Dunbar   Public Health Field Nurse Consultants
Mary MacAravey

Milton I. Levine, M.D., Pediatric Consultant

The story of those first few years was told in a pamphlet published in 1946, entitled "The Day Care of Little Children in a Big City." [2] With courage, determination and considerable trepidation, the staff began its work of observation, evaluation and interpretation, seeking the best possible ways and means of improving conditions for young children in daytime group care, by putting the new code standards into effect, city wide. The code defined "a group" as four or more children. The opportunity of looking at all these children through the tripartite lens of health, education and welfare meant that the entire field of day care in New York City would be viewed and evaluated as appropriate to the growth and development of the child, in more meaningful and comprehensive terms than ever before. This opportunity (and obligation) to observe at first hand and often for the first time, hundreds of differ-

---

2. "The Day Care of Little Children in a Big City" written by Dr. Leona Baumgartner, Cornelia Goldsmith and Yetta Bokhaut. It was published by the Child Welfare League, Inc., in May 1946. Although out of print it is on file in the libraries of the Department of Health, 125 Worth St., New York City 10013 and of the Child Welfare League of America, Inc., 44 East 23rd St., New York City 10010.

ently organized and motivated day care groups, through such a precise and effective tool as the revised health code regulations, made a powerful and inescapable impact on the day care unit staff as well as on the community. To see thousands of young children, eager and alive, across the busy, bustling span of the city's five immense boroughs, in a variety of neighborhoods with differing economic, social and ethnic backgrounds, presented challenges of infinite variety and complexity. The staff responded with enthusiasm and alacrity, as did the majority of the day care operators. A pioneering spirit invaded the field of day care.

To focus always on the needs of the children themselves was the primary motivating force that sustained and rewarded the staff's unflagging interest and drive throughout the first two decades as described in this book and for years beyond. Constant improvement of skills, insights and procedures was essential. Severe staff limitations made it necessary to seek, recognize and use indigenous talent and leadership, wherever it could be found. Such individuals became a major strength in the community's struggle to improve the conditions and services provided for its young children.

Additional strengths lay in the active cooperation of state and local governmental agencies, particularly in the availability of rich and varied resources within the Health Department itself. Such a wealth of resources meant there could never be a dull moment in the tiny office of the Day Care Unit. As constant and perplexing problems came in from all directions and at all hours, staff ingeniously sought answers. Again and again the close partnership of the multiprofessional consultant staff proved that two or more heads were better than one. In such a setting no one could get into a rut or draw hasty, undigested conclusions. Working side by side with persons having different professional training and experience in regard to young children kept everyone sharing and learning. It opened a wide variety of possible solutions to each perplexing problem, making it necessary to give careful thought to selecting the best. Neither pioneering nor creative thought or effort was deterred by the complexity and necessary "red tape" implicit in the structure of so large a city department.

In spite of all the changes and turmoil, reliable, objective and effective procedures were developed in the effort to assure consistency and fairness to all day care operators. Although the Day Care Unit staff was constantly increased in numbers, it never became sufficiently large to cope fully with the ever-expanding needs and services in the rapidly growing day care field. Even so, tremendous gains were made.

The struggle to achieve and maintain an advancing quality of service in the day care programs in New York City meant constant reevaluation of priorities in the use of staff time and effort. To recapture in words the drama involved in this effort over its first two decades and during the urgency of a wartime situation is an all but impossible task. Nevertheless it should be told and is herewith attempted.

Cornelia Goldsmith.

PRELUDE

The time was October 1943.

For me, personally, the idea of licensing all nonpublic groups of young children in New York City was plummeted dramatically and unexpectedly into the middle of the tense and anxious atmosphere of the Second World War. It happened on a particularly beautiful Sunday afternoon. The fall semester had just begun at Vassar College, Poughkeepsie, New York. I was teaching in the Department of Child Study, where Mary Shattuck Fisher (Essex) was the department head.

World War II, weighing heavily on the minds and hearts of everyone, filled the days and nights with wartime activities and strain. Yet, in Dutchess County, New York, on the shore of the Hudson River, nature seemed oblivious to man's suffering. Indian Summer had brought gay, brilliant foliage of compelling beauty. A prolific harvest of orchard, field and garden was being gathered. My phone rang. It was Dr. Alice Keliher, professor of education at New York University, to ask whether I would be interested in coming to New York City to direct a new project being undertaken by the Department of Health under Dr. Leona Baumgartner, then Director of the Bureau of Child Hygiene.[1]

The idea that Dr. Keliher propounded over the telephone was electrifying! What an opportunity it presented and what an irresistible challenge. Action had to begin at once.

An immediate decision was made. I was promptly released, as requested, from all college responsibilities. By the next evening, I was

---

1. Later Dr. Baumgartner became Commissioner of the New York City Department of Health.

in New York City meeting with the members of the advisory committee to a newly formed Day Care Unit. Thus began the first amazing year in a succession of 20 fast-moving, incredible years as head of the Day Care Unit of the New York City Department of Health. Every iota of knowledge, experience, imagination and wisdom, garnered from 30 preceding years of study, teaching, directing schools and a summer camp for young children, working with teachers, parents, students and volunteers as well as with children themselves, was called into play.

The structure of the new project had already been formulated and the other staff members of the multiprofessional team of consultants assigned. Its purpose was to take responsibility for the evaluation and standard raising of all daytime group programs for children under six years of age, regardless of the type of agency, its location, size, goals, hours of operation or the auspices under which it operated. This included those agencies serving children of all ethnic groups from all economic levels and regardless of the name by which they were called, whether school, play group, day camp, day nursery, child care center, day care agency, kindergarten or nursery school.

INTRODUCTION

The 1970's are seeing a renewed surge of interest in day care for young children. Many forces are involved: the push to get families off of welfare rolls, to help working mothers with small children, the smaller living quarters that do not provide space for the older relatives who used to be relied on, the lack of and increasing cost of domestic help, earlier marriages, the desire of and better education of younger mothers for a life outside of the home, and the growing body of scientific evidence which shows that experience in the early years (nutrition, activity, stimulation, relationships with peers and elders) all leave their indelible mark on the development of the child. It is now supposed that the individual's intelligence is much more subject to modification than is his personality.

The more recent research is turning away from the behaviorists among American psychologists who are more and more associated with research on cognitive development, with expanding boundaries for psychological research and more expert information on brain function. New technology has developed new methods of approach—computer simulation, chemical and electrode stimulation of brain centers, processing of large amounts of information and the post-Sputnik examination of the American educational system. These and many other developments have led to a new look at education and the development of children, particularly the preschool child. They seem to point to different types of programs for different children, and certainly point to the need for working with parents, particularly the disadvantaged.

Politically many forces are at work: Women's Lib, labor unions, managers who need experienced women to help their businesses, hospitals and institutions operate, the many years of demonstrations of the need for day care, the future professionalization of those who worked with families and children, and the several lobbies and individual politicians who have pushed for day care as a right not a privilege. Once this had been little more than a dream of the Children's Bureau, of the federal government and a few private groups. And finally, a separate office, in the office of the Secretary of Health, Education and Welfare, for child development led, in 1971, to the enactment in the Congress of the Comprehensive Child Development Bill (S. 2007) and its veto by President Nixon. (H. Doc. No. 92-48) Yes, day care is on its way up—still by slow steps perhaps, but with ever-increasing vigor it moves into the establishment of the social, health and educational services that our society is accepting as important to the well-being of family and national life.

This book does not talk of the 1970's, but of the 1940's and 1950's. Nevertheless it is of real importance to the developments of the 1970's for it gives a picture of the way in which government can help meet local needs, using local facilities and people in a flexible fashion with the full cooperation of the private sector. It shows how governmental engagement is essential; how licensing, so often thought to be restrictive, can be used creatively to help others to help themselves in giving better service; how important the flexibility of governmental cooperation can be. It shows how governmental and private agencies can be changed and made into newer, greener fields where their joint skills are needed.

It shows, too, how joint efforts of the vested interests of different hidebound professional groups also can be melded into common goals, just as governmental and private groups were "melded." And perhaps, most importantly, it shows how the imagination, the creativity and the patience of a few leaders can leave a mark on hundreds of agencies and, best of all, on the lives of the thousands of children they "care for."

This particular experience in the Day Care Unit of the New York City Department of Health is told largely through the eyes of the educator. This is inevitable, for Miss Goldsmith is a pioneer in the "early childhood education field," who worked in the experimental Walden School in New York City and with Mary Fisher (Essex) in the Vassar preschool experiment, operated one of the first interracial summer residential camps (which took some handicapped as well as normal children) in the country, and went on to view the national scene as executive director of the National Association for the Education of Young Children. She is the mother of two children and the grandmother of six. An infectious gaiety and optimism cover an easily outraged anger at anything, any person, any regulation which hampered the development of the young child. The story of her standing in the wings of a theater to serve a warrant on a member of the cast who was also a greedy operator of a day care center and whose exploitation of several hundred children had long offended the neighborhood, is true. And she had the legal evidence necessary to put him out of business. Challenged by court action only 10 times in 20 years, the department's actions were always sustained. But such incidents were rare. The story was essentially one of growing cooperation, of better lives for children.

Some contributions are touched on relatively lightly, such as the consultation services of the Health Department pediatricians, nurses, nutritionists and sanitarians. Another is that of the social worker. As a member of the staff, she worked closely with the Department of Welfare, which finally took over the management of the city supported day care services for children of working mothers, with a large staff of social workers and early childhood educators. In the Health Department's Day Care Unit, the social workers were always a part of the team. Another point that some may find underemphasized is that the focus is primarily on the child and his development rather than on the family and its problems.

The refusal of New York City's Superintendent of Schools to allow public school buildings or playgrounds to be used for the care of younger children and to take over the program was regrettable. Had the public schools been willing at that time, as in Europe, to share the responsibility with the Health Department, the story might have been quite different. Not until Head Start and its related programs such as "Upward Bound" and the "Four C's" were established, did public education begin to become truly involved. These programs, as the welfare programs for working mothers, were for the poor. Though the poor and the children have always been with us, they somehow were rediscovered in the 1960's—as they had been earlier in the century. Of course, the poor need help desperately. But many more fortunate children need day care, and the protection the poor got.

It is interesting to realize that this affluent country could not fully recognize the social benefits of better opportunities for *all* children to be integrated in their preschool years, in programs dominated by the desire to help each child of every social, racial, and economic group to maximize his or her potentialities for growth and development. Education and health departments have dragged their feet as Miss Goldsmith's figures (see Chapter Two) show. The nation's first major current efforts are focused on the poor, who indeed deserve priority. With a little effort, however, governmental agencies with overall licensing responsibilities can help all groups, and perhaps in the next 20 years bring better programs for *all* children, as this book shows.

Another noticeable difference between then and now is the relative silence of militant parents and other groups in the earlier years. Having consumers part of the action is new. But even in the earlier experience, parents did help build some programs as real planners and leaders. It would be interesting to study their reactions and those of similar groups today. It seems fair to assume that the greatest difference is that day care is seen today as a right, not a privilege.

These are but some of the questions raised by this fascinating and timely story. Miss Goldsmith's book is a must for leaders in the day care field, not because it is an exact blueprint to be followed today but because the experiences gained in the 1940's and 1950's are relevant to today's programs. Just as programs then demanded infinite patience, toughness and imagination, so do today's efforts.

Leona Baumgartner, M.D.
Visiting Professor of Social Medicine
Harvard Medical School
Formerly Commissioner of the
New York City Department of Health

February 4, 1972

CHAPTER I

DAY CARE IN NEW YORK CITY
A New Role for the Department of Health

Before October 1943 a representative multiprofessional committee of high competence had been at work and had accomplished several essential preliminary tasks. A code revision committee had labored long and hard at revising and implementing an old, unsatisfactory, outmoded section of the Sanitary Code[1] (Section #198) pertaining to limited aspects of certain preschool programs for poverty children. Their recommended revisions and amplifications had been reviewed and approved officially by the Board of Health, thus becoming mandatory as of February 23rd, 1943. A new era in day care was about to begin.

The quality of insight and leadership provided by the members of the Advisory Committee gave assurance that the Day Care Project would be undertaken in depth, focussed on finding the best possible means by which all young children in group care would be safeguarded and their programs improved.

A first all-inclusive survey of agencies giving group care to children under six had already been undertaken. It included all agencies operating in the five boroughs of Metropolitan New York regardless of the names by which they were called. The survey had been completed during 1942 by the Bureau of Child Hygiene,[2] with the cooperation of many interested private organizations and citizen groups. Before that no one had known the number of operating groups serving young children, nor the number of children attending such groups. This initial survey revealed over 400 operating groups, in addition to those in the

---

1. Later called the Health Code.
2. Later called the Bureau of Child Health.

1

public and parochial kindergartens and nursery schools. Of these 400, nearly half had never been in touch previously with any official or professional agency, not even with the Fire Department. They were of every conceivable type and description. Some had been in operation practically unchanged for nearly a hundred years, while new ones were opening almost daily.

A 1938 "Report of Sanitary Inspections of Agencies Giving Day Care to Children" stated that only 103 Sanitary Permits were in force at the time. Such permits indicated merely that an inspector had made a visit during the past year to check on the physical and nutritional condition of the children, to ascertain that they were free from contagious disease and had the proper number of toilets and of fire extinguishers.[3] They never looked for newly opened agencies.

A "Survey Guide"[4] had also been developed as an instrument for the evaluation of day care programs. It was intended to be used for self appraisal by operating boards and staff members, as well as a guide for anyone planning to open a new service. Here was a valuable interpretive tool to help those directly involved, as well as to inform and stimulate interested parents and others to understand the new regulations and to make them aware of their obligation to help meet them.

The initial funding of the Day Care Unit was achieved in two ways. Financing of the first three years (1943-1946) was made possible through a grant of $12,500 from the New York Fund for Children, granted with the understanding that it would be terminated as soon as the city took full responsibility for the financing of the Unit. To supplement the grant the Health Department assigned certain civil service personnel such as the public health nurse consultant, the three public health nurse field workers, a secretary and the pediatric consultant, as well as making available the necessary office space and equipment. By this joint public-private financing it was possible to get started promptly. In 1946, after three years of trial (in 1946), after the war had ended the Unit was finally fully accepted as a necessary and continuing responsibility of the Department of Health and was budgeted accordingly. The city authorities were finally convinced of the urgent, on-going need for the

3. Sanitary Inspection Report by Walter A. Foley, Chief Clerk of the Sanitary Bureau to Dr. Oberwager, Director of the Bureau, July 12, 1938.

4. "The Survey Guide for Evaluating Health Services in Centers Providing Day Care for Children," by Ernest L. Stebbins, M.D., Commissioner of Health and Leona Baumgartner, M.D., Director of the Bureau of Child Hygiene, and Amelia Grant, R.N., Director of the Bureau of Nursing. Mimeographed December 31, 1942 by the New York City Department of Health.

service even though the war had, by now, come to an end. It had become obvious to many that young children needed care and protection, whether the country was in or out of war.

Back in October 1943 the stage was set for progress—the time was ripe. With the newly designed and sharpened tools of the revised Sanitary Code, the preliminary survey completed, funds assigned and a multiprofessional staff employed, a task without precedent was about to be launched. At long last the young child in daytime group care was to be recognized as a person with rights and potentialities, an important member of his peer group, his family and his community. A new look was to be taken at the whole child in his full dimension, responding to his entire environment. The work of observation, evaluation and consultation was about to begin. The task requiring a new combination of skills and insights was now to be undertaken. Some organizations wanted help, others resented it. The staff needed a goodly measure of caution and courage, humility and audacity, flexibility and assurance.

Strong community support came forward almost immediately and from many sources. Resistance too, from a minority, became increasingly vocal and determined. The protestors were primarily those who found, quickly enough, that compliance with the regulations disallowed overcrowding and forbade the use of inappropriate and unsafe equipment or inadequate premises. It would now no longer be possible to use shortcuts in the number of staff employed or by other means put unfair profits into the pockets of operators at the expense of the children. The results of such practices were equally harmful and sometimes even disastrous to the children, whether they were due to ignorance or to deliberate and malicious exploitation.

Growing citizen concern about the deplorable conditions under which many young children were found to be living had now reached newspaper headlines. During the months of preliminary work on code revision, on preparing and circulating the Survey Guide, the number of interested and aware citizens had constantly expanded. Through Health Department employees alone (numbering some 3,328 in 1945) information about the Day Care Unit's commitments and goals reached into all the District Health Centers throughout the five boroughs. The officials and employees of other public and private organizations throughout the city, also troubled about the neglect and exploitation of large numbers of young children, helped to spread the word. The New York State Departments of Health, Education and Welfare were also seriously concerned about the increasing numbers of fly-by-night nurseries opening in hidden garrets, dank cellers and barren, vacant store fronts.

3

Although this seemed to be happening in all large cities, it was apparently particularly true in New York City. Or could it have been that New York City was awakening to the situation before most of the other big cities across the country?

Those college and department heads and faculty members in the universities offering courses in teacher training also gave ready and invaluable cooperation by assuring that every student of early childhood education became fully cognizant of the new code regulations in detail and understood the work the Day Care Unit was launching. In this way the code regulations were studied, discussed and interpreted as part of the college curriculum of those preparing to become nursery school or kindergarten teachers or directors. Members of the Day Care Unit staff were frequently asked to address college classes on code requirements and to lead discussion groups on the subject.

Fortunately, a new and growing realization of the nature and meaning of human growth, development and learning in the early years had already been making headway. This was attested to by the researchers and other professionals in such related fields as psychiatry, psychology, sociology, mental health, public health, pediatrics and cultural anthropology. Over and over findings indicated that the mere custodial care of infants and young children was not only undesirable but often seriously harmful and not to be condoned under any circumstances. Providing children with food, clothing and shelter, while it sustained life, gave that life neither benefit nor value. The Day Care Unit staff called this form of minimum care "Zoo Care," fit for animals, perhaps, but not for people. Even when provided as a voluntary charity by generous and well-intentioned people, it was actually a disservice, even to "the poor children of the poor."

As the unit began its work, great expectations and enthusiasm on the part of the staff were mixed with considerable uneasiness. Could the challenge of this promising new frontier be met? Would the tools prove sufficiently precise, sturdy and yet flexible enough to meet and cope with the infinite variety of situations that would be encountered, without producing fresh stereotypes? Could the close coordination of different professional skills work wisely and well? Did the staff members have the ability, creativity, patience and dedication to win each other's respect and the respect of those they worked with and to carry out their stated goals? Would the community respond positively and give support? Only time would tell.

The "First Progress Report" from the Head of the Day Care Unit to the Advisory Committee captured the flavor of those early efforts:

4

On July 1, 1943 there were 409 operating day care units known to the Bureau of Child Hygiene. Between July 1 and October 1 of that year, approximately 50 of these were discontinued. The majority were small groups operating on a part-time basis. They failed to reopen after the summer because of difficulties in employing qualified staff, or for financial reasons, or because of internal difficulties, lack of leadership and so on. A few, in which really serious situations existed, involving neglect of children, were persuaded to go out of business voluntarily.

At the same time approximately 90 individuals and/or groups have applied for a permit to open a new unit. Less than 10 percent of these have personnel with any training or experience in the care of young children in group situations. And additional applications continue to come in almost daily.

During the month of October 1943 the three public health nurses visited a total of 79 child care centers and wrote up their reports on the backs of the application blanks. We have organized regular weekly staff conferences to go over the data thus far gathered from all sources, to reach common agreement as to the best course to pursue in each instance. These are challenging and stimulating conferences and are the test of our ability to make our various contributions count . . . for the benefit of the unit (program) under consideration.

We are also attempting to establish working relationships with other groups responsible for child care in New York City and have made contacts, and the beginning of a working plan, for sharing information and for avoiding overlapping of work in the field.

We are in contact with the State Department of Education, the Mayor's Committee for the Wartime Care of Children, the New York Kindergarten Association, the State Advisory Committee on Nursery Schools, with Catholic Charities, the Contributor's Information Service of the Welfare Council, the New York City Board of Education and the Visiting Nurse Service of Henry Street.

With the help of Dr. Baumgartner and Helen Harris we are attempting to create the machinery necessary for moving the wheels of government more smoothly, to facilitate and speed up the process of granting permits to those that are ready for them and to avoid the innumerable and unnecessary delays that hinder the program.

We are taking time with all new applicants for permits, to go over the code requirements with care. These are time-consuming interviews but they nevertheless represent time well spent. In this way we help each to build the best possible organization and to discourage the wrong kind (slipshod, superficial or misguided) before they even get started.

We are planning with the help of Amy Hostler's [5] students from Mills college, to make a large book of borough maps and to spot them for all services available to young children in New York City.

We are planning, with the help of the Community Defense Volunteer Association (CDVA), to create or find some group that would undertake to organize a toy exchange and equipment center. It would also be a demonstration center for people who need help in deciding what type of toy or what piece of equipment suits their needs best. High school children might come to such a center with their shop teachers to discuss what they would like to make for younger children and whether they had an appropriate group in mind.[6] Soldiers and sailors with free time on their hands might be glad to repair used toys and equipment. . . . Low cost materials could be demonstrated to help agencies that are functioning with no equipment whatever to realize how much could be done with little.

It seems that many parents need simpler reading materials about the needs of children than is available to them.

We are sometimes overwhelmed with the magnitude of the task before us, and sometimes deeply depressed by the sights we see. But we are also challenged and stimulated by it all and are encouraged by your support and your understanding of the many problems confronting us.[7]

More publicity was needed. It became increasingly apparent that more widespread interpretation of the work of the Day Care Unit, on a broad community basis was needed. High priority was given to the dissemination of such information in every way possible. Copies of the revised section of the code were mailed to those known to be operating or planning to operate a day care agency. Copies were also sent to every community agency and in response to every inquiry, no matter what the nature of the inquiry, and whether received by mail or telephone. A friendly covering letter accompanied each copy inviting the recipient to an office conference to discuss any questions, problems or plans he might have about group programs for young children.

To better inform the public, an educational campaign via press and radio was then carried out. Printed materials were prepared and distributed by the City of New York Department of Health, such as a pamphlet on "Choosing a Day Care Agency for Your Child." These were made

---

5. Dr. Amy Hostler, then President of Mills College, New York City and member of the Day Care Units Advisory Committee.

6. This was later achieved by Joe Bohmer at the Walden School.

7. From a mimeographed Progress Report from Cornelia Goldsmith to the Advisory Committee of the Day Care Unit, dated Nov. 12, 1943. On file in the New York City Department of Health, 125 Worth St.

available to parent-teacher associations in great quantities. Other pamphlets were entitled "Children's Nutritional Needs," "Pointers for Parents About Day Camps for Children" and beginning in 1950 a "Directory of Day Care Services in New York City" was published every two years. One of the most popular pamphlets, which was rewritten and republished repeatedly was the "Guide for the Health Program in the Day Care Center." All were made available to the public free of cost and in reasonable quantity. Requests to the staff to address meetings and discussions of parent-teacher groups were frequent and were fulfilled as far as possible. And so the good word spread.

A Day Care Quarterly was issued in 1946 by the Bureau of Child Hygiene and sent to all day care operators and other interested persons. Later it became a regular Day Care Newsletter, used as a lively medium of exchange and information between the operators and the Day Care Unit. In the second issue of the Day Care Quarterly Dr. Baumgartner wrote:

> There is a widespread movement and growing interest in the fields of health, education and welfare to further adequate legislation for the protection of all young children living in groups during the day, outside the home. We have received many requests for information from all over our own country and abroad, from as far away as South Africa, from as near as New Jersey, Massachusetts, Alabama and Maryland. There are many questions asking how standards are being raised in the day care agencies in New York and how the Sanitary Code operates.

> It is encouraging to know that standard raising efforts in New York City have been instrumental in stimulating other similar efforts throughout the country. And it is through continuing cooperation of all concerned that further progress can be made.

In every conference held in the Day Care Unit office, code regulations were repeatedly reviewed, interpreted and discussed. Although time consuming, such face-to-face conferences helped to a considerable degree to clear away misunderstandings and to eliminate the too frequently ugly picture in the minds of certain segments of the public of another governmental authority imposing its will arbitrarily on the helpless citizen. In such cases, mutual open and frank discussion usually brought about reciprocal understanding and trust. There were of course some instances where the hostilities refused to melt.

Apparently, in the minds of some, the previous public image of any city department's role had too often been that of an official agency concerning itself primarily with its preemptory legal authority and power. In regard to the Health Department, there seemed to be particular resentment about the numerous, detailed sanitary requirements. When the reasons for these requirements were explained, they seemed less onerous.

The full cooperation of the State Department of Education (Bureau of Child Development and Parent Education) and of the State Department of Social Welfare, were of inestimable help to the Day Care Unit at this time. All private schools for young children in New York calling themselves nursery schools or kindergartens, were required at that time to be registered with the State Education Department. Although the state regulations requiring such registration were abrogated in 1948 by order of the New York State Supreme Court, the state's standards for the registration of nursery schools and kindergartens had until then been similar in most respects to the Health Department's day care regulations. This consistency was beneficial to both city and state in helping to forward the standards of both. The Bureau of Child Development and Parent Education of New York State had been handicapped in achieving full compliance with its standards due to a lack of sufficient staff to assure such compliance. Now, under the direction of Dr. Ruth Andrus, Chief of the New York State Bureau of Child Development and Parent Education in Albany, it became policy to make New York City Health Department licensing of any nursery school or kindergarten a prerequisite to state registration. This strengthened the cause of city licensing greatly. In lieu of a field staff for New York City, Dr. Andrus had used a carefully selected voluntary New York City committee of experienced and fully qualified nursery and kindergarten directors. They visited and appraised certain private preschool groups at her request and submitted their findings in written reports. These detailed reports of some 47 visits to private schools in New York City were now turned over to the Day Care Unit as a basis for further follow-up. The members of the New York State Evaluating Committee (as the group was called) some ten in number then offered their services to the Day Care Unit on a voluntary, part-time basis. Since the Day Care Unit was also suffering from acute staff shortages, the offer was gratefully accepted as a temporary expedient. Their assignments for field observation were made to carefully selected agencies that needed and welcomed their help. Their services were terminated as soon as it was possible to replace them with regular full time civil service consultants in early childhood education.

The State Department of Social Welfare, also critically short of field staff, had until now supervised all the day nurseries and child care centers in New York City that were incorporated as charitable institutions. Their state standards were meager, showing little concern, if any, for the educational aspects of the programs. Consequently the Welfare Department too, turned over its evaluative and supervisory findings and reports of observations regarding some 80 long-day child care programs, to the Day Care Unit for follow-up and licensing. It was recognized that the young children in these programs would be greatly benefited by the new plan and that the double jurisdiction of the past had been wasteful.

A complete and comprehensive file for each operating agency and each prospective agency, was set up in the Day Care Unit office. Before a field visit was made or an office conference held, all available records, from whatever source, were reviewed by the Day Care consultant assigned to the case. In difficult situations, where standards fell seriously below acceptable practice, a representative of the appropriate state department often joined the Day Care consultant to review the total situation in order to reach agreement on the most essential and effective next steps to be taken. Such joint observations and discussions between state and city workers were most productive. They often helped to convince negligent and indifferent operators that unless hazardous and unsatisfactory conditions for the children were promptly eliminated and code violations removed, their right to operate was in jeopardy.

Approvals of day care premises by a number of city agencies were now a prerequisite to Health Department licensing. This meant preliminary visits by inspectors from the Fire Department, the Department of Housing and Buildings, and by Sanitary Inspectors and nutritionists from other bureaus of the Health Department. Having to deal with several inspectors, each with a special responsibility and a particular legal jurisdiction, confused and irritated some operators. To them each such visit meant another contact with "officialdom." Misunderstandings, inconsistencies and apparent contradictions often brought conflict or confusion, not only to the day care operator, but also between the representatives of the different departments and bureaus. A large part of the problem was resolved when Dr. Baumgartner requested the mayor to call a meeting of the three commissioners of Fire, Housing and Buildings, and Health to clarify their interrelated roles in regard to the inspection and supervision of day care agencies. The meeting was held in the Mayor's office and satisfactory plans and procedures were agreed upon. From then on each department kept the others fully informed as to visits, findings and recommendations. Contradictions and misunderstandings were greatly lessened. One complication after

9

another was untangled. Yet no day dawned without its problems, old and new, major and minor. The Day Care Unit staff continued to find that there was never a dull moment on any day.

Semantics presented a problem at times. As the types of day care service changed, old titles were transferred to new or changing forms. Some new terms were invented. "Preschool" for instance lost its validity as more and more children under the age of six (previously considered to be the age of entrance to "regular" school when "real" education presumably began) were now attending school groups. The term "day care;" in its generic, legal and logical sense, was an inclusive, umbrella term covering all types of daytime, group care programs for young children. Nevertheless the Day Care Council and the New York City Department of Welfare assumed that the term was limited to their particular long day, child care center program for the children of working mothers, and/or to poor and handicapped mothers. This created confusion in the minds of many. In general parlance a new term entitled "early childhood education" was replacing what had been previously known as "nursery," "kindergarten" and "primary" education. It gave meaning and continuity to the concept of "young children" and recognized the validity of education as a continuing process throughout the early years.

The Day Care Unit staff found serious incongruities between the needs of young children and the pressured life of the large city. The very thought of so complex, immense and sophisticated a city as New York and the many thousands of eager, viable and vulnerable young children in the process of growing up in it seemed not only inharmonious but too often unsuitable and irrelevant. The sense of incongruity increased as more and more children, growing up in so tightly packed and highly complicated a city, had no choice but to accept limitations and restrictions, having no other recourse, no other possible way of life.

Unlike the young children of previous generations, relatively few of these young children in group care had known the sure and stable life in a secure community, or being part of a well rooted family in a familiar neighborhood. For them, freedom of movement, direct access to open play space, easy contact with other children, could no longer be taken for granted. Obviously day care agencies had to provide children with opportunities to become directly familiar with water, earth and sky, with live and growing things, with stimulating and enjoyable activities with their peers, in a safe, ample and well-equipped environment, and with rich opportunities for intellectual, emotional and physical gains. Day care programs had to take responsibility for satisfying the young child's unmet needs, in the city's increasingly harassed adult world.

Of all this the Day Care Unit, through its consultant services, took cognizance. Whenever possible, children were given opportunities to have and to care for pets in their day care facilities; to do planting, weeding, watering and even harvesting in some part of their playground as well as indoors; to take trips to nearby farms and zoos; to make opportunities for climbing trees and hills; to enjoy weather and seasonal changes; to follow nature paths where wild life could be observed at close hand; to enjoy the sky and cloud movements, water and boating and wide open spaces.

CHAPTER II

THE ORIGIN OF CHILD CARE CENTERS IN NEW YORK CITY
One Form of Day Care

With the new emphasis on better care and education of young children springing from so wide a variety of sources and forces, no single type of program or service could be labeled as the one and only "best" for all children under all circumstances. As general dissatisfaction with old, traditional methods and goals was mounting, there was no consensus about any single specified goal or set of procedures by which to replace them. Criticism of the past and adjustment to a rapidly changing present brought both discontent and a new hope for a more promising future. Many were stimulated to delve into the dynamic search for new and better theories and practices that might assure the optimum development of the young child in all aspects of his growth. Widely differing and sometimes confusingly similar approaches brought different styles and ideologies into use. Old terms were used with new meanings. Some terms were used interchangeably, further confusing the picture.

The same terms often meant different things to different people. For example, "day care," actually a generic term had its origin and context in welfare covering all types of daytime services for the group care of young children, and appropriated by some to refer exclusively to the full-day programs set up for children of working, impoverished or handicapped mothers. The word "care" became associated, in the minds of many, with the need to supplement inadequate parental care in poverty families requiring welfare aid. The term "school," on the other hand, became associated exclusively with those half-day programs having education as a major focus. The earlier lack of communication between the two fields led to the impasse between them.

In the child care centers and the day nurseries, the concept of health, education and care as an essential blend of primary ingredients in all programs and for all children was quite unrealized. Education and care seemed rather to be in competition. The importance of physical health for all children was readily recognized, but emotional and social health still lagged behind. By categorizing "education" and "care" separately, it seemed easier to justify keeping the children of working mothers in a center for eight to ten hours a day primarily because they lacked maternal care at home. Education was thought of as desirable but not essential, diminishing the urge to provide a variety of enriching educational opportunities and experiences of value to all children in every center. It was in June 1942 that Mayor Fiorello H. LaGuardia requested the Commissioners of Health and Welfare to meet with the Superintendent of Schools, John Wade, to determine the needs of young children in New York City in the light of the wartime emergency. He was particularly concerned about the availability of programs offering long hours of daytime care to the children of the growing numbers of working mothers.

On October 20 of that year, the three commissioners reported to Mayor LaGuardia as follows:

> At the outset, we would like to say that we did not wish to urge or lend encouragement to mothers leaving their homes and their children for employment, as long as sufficient workers are available to meet war needs. It is only as available manpower, including unmarried women, is exhausted that the employment of (married) women should be resorted to. . . .
>
> You asked that the Committee report on the needs in New York City along these lines, the projects that ought to be established to meet such needs if they existed, and the extent to which federal aid might be secured to assist in the financing of such projects. Your Committee has . . . reviewed much of the available material, particularly the reports from the Federal Security Agency and from the Division of Research and Statistics of the United States Employment Office. We have made some study of existing facilities for the daytime care of children and have sought to form some opinion as to what present and future needs will be . . . it seems clear that the employment of women is increasing rapidly throughout the country. As war industry expands and more women workers are mobilized there will be an increasing need for daytime and after school care for children. The facilities for this task must be operated on good standards of health, education and social service— the standards now achieved by the best organizations in the field and in accordance with the official requirements of the public departments having legal responsibility in these matters.

While the national need for daytime care is clear . . . our immediate concern is the nature and extent of the problem in New York City. The Committee has not been able to secure as complete and comprehensive data for this city as it would like. . . . Some of the data are simply not available.

We do have some facts which suggest what the needs are at this time and we are convinced that in six months from now we shall be faced with a very serious problem. We know from the federal census table that 34 percent of all women in New York City, of working age, were in the labor force—that is, employed or looking for work, as of April 1940. This is higher than the national average which was 31 percent for urban areas and only 25.5 percent for the entire country. The largest percentage of women in the labor force includes those 20 to 44 years of age.

The conclusion is inevitable that this increase in the employment of women will require greatly extended facilities for the care of children of married women who are or will be employed. The service should not be regarded as a charitable one, because many employed mothers are willing and eager to pay for it and the cost of operation of new facilities can be met, in part, from fees.

So far as we can learn, there are slightly less than 400 places for the care of young children in the City of New York:

    221 in Manhattan
     49 in the Bronx
     75 in Brooklyn
     45 in Queens
     10 in Richmond (Staten Island)

These include small units run as home industries, many supported by private philanthropic contributions, some by WPA (the Works Progress Administration) funds. They enroll from 4 to 200 children per unit and, according to their statements, could care for an approximate total of 7,000 children. However, the geographical distribution is such that the service is often not located where it is needed.

Out of the approximate total of 400, 243 are either licensed by the Department of Health, registered by the State Department of Education or inspected by the State Department of Welfare. We have discovered at least 145 unlicensed groups and there are probably more in existence. There are many well established and efficiently operated organizations under the auspices of both sectarian and nonsectarian agencies whose work needs expansion and further coordination into a city-wide plan.

The largest single public operation for daytime care is under the joint auspices of the WPA (the Works Progress Administration) and the New York City Board of Education. There are 32 such nursery schools now maintained by the Board which care for about a thousand children daily. They have been open from 9:00 A.M. to 3.00 P.M. but the hours are now being extended from 8:30 A.M. to 5:30 P.M. In the past only children having actual relief status or its equivalent have been received for care. We are advised that working mothers without relief status can apply for the admission of their children during the day, but the facilities are too limited to care for many on this basis.

The nurseries are located in various buildings, such as settlement houses, previously established day nurseries, social agencies, etc. In addition to housing, the local organization provides equipment and in some instances, food. Food supplies are also provided from the surplus given to New York City by the Department of Agriculture.

The big problem in these WPA nurseries is the question of standards of personnel, both in quantity and quality. The employees are recruited from the relief rolls with the exception of a 5 percent exemption for supervisors. A request to increase the exemption for nonrelief personnel from 5 percent to 10 percent has been made because trained supervision is indispensable, if proper care is to be given. It is increasingly difficult to get the proper number of supervisors or an adequate number of workers with the kind of background or training which qualifies them for this work. Some way of providing better personnel must be found and we believe the CDVO (the Civilian Defense Volunteer Organization) can be of real assistance here through its training program.

It is important that all persons or organizations meeting standards in this field be properly licensed as soon as possible. Provision should be made for the remainder to be brought up to that within a reasonable period of time or closed.

On the basis of all available evidence we are of the opinion that there will shortly be, if there is not already, compelling necessity for improving and increasing facilities for the day care of children in this community and this is the time to plan for future needs. The matter of relocating these facilities will have to be determined by further study and experimentation.[1]

Following this report specific recommendations were made by the Commissioners to the mayor:

1. ... every effort should be made to provide a minimum of 40 nursery school centers and a steady increase above this minimum to keep pace with the need.

---

1. From Report to Mayor LaGuardia from William Hodson, Commissioner of Welfare, Ernest Stebbins, M.D., Commissioner of Health and John Wade, Superintendent of Schools, October 20, 1942. Mimeographed, five pages, New York City Municipal Reference Library, Municipal Building, New York City.

Since the demand for properly qualified nursery school teachers far exceeds the supply, consideration should be given to training teachers through in-service training courses, improved supervision and scholarships in recognized training schools. Private day nurseries and nursery schools can be helped and encouraged to expand their work as needed.

2. If possible the Board of Education should extend its present after-school programs for (school-age) children, particularly in the areas of the city where there are no existing facilities.

3. There should be established for New York City an office of information, advice and consultation where mothers could go and talk over their problems. . . .

4. We recommend the establishment . . . of a central coordinating committee, . . . a permanent committee on Wartime Care of Children, consisting of at least nine persons, three to represent the Departments of Education, Health, and Welfare; four to represent private agencies, religious federations and interested civic groups, including at least one large employer, . . . a representative of the Civilian Defense Volunteer Organization, and two to represent organized labor in the city. A representative of the WPA should be an ex officio member of this central coordinating committee.

This committee could assume responsibility for the coordination and extension of existing operations under the various city departments and among the private agencies and the preparation of new projects requiring local, state or federal action.

A small experienced staff would be essential to the success of such a plan. . . .

Within three days after the joint Commissioners Report had been submitted to the mayor, on October 23, 1942, a 14-member Mayor's Committee on Wartime Care of Children was appointed by the mayor. Broadly representative of the total community it included:

William Hodson, Commissioner of Welfare, Chairman
Ernest Stebbins, M.D., Commissioner of Health
John Wade, Ph.D., Superintendent of Schools
Major Irving Huie, Commissioner of Public Works
Monsignor Robert Keegan, Executive Director, Catholic Charities of the Archdiocese of New York
Mark Starr, Director, Division of Education, International Ladies Garment Workers Union
Alice Keliher, Ph.D., Chairman Child Care Program, Civilian Defense Volunteer Office of New York

16

Beatrice Abramson, Chairman Women's Auxiliary, New York Congress
  of Industrial Organizations
Eunice Barnard, Education Director, Alfred P. Sloan Foundation, Inc.
Reverend John Johnson of the Church of St. Martin
Reverend Edward Swanstrom, Associate Director, Division of Children,
  Catholic Charities of Brooklyn
Mrs. Lawrence M. Orton, President Colored Orphan Asylum
Mrs. Peter Abeles, Advisory Council, Federation of Jewish Women
Justice Stephen Jackson, New York Court of Domestic Relations

In December of that year (1942), Miss Helen Harris was appointed by
the mayor as Executive Director of the Committee on Wartime Care of
Children. An interim progress report,[2] submitted to the mayor in that
same month by the chairman of the committee, indicated that substantial
progress had already been made:

Seven subcommittees have been appointed—
  1) Extension and supplementation of the WPA Projects
  2) Extension of After-School Projects
  3) Advice and Information Service
  4) Training (of personnel)
  5) Health aspects
  6) Harlem needs
  7) Cooperation with private agencies

We have received an excellent report from the Department of Health
which lists all known facilities . . . subject to license. . . .

Existing studies and surveys do not give a clear picture of what the needs
are . . . the committee must undertake a quick sampling study of blocks
throughout the city to get reliable information. (This) will provide the
first reliable and comprehensive information as to our needs here in New
York City, and . . . should constitute a unique contribution. . . .

One of the major needs . . . is a service of advice and information (to)
mothers employed or about to be employed. . . .

Every effort is being made to increase the number of Works Progress
Administration Nursery Schools (WPA). The Committee hopes . . . that
after-school care (of school-age children) will be provided on a broader
basis than has been possible up to this time.

                              (signed)
                              William Hodson
                              Commissioner of Welfare

Obviously new thinking and activity were astir. Overriding wartime pressures, creating critical family needs, had broken through public

---

2. Report available in the Municipal Reference Library, Municipal Bldg., New
York City. Three mimeographed pages, dated Dec. 2, 1942.

indifference. Steps were being taken toward broad community planning and cooperation in an attempt to resolve the acute family problems involving young children. By 1943 six information and counseling offices had been opened in various parts of the city by the Department of Welfare [3] to advise mothers about their child care problems. The first such office was located in the Harlem Health Center, opening in January 1943. The others followed: Ft. Greene and Bay Ridge in Brooklyn, Long Island City in Queens, Tremont in the Bronx, and the Lower East Side in Manhattan. By January 1946 nearly 20,000 mothers had sought help through these centers regarding some 27,000 children. Unfortunately and all too soon (for budgetary reasons), they were consolidated into a single Manhattan Center, greatly curtailing the accessibility of this resource to mothers in the other boroughs. By 1954, the only remaining vestige of this invaluable service was in the hands of a single social worker who conducted the service alone with the help of a telephone. Responding to some 4,000 inquiries annually, mothers' questions were answered and factual information given, but skillful guidance and individual counseling were no longer possible. Federal funds had not been made available for child care centers in New York City because New York was not classified as a war impact area by the Federal War Manpower Commission. When the city found itself without any allocation of federal funds for child care center programs, other solutions had to be found.

In March 1943 the New York State Legislature appropriated funds for child care to the New York State War Council to aid communities not eligible for the Lanham Act federal funds. A tripartite financial plan was then evolved for the child care centers of New York City. The State War Council, by authority of the Moffat Act of 1942 paid one-third of the cost, the city of New York paid another third through the Department of Welfare and parent fees plus contributions from board members constituted the final third. On March 3, 1943, Mr. Leo Arnstein, successor to Mr. Hodson as Commissioner of Welfare and then Chairman of the Mayor's Committee on Wartime Care of Children, wrote Mayor LaGuardia that $360,000 would be needed to serve the 1,000 young children enrolled in the WPA Nursery Schools. The tripartite financial plan continued in effect for the duration of the war, being officially terminated September 30, 1947.

In a resolution adopted May 28, 1943 the New York War Council had certified to the Board of Estimate of New York City that the

---

3. Later called the Department of Social Services.

employment situation in the City of New York indicated the need for the furnishing of care for the children of mothers employed in war work, that available facilities were inadequate, and that the following child care projects would help to meet such need:

Union Settlement
Regina Day Nursery
Recreation Rooms and Settlement
Prescott House
Juvenile House
Hebrew Kindergarten and Infants Home
Hamilton House
Grand Street Settlement
East Calvary Methodist Church
Church of All Nations
Council House
Children's Aid Society
Brooklyn Urban League
Bronx House
Bread Donor's Day Nursery
Aheveth Cheses Day Nursery
East House

These 17 nurseries,[4] operating under the sponsorship of private boards, agreed to keep open six days a week for ten to twelve hours a day. The transitions made by many of these centers between their origins in the mid-nineteenth century to serve the changing community needs and the goals of the mid-twentieth century were indeed remarkable. They formed the nucleus from which the New York City Child Care Center program and the Day Care Council eventually grew. The problems and difficulties encountered were tremendous. Fortunately, under the leadership of Helen Harris, the difficulties became challenges rather than defeats. Effort and determination to succeed seemed to increase with each obstacle. The broadly based support from both public and private organizations and active community involvement in the program proved to be a greater and more lasting asset in the long run than the temporary Lanham Act funds alone could possibly have achieved. The community was aroused and involved. Fortunately racial

---

4. See Resolution of the New York City War Council, in the files of the Mayor's Committee on Wartime Care of Children, Municipal Archives and Records.

integration was required in all child care centers in receipt of public funds, so this was established from the beginning. Unfortunately, however, due to the priority of need, the segregation of children from families of poverty from children of other social classes, became a prototype.

In most large cities across the country, with the exception of San Francisco, the withdrawal of Lanham Act funds at the close of the war terminated their federally supported child care center programs. In New York City, forced by circumstances to work out its own day care destiny without federal assistance, day care had gained sufficient strength, know-how and community support to survive at the end of the war. Increasing numbers of citizens had become convinced that the urgent need for the child care programs did not stop at the war's end, but rather that it needed expansion and further improvement. Not only was the program valued by the parents of the children who attended, by the board members responsible for each operation, by the teachers, directors and other employees directly involved, but also more and more by the citizens at large. And so, in spite of frequent setbacks, continuity and progress were assured.

In April 1948, a membership organization called the Day Care Council was formed with Helen Harris as chairman.[5] The governing board of this Council was comprised of representatives from each of the operating agencies. Close liaison was maintained with the Department of Welfare and other city-wide organizations toward continual improvement and expansion and toward meeting the licensing requirements of the Department of Health. In January of that year state funds were withdrawn. The New York City government then agreed to assume the state's financial share in addition to its own. In other words, from then on, two thirds of the total child care budget was administered through the New York City Department of Welfare. The Commissioner of Welfare was asked to appoint representatives of his department to meet with the Day Care Council in order that policies and procedures be considered and developed jointly.

A Day Care Manual, published May 1, 1961 by the Day Care Council reviewed the history of the Child Care Center program in New York City, its purposes and structure. To quote:

> One of the unique features in the program is the pattern of public-private cooperation. This has been present both in the relationship of the indi-

---

5. Elinor Guggenheimer succeeded Helen Harris. In 1960 Nancie Stewart became chairman of the Day Care Council.

20

vidual agencies and the staff of the Department of Welfare, and in the relationship built between the Day Care Council which represents the operating agencies and the Department of Welfare's Bureau of Child Welfare and its Division of Day Care.

At the present time, the majority of centers provide care for children between the ages of three and six. Some centers also have school-age programs for children between the ages of six and eight.

The purpose of the program is to provide the best possible care for those children who for one reason or another cannot be cared for adequately at home during the day. The effect of this in some cases has been to enable children who otherwise might have had to be placed away from home, to remain with their families; it has enabled families to secure good care for their children instead of relying on makeshift arrangements; and it has made it possible, in many cases, to identify the specific problems of children and/or their families and to make plans to deal with them.

Through the efforts of the Day Care Council, Mayor Robert Wagner agreed to help focus public attention and concern on the child care center program by declaring one particular week each spring to be Day Care Week in New York City. Special programs and publicity during this week brought the program dramatically to the attention of legislators and community leaders at the local, state and federal levels, as well as to the public in general. Active interest and support were stimulated. Twenty-five percent of all children attending daytime programs were enrolled in this long day service, under the aegis of the Welfare Department. Seventy-five percent attended programs under other auspices such as parent cooperatives, church groups, private nursery schools and kindergarten, demonstration, training and research centers in some universities and hospitals. Slowly but surely the number of full-day child care centers for the children of working or disadvantaged mothers increased year by year. By 1954 there were 65, serving 3,496 children under six years of age and 1,673 older children (between six and twelve) during their out-of-school hours. At that time there were some 2,000 children on the child care center waiting lists. By the end of 1963 there were 85 such centers in operation throughout the five boroughs, serving 5,030 children under six and 1,259 over six. The number on waiting lists had also increased to some 4,506 children. The annual Welfare Department's budget in support of this program had climbed to $7,407,203. The partnership between public and private effort in funding sustained and strengthened the program. It had proven to be workable, even though it continued to present many complex and knotty problems.

During the war, sample block studies, undertaken by the Department of Welfare in needy areas of the city, determined the extent of need for the opening of new centers. In some areas, special registration of eligible mothers was conducted before a new center was opened. The mobility of families and the rapidly changing characteristics of many neighborhoods made area selection difficult. Safe and appropriate premises were also hard to find.

During the war too, the lack of qualified personnel to work with young children presented an acute problem. A program was no better than its professional leadership. The Civilian Defense Volunteer Organization (CDVO), through its Greater New York Child Care, Development and Protection Program, held weekly meetings at City Hall. It provided an intensive six week training course for volunteer child care assistants. Miss Jessie Stanton, consulting director of the Harriet Johnson Nursery School of the Bureau of Educational Experiments and lecturer on Child Development at New York University, served as chairman of the preschool training program. The course consisted of 36 scheduled hours of observation in selected day care programs and 36 lecture hours under qualified and experienced nursery school teachers and directors, as well as lectures by pediatricians and psychologists. The movement by colleges and universities to offer specialization in the new field of "early childhood education" was greatly accelerated. It included the sequence of nursery, kindergarten and primary training. By 1957 degrees in early childhood education were being granted by:

Adelphi College, Garden City, N.Y.
Bank Street College of Education, 69 Bank St., N.Y.C.
Brooklyn College, Bedford Av. & Av. H, Brooklyn, N.Y.
Columbia University, Teachers College, 120th St., N.Y.C.
Hunter College, 695 Park Av., N.Y.C.
Mills College of Education, 66 Fifth Av., N.Y.C.
New York University, School of Education, Wash. Sq., N.Y.C.
Queens College, 65-30 Kissena Blvd., Flushing, N.Y.
Saint Joseph's College for Women, Convent Av., Brooklyn, N.Y.

Summer and extension courses in early childhood education were also offered at that time at City College, Convent Av. and 139 St., N.Y.C. After the termination of the war, as doctor's services again became more readily available, Dr. Leona Baumgartner (having become the New York City Commissioner of Health) was finally able to carry out a plan for health care which had been held in abeyance for a number of years. She now authorized the Day Care Unit of the Department of Health to offer a direct and comprehensive health service to any nonprofit day care agency in New York City whose board officially requested it. The child care centers were all nonprofit agencies. Very few of the families whose children attended them could afford the services of private physicians. Clinics and child health stations were overcrowded, necessitating long hours of waiting. This was a particular hardship for the working or ill mother or one with a large family. Consequently their children received little, if any, regular health care. The responses of the child care center boards to Dr. Baumgartner's offer were immediate and enthusiastic. A Senior Pediatric Consultant (Dr. Hugh Chaplin) was assigned full time to the Day Care Unit to take charge of this program. Assisting him were a number of physicians and an experienced and dedicated consultant public health nurse, Mrs. Mabel Davis. Together they set up and supervised a new and unique health program. A physician was assigned to each Child Care Center and his work carefully coordinated into the day-by-day operation of the center. The health education of both parents and staff was undertaken in cooperation with the center director. A comprehensive health service was provided to every child. Without cost to the family, each child received a regular and complete six-month physical examination and necessary inoculations. A thorough health history was obtained. A mother was invited to be present whenever her child was examined by the doctor and usually came. Follow-up on recommendations was done by the part-time nurse employed by the center. Her hours coincided with those of the doctor. In this way any remediable defects were more likely to be found and promptly corrected. As the program developed, both eye and hearing examinations of every child were added to the routine. In this way no child entered the first grade without glasses if he needed them and no child with a hearing loss could be misdiagnosed as mentally retarded because he had not been able to hear what the teacher said. Thus the public health component in the group life of these vulnerable young children became an intrinsic and important part of the total child care center program. The health findings and recommendations for each particular child were fully discussed with his parents, questions were answered and guidance given. The physician, who had been selected and assigned by the Health Department was also supervised and paid by that department. The doctor, as well as the nurse, were available for parent-teacher conferences, as well as for staff or parent meetings.

By September 1960, the health program was established in 70 centers, serving 4,300 children. A staff of some 40 practicing physicians were using part of their time to conduct these programs. Unfortunately the expanding services never caught up with the ever more rapidly growing waiting lists. As the Welfare Department assumed increasing financial and procedural responsibility, it also assumed more and more control of the total operation. This, to some degree, reduced the initiative, involvement and enthusiasm of some board members, tending to reduce innovation and to encourage stereotyping. Nevertheless many hurdles were surmounted and real contributions made to the children themselves and to the peace of mind of their parents. Yet far, far more remained to be done for the children, their families and particularly for the younger siblings (those under three) for whom no program of adequate daytime care was available.

CHAPTER III

THE CODE ITSELF, A BASIC TOOL
The Guarantor of Children's Rights

The story has often been told of the church worker in 1874 who while visiting an aged woman in a tenement learned of the brutal mistreatment of a child by her foster mother. Already weak and ill as a result of long abuse, Mary Ellen was chained to a bed and fed only bread and water. However, the church worker found no way to intervene on behalf of the child. The police, the district attorney and various agencies in the community could not, they felt, intercede where the primary rights of parent or guardian were involved.

There had been created in the previous decade, in Manhattan, an American Society for the Prevention of Cruelty to Animals, patterned upon an animal protective society established in England in 1822. The mission worker argued that surely a child was a member of the animal kingdom and merited protection, at least as much as a cat or a dog. Thus, on the petition of the Society for the Prevention of Cruelty to Animals, the suffering child was brought to court and the foster parents were jailed.

New protective societies were then created to work on behalf of children, while others which had animal programs revised their charters to create children's divisions. New York County's Society for the Prevention of Cruelty to Children (was) founded in 1875.[1]

Where do standards come from? We accept standards as part of our regular way of life, as both necessary and useful. Woven into the day-by-day pattern of common usage, their existence and reliability are taken for granted. Established by a recognized authority, they serve as a rule for such measurements as time, temperature, weight, money, distance, quantity. We have standard wavelengths, candle power, units of electrical energy, speed, atomic power, etc. Standards relating directly to human behavior are perhaps the most subtle and complex.

1. "Protecting New York City's Children" by Alfred J. Kahn. Published April 1961 by the Citizen's Committee for Children of N.Y. Inc. 48 pages $1.00.

25

146848

Every regulatory standard has been created out of a recognized need, followed by an effort to meet the need. Success or failure in overcoming the often troublesome problems that are encountered become the measure of progress. A standard-setting process might be initiated by the coming to light of a new idea, by the reawakening of an old dream whose time had come for realization or by the pressure of changing conditions upon the lives of people. Its success was inevitably related to the readiness of the people affected by it, to accept and use it. Such stirrings became useful to the degree that they were in accord with the needs and wishes of the people concerned. Imaginative, aware and inventive leadership, able to rally community support, usually provided the impetus that moved society toward its acceptance.

So it was in 1942-43 that day care standards became a reality in New York City. An acute need, a growing public awareness and dedicated, skilled leadership were present and the community responded. This did not mean that the sailing was smooth. Ways had to be found to make the newly revised code a fully effective tool to guarantee the recognized rights of all young children in group care.

Concepts of public health were changing. Although the Bureau of Child Hygiene had been established in the Health Department in 1908, it was not until 1914 that children in day nurseries were required to be examined regularly by a licensed physician. Some programs for groups of children had come under the regulations of the municipal sanitary code as early as 1895, but only those that happened to apply voluntarily to the Health Department for a permit were ever visited by a health inspector. This was also true in regard to the fire inspector.

The new day care code regulations came into being at a time when major public health trends were being directed toward the conservation of health and the prevention of illness and disease. Earlier emphasis had been primarily on combatting contagious and infectious diseases and on meeting emergencies. Changing attitudes were leading toward a new era in public health. Communicable diseases were disappearing one by one as research and its application allowing for effective prevention in other fields gained headway. The new concept of public health encompassed not only man's physical health and the hygiene of his environment, but his mental and emotional health as well. The earlier focus on an individual and possibly on the members of his immediate family, now broadened to include also the community in which he lived. What a propitious time for a day care licensing program of new dimensions to come under the aegis of so forward-looking a Department of Health.

Citizens too were becoming aware that the spirit of a law was as important as its letter. Children, it seemed, were as dependent on the intangibles as on the tangibles in their environment. Both the content, the method and the spirit of conducting a program were crucial factors in its success. Only through genuine understanding and support could children respond and learn. Could the code now be used both as a stimulant and as a measuring device to bring about a better way of life for the children? If so, by what methods?

On March 1, 1943, Commissioner Ernest L. Stebbins, M.D., sent out the first official letter informing all known day care operators of their new responsibilities. A copy of the new regulations and of the "Survey Guide for Evaluating Health Services in Centers providing Day Care for Children" was enclosed. The commissioner's letter read, in part:

> I know that you will be interested to know that Section 198 of the Sanitary Code, under which you now operate, was revised by the Board of Health at a meeting on February 9, 1943. I am enclosing a copy of these new regulations. In the course of the revision of these regulations, many individual agencies and all of the standard-setting and coordinating groups interested in the promotion of good standards in child care in the city were consulted.
>
> You will note that permits, contrary to previous practice, are now good for only two years and if your agency was given a permit more than two years ago, it will be necessary for you to have a new permit. Later on in the year you will receive an application blank to be filled out and returned to the Health Department. In the meantime, we believe you will wish to study the new regulations.
>
> The wartime emergency has focussed our thinking on the care of children, and the "Survey Guide," which I am also sending you, is intended to assist you in checking the quality of the health program in your unit. This has been based on the best thinking of the leaders in the field of child care and I hope you will find it helpful.
>
> It is the concern of all to make it possible for children to live and grow under happy, healthy conditions and I appreciate the efforts you have been making to maintain these good standards of care. The Bureau of Child Hygiene of the Department of Health stands ready at all times to assist you with the problems which may arise in connection with your service.

The code's broad and inclusive definition of a "day care agency" deserves first mention here. The opening paragraphs made it immediately clear that it was unlawful to operate a day care agency without a permit. Such an agency was then defined so broadly as to include every type of daytime group service for children under six years of age. This in itself was history making! The standards were to apply to all groups and to all children alike, whether rich or poor and regardless of race, color, creed or place of origin. The definition read:

> The term agency giving day care to children shall mean and include, (a) any institution or place, whether known as a day nursery, nursery, school, kindergarten, child play or progressive school, or *under any other name,* which for compensation or otherwise, receives for temporary custody, *with or without stated educational purpose,* for all or part of the day, apart from their parents, four or more children not of common parentage; (b) any person who holds himself or herself out for hire to care for four or more children under six years of age and not of common parentage, separate and apart from their parents and elsewhere than at the home of one of them during all or part of the day.[2]

To avoid jurisdictional conflict between the city departments and between church and state authorities, nursery schools and kindergartens operating as part of an elementary school were not required to obtain a permit. Nevertheless they were to be maintained in conformity with the code regulations (presumably under their own recognizance). It was under Section 200 of the code that the elementary schools were already governed, as far as the Health Department's authority was concerned. However, any such nursery school or kindergarten which voluntarily applied to the Health Department for a permit, even though not required to do so, received consultative service and was granted a permit as soon as requirements were met. A number of such requests were received from religious institutions, but none from the Board of Education.

Once a permit was granted, it was to be "posted in a conspicuous place in the entrance lobby or the reception room of the premises to which it applies" for all to see. There was no longer an escape from the knowledge as to whether an agency did or did not have a permit. There was nowhere to hide, as far as the public's right to know was concerned, The basic rights of all young children were at last to be recognized and upheld.

The Day Care Unit's first direct contact with an existing or prospective operator was usually when his application for a permit was received. How wise the codemakers proved themselves to be when they stipulated that an application for a permit had to be made in person. No better way could have been devised to prevent or resolve

---

2. Italics are the author's.

misunderstandings and confusions than to meet face-to-face for the free discussion of any and all matters of concern. These initial conferences covered all phases of day care operation including the motives and goals of the operator, the nature of the premises and their intended use (both indoors and out), budgeting, staffing, programing, grouping of children, intake procedures, choice of equipment and supplies, plans for health protection, safety, maintenance, parent involvement and participation, and the handling of emergencies. Step-by-step licensing procedures were further clarified at each conference.

To the initial conference the operator was asked to bring:

a) A floor plan or sketch of the premises, with accurate measurements of all space to be used for child caring purposes.

b) A written statement of purpose and a description of the program and activities designed to carry out their stated purposes.

c) A statement of the method to be used in admitting children for care.

d) Reasonable evidence of a secure financial position to permit compliance with the code regulations.

e) A copy of the proposed annual budget for the coming year.

All this gave not only an opportunity for detailed and comprehensive review of an applicant's thinking and planning, but it revealed also his quality of concern for the children themselves. Too often, poorly prepared and misguided operators expounded at length on their love and devotion to children while no shred of such evidence was observable in their attitude or planning. The true extent of an operator's knowledge and skill about conducting a good program, or his lack of it, usually became discernible during the course of such a conference. Until a complete and proper application with the necessary accompanying data, as described, had been received, no decisions or recommendations could be made.

An early field visit to the actual premises to be used was made by the consultant assigned to that agency. Permission to enroll children was granted only after the premises had been inspected and approved in writing by representatives of the Fire Department, the Housing and Buildings Department and the Bureau of Sanitary Inspections of the Health Department. No room was to be used regularly for child caring purposes unless one or more windows opened upon a public thoroughfare, yard or court, not less than ten feet in depth and extending the length or width of the building. No room could be so located that the floor on any one side was more than three feet below the surrounding ground area. Nor could a day care service be conducted above the third floor unless an elevator was provided. Having young children in cellars or basements was generally considered undesirable. Conducting a day care agency in a factory, mercantile or business building was disallowed.

Precise floor space allowances per child were spelled out. Proper lighting, heating, ventilating, refrigeration and food storage were necessary. Water purity, standard dishwashing facilities, accessibility and sufficiency of toilet and washing facilities, provision of individual cots with sheets and blankets as needed were all required. The premises had to be hygienically maintained. Equipment and play materials had to be safe, appropriate and available in sufficient number and variety to meet the growing needs of the children. Furniture was to be child-sized.

Food and nutrition requirements were as follows:

> Nourishing food following a standard dietary acceptable to the Department of Health and adapted to the different age groups shall be provided at intervals not exceeding four hours. If an agency provides care for more than six hours, a hot meal served at noon and a daily allowance of at least a pint of milk a day are required.

The Bureau of Nutrition of the Health Department offered the cooperation of its nutritionists under the excellent guidance of its head nutritionist, Dorothy Williams. They evaluated the menus and the total food service in each day care agency as requested either by the day care consultant or directly by the agency director. Sometimes the cook or the nutritionist of an agency took the initiative in seeking guidance.

Once a program was in actual operation, the Health Department nutritionists made one or more field visits to observe the entire food program from the preparation of the meal through its consumption by the children. They gave expert advice on food purchasing, menu planning, food storage, food preparation and serving, including the midmorning and the midafternoon snacks. The Bureau of Nutrition prepared food guides and helped to solve innumerable dietary and budgetary problems. Where food problems remained serious or unresolved, joint conferences were sometimes held with the agency director, the cook or food planner, the Health Department nutritionist and the Day Care Unit consultant. By this means, answers were usually found. In an early contact with an agency, the director was requested to submit in triplicate typical daily menus covering a three week period. These were then carefully evaluated by the nutritionist and a copy returned to the operator with comments, criticisms and suggestions; a second copy went to the day care consultant.

Midmorning and midafternoon snacks of milk or of citrus fruit juice served with a crisp chewable wafer or cracker, a piece of celery or raw carrot became the order of the day in all agencies. Such snack-times provided a needed and welcome pause in the day's occupation, a relaxed and refreshing social interlude for both the active energetic children and for their busy teachers. The directors, following recommended practice, posted each week's menus in advance, to help the parents in their menu planning for the children's home meals. Non-profit agencies were helped to obtain available supplementary surplus foods from the government. All food handlers and/or planners were educated as to food values, on how to prepare food so as to retain its nutritional benefits, and also on how to make it palatable to the children. The enjoyment of their meals and snacks undoubtedly aided the friendly relationships of children and adults, as well as their digestive processes.

The physical health of each child and of every adult who came in contact with him, was protected by regulations numbers 7, 8 and 9 of the code. These had many important ramifications:

A complete medical examination of each child by a physician, before his admission to a day care agency and of each adult before his employment, was required. The children were to be reexamined every six months and the adults every two years.[3] The written record of each medical examination was to be kept on file in the agency where it might be reviewed by the consultant.

Data for each child was to include certification of freedom from communicable disease, measurement of height and weight, recommendations for any necessary medical treatment and any special regimen as to diet, rest, etc. Children with frequent epileptic seizures or a handicapping physical or mental condition might not be admitted.[4]

All adults, when appointed, were to submit a certificate from a physician certifying them to be free from disease in communicable form. Such certificate was to be based on a medical examination and chest X-ray, with such laboratory tests as might be indicated, and to be kept on file at all times in the agency.

A daily record of the children admitted was also to be kept, as well as a permanent register giving the name, home address and birth date of each child with the date of his admission, the date of his discharge and the reason therefore; the name and home address of his parents or

3. The 1959 code revision extended the required interval for the physical examination of all adults who came in contact with the children to three years, to make it consistent with Section 200.
4. This regulation (number 6) was deleted when the code was revised in 1959. See Article 47.07 of the revised code.

guardians and the address and telephone number where a parent could be reached during the day in case of any emergency.

Printed health forms were made available in quantity, upon request, for the full recording of each child's complete health data, during the entire time of his attendance in the agency. These were distributed free of cost to encourage their use. Respect for the medical profession, already inculcated in the mind of the public, greatly encouraged compliance with the health regulations. Record keeping moved forward apace. Unfortunately, in too many instances, it remained true that the mere keeping of health records in no way guaranteed that the recommendations were being carried out. Too often they were merely kept on file to be available for inspection without benefit to the children of any followup whatsoever. Consequently the consultant had to interpret and reinterpret the full intent of the code in regard to record keeping, interpretation to the parents and appropriate followup.

First, last and all the time, the staff was unquestionably and invariably the primary and most important factor in determining the degree to which children derived, or failed to derive, benefits from their group experiences! The ability, skill and perceptiveness of the director and the other staff members, the quality of their concern for the children's well-being, ascertained the true value and the basic nature of the program, regardless of all other considerations. Professional training in early childhood and experience with young children for the person in charge were recognized as essential. Yet it was also recognized that integrity, understanding and genuine concern for the healthy, happy growth and development of the children were even more important, though far more difficult to legislate. The code put it this way:

Constant and competent supervision must be provided for all children.

The executive in charge should be a competent administrator with a knowledge of child development and behavior and shall have the capacity and responsibility for training other members of the staff. Training should include work with the children under professional supervision, work with parents, a knowledge of community resources and how to use them. Such executive should also have demonstrated ability to make practical use of such training.

All members of the staff should be friendly and emotionally stable and have a sympathetic understanding of family and children's problems.

These statements deserve a resounding "bravo"! Just as a stream of water cannot rise above its source, so the quality of care received by any group of children could not rise above the level of the professional skill, awareness and dedication of the director and the staff who were in direct and constant contact with the children. The educational leader, supervisor and administrator as well as the director set the tone of the agency. The importance of this role cannot be exaggerated.

Without an official, objective standard to go by, how was the competency of a director and her staff to be evaluated by the Day Care consultant without personal bias or prejudice? Fortunately such aid came in the form of a new regulation of the New York State Education Department, officially establishing for the first time (in 1945) the requirements for the training and experience of teachers and directors in the field of early childhood education (including nursery, kindergarten and primary years) throughout the state. Another milestone had been reached! Professional recognition of the "preschool educator" had been achieved at last, giving the continuity of learning throughout the early years a new impetus. The new state requirements were equivalent to those for a degree in any other teaching field, regardless of the age of the children taught. In the past it had been customary to require comparatively more in training for teachers preparing to work with older children. Now a college degree in early childhood education was to be recognized as objective evidence of a person's professional training and competence in that field. It was still necessary, however, for the executive in charge to demonstrate his or her ability to make use of such training.

Fortunately, an administrative procedure was worked out with the Bureau of Child Development and Parent Education of the State Education Department whereby time might be allowed to those partially qualified, if they were on their way to completing their training. This helped to prevent any loss of work and income. No one willing to complete his training was arbitrarily excluded from work with young children. An evaluation of each individual's training and experience now became necessary. This could be done either by the office of Instructional Supervision of the State Education Department or by any of the colleges with accredited departments of early childhood education. Each teacher or director whose training had not yet been completed, submitted an official, detailed statement to the Day Care Unit indicating what work still remained to be done, accompanied by a signed letter indicating the date by which the necessary training would be completed. There was much variation and flexibility in regard to the date by which the necessary credentials would be completed. So it was that young and old returned to college with a new respect for their rising professional status. Most went with enthusiasm, some with resistance. One by one, almost every New York City college, public or private, established a state-approved Department of Early Childhood

Education. To accommodate the many students of all ages who were at work in day care agencies during the day, evening and Saturday courses were offered. Still the gradually increasing supply of qualified personnel could not fulfill the growing demands, and shortages continued.

By 1950 there were over 1,000 fully accredited teachers and directors in the 500 operating day care agencies in New York City. Hundreds more were studying to become qualified. Their distribution was uneven, but more than any other single factor, the professionalization of the early childhood field slowly but surely moved the operation of day care to a new level. Much had been achieved, but again, much more remained to be done. Unfortunately, becoming qualified did not always, by and of itself, bring quality teaching in its wake. The degree alone was not the entire answer. Some colleges admitted every student who applied, even though of poor caliber or character. Some offered weak courses that left much to be desired. As in other professions, the degree did not invariably guarantee superior performance nor assure integrity.

A key provision of the code was the "exception clause" (regulation 12) entitled "Discretion of the Board." In accord with its general law enforcement policy, the Health Department made specific allowance in Section 198 for desirable flexibility and diversity by allowing an exception to the regulations under unusual and well justified circumstances:

> "If there are practical difficulties or unnecessary hardships in carrying out the strict letter of these regulations the Board of Health in its discretion and in a specific case, may modify any provision *in harmony with their general purpose and intent* and upon such conditions as *it may deem necessary for the children's welfare.*" [5]

The "exception clause" was meticulously guarded and cautiously used. There might otherwise have been a danger that allowing an exception might become the rule, a convenience to the operator rather than a benefit to the children. Requests for exceptions, therefore, were not treated lightly nor allowed to become an expedient for code evasion nor a mere convenience to a maneuvering operator. When pressure or political influence were brought to bear on the Day Care Unit to win a questionable favor, as happened occasionally, there was no success. Specific exceptions were allowed from time to time, after careful consideration and when beneficial to the children's welfare.

A Board of Review in the Health Department held informal, semi-official hearings on unresolved controversies between an operator and the Day Care Unit and on official requests for an exception to code

---

5. Italics are the author's.

regulations. Chaired by its legal counsel,[6] the Board of Review submitted a full report with its recommendations to the Board of Health through the Commissioner of Health. Final authority was vested in the Board of Health which then officially notified both the applicant and the Day Care Unit of its decision. Beyond this there was no further recourse except through the courts.

The majority of requests for exceptions to the code dealt with an operator's being allowed to conduct a day care service in premises that were more than three feet below the surface of the ground surrounding the building. The Board of Health was making every possible effort to get young children out of dark, damp cellars and basements, often difficult of access and lacking the required two means of egress to assure fire safety. When no more desirable, available facilities could be found and when the basement premise was dry, safe, well lighted, heated and ventilated, the exception was reluctantly granted. In such instances, the day care consultant urged the operator to continue a relentless search for more suitable premises above ground. Although desirable space in the city was at a premium, in the end they were usually successful.

There was no attempt on the part of the Day Care Unit staff to stereotype agency programs into any one preconceived pattern, nor to interfere with the philosophy, pattern or stated goals of the sponsor under whom they were to operate. A more creative approach was taken by helping operators to evaluate their own goals and services, assessing the child care needs in their communities and reviewing their own competencies to serve that particular group of children well. It became quickly apparent in every case brought to court, that the code requirements were unquestionably essential for the protection, health and good living of every group of children, no matter how varied in philosophy or program.

Some agencies patterned themselves according to the beliefs of Froebel, Montessori, Gesell, Dewey and later Martin Deutsch or Bereiter and Engleman. Some focussed entirely on research, experimentation, demonstration or teacher training; others served only gifted or handicapped children. Such wide variety helped to stimulate innovation and gave parents a wide choice to select from. No controls were exercised in regard to the size of an agency as long as adequate space, staff and equipment were provided for the number of children to be enrolled. Expanding the size of an already operating center was discouraged

---

6. Christine Kefauver was succeeded by Harry Hollander as Legal Counsel on July 1, 1948.

until and unless code requirements had been fully met and sustained for the original number.

Hours of operation varied too. A full day program might operate for from five to ten hours daily, including lunch. Others might operate mornings only or afternoons only, with or without lunch and with or without offering transportation. Some programs served children only on certain days; others served different groups of children on different days. Some accommodated their hours to suit the convenience of the parents, disregarding the needs of the children. Others did the reverse.

Types of applicants for licensing also varied tremendously. An application could legitimately be made by an individual, a partnership, an incorporated or unincorporated board, a cooperative group of parents and/or teachers, a community agency (public or private), an association or society (philanthropic or commercial), a church, a hospital, a college or university.

As goals, hours, fees, size, ages of children, location, quality of leadership, type of organization, auspices and sponsorships varied, so premises too varied greatly. Interestingly enough and to the surprise of many, little relationship was found between the fees charged and the quality of the service rendered, nor between the type of premises occupied and the fee. Some low cost programs offered the children an experience "par excellence," some expensive, top fee charging agencies gave miserable, meager care to the children. Some groups housed in palatial, impressive quarters provided the children with the barest "vacuum care," while others, perhaps in the same community, offered superior programs in modest and simple premises. These discrepancies occurred regardless of whether a program was conducted under private, public, religious or philanthropic auspices, whether it was the concern of a single purpose agency (interested in day care only), or of a complex multipurpose agency. There were good, bad and indifferent day care programs under all types of auspices.

The group care of infants was not disallowed in the 1943 revision of the code.[7] It spelled out in considerable detail the regulations concerning children under 18 months of age. By October 1943, the Day Care unit staff had found seven agencies that were enrolling infants from two weeks to two months of age. Soon an additional 21 agencies

---

7. Section 53.07 (C) of the 1959 code revision required for the first time that a certificate of approval from the Health Department be granted to allow any unrelated persons to give regular daytime care to not more than two children under two years of age.

were found to be accepting infants between six and eighteen months of age. These programs were firmly entrenched in the practice of giving custodial care only; in none were the conditions satisfactory; not one met the basic needs of the infants. Even when consultants were assigned to help directly in the agency, bringing some temporary improvements, they were not sustained. Some operators, conducting hopelessly poor and often hazardous programs, were promptly reported to the Society for the Prevention of Cruelty to Children so that the parents could be notified, the children removed and the agency closed. It was obvious that infants could not thrive in such centers. Better solutions had to be found for these very young, highly vulnerable children requiring care outside their own homes.

In a city the size of New York it was impossible to prevent all dishonest and maneuvering operators from camouflaging unsavory child care efforts behind an attractive facade where their operations gained a foothold and parents were misled. Evidence of code violation in such situations was often difficult to obtain. Yet it had to be obtained if public confidence in the code was to be upheld and if the children were to be protected. As false, undercover and unreliable operators appeared from time to time, their surreptitious activities often came to light through a complaint. Promptly, the ever-watchful eye of the day care consultant, looking behind the facade, verified the true facts and through the authority of the code took appropriate action. Without the code, without an alert and concerned public, and without a vigilant frontline staff in the Health Department, malpractice in day care could not have been prevented.

As the work of the unit became better known, more and more complaints were received. Whether anonymous or identifiable, whether received by mail, phone or in person, they received prompt attention and follow-up. Either an unannounced visit was made by the assigned consultant or the matter was referred to the public health nurse in the district for investigation and report. Every effort was made to verify or disprove the complaint as objectively and fairly as possible. The operator was frankly told the nature of the complaint, but not its origin. Depending on the nature of the findings, action was then taken. Immediate closing was sometimes the only possible solution. False complaints and misunderstandings were cleared, minor difficulties overcome and major problems handled.[8]

Keeping a meticulous record of all complaints often made it possi-

8. See Chapter VI, "Coping with Exploitation."

ble to identify a "cheating operator" who changed his name, address and the name of his agency as he moved from place to place, while he carried on miserable unlicensed services, one after another, until caught. Such persons were usually unqualified in every way to work with children even when, as occurred in a few instances, they had earned a university degree. Where there was continuous overcrowding of children, deliberately deceptive record keeping, insufficient food, diluted milk, hostile, incompetent staff, it was often found that the owner and/or operator had serious personality disorders which made the situation extremely difficult to handle and of dubious value to the children.

Whenever there was both the possibility and the desire to overcome violations, an application was allowed to remain pending for a reasonable length of time to give the operator an opportunity to remedy his mistakes and to demonstrate his sincerity. Affording this leeway nearly always brought about gains and mutual confidence between the operator and the consultant.

By January 1944, 46 day care agencies had closed their doors because of inability and/or unwillingness to overcome serious deficiencies. The scarcity and heavy cost of equipment and toys, of materials for building repairs during wartime, as well as the finding and employing of qualified staff in sufficient number was sometimes an almost insurmountable barrier. Ignorance and ineptitude were often equally insurmountable.

The majority of complaints came from three sources:
1. from neighbors, who saw the day-by-day happenings from outside the school;
2. from reliable teachers who had been employed to work in the school where they saw shocking happenings;
3. from the parents of children who had been enrolled in the school without having made sufficiently careful investigation.

Occasionally complaints came from competitors who wanted to damage the reputation of a nearby school in order to swell their own enrollments or from malicious trouble makers with a personal grudge. Sometimes teachers as well as parents with legitimate complaints, were reluctant to become involved, fearful that they would become targets of an operator's malevolence. It was hard for them to realize that without their help as witnesses, the Health Department was frustrated in its attempt to protect their children as well as those of others. Fortunately some complainants saw their roles differently and volunteered to help in every way possible. Many soundly based groups operated year in and year out without having a single complaint filed against them. This usually meant that not only was a satisfactory program being operated but also that good relations had been established with the parents and in the community. In other situations, where repeated and never-ending complaints were received from a wide variety of sources, an agency was kept under constant and close surveillance. The natural, gay sound of children's voices during their outdoor play time was sometimes disturbing to elderly, invalid or querulous neighbors, who wanted quiet above all else. The operator and the complainant were then brought together to discuss possible adjustments, but it was made clear that young children were not puppets who could be bottled up in silence for they too had their rights.

From the beginning and as the years passed, the validity and soundness of Section 198 of the revised code were tested in a number of court actions taken by the Department of Health against operators who were found to have neglected, abused or exploited children, and who still refused to close shop. When they continued their questionable activities, even after the Board of Review had held hearings and recommended their closing, court action became necessary. Of the ten such court cases, none was lost by the Department of Health and only one withdrawn. Each had its unique aspects and ramifications. Each in turn threatened to undermine the Code's effectiveness should the case be lost. Since the regulations were new and therefore as yet uncontested in the courts, the judge's decision in each case was critical to the entire work of the Day Care Unit.

Lawyers and judges often seemed unconvinced of the soundness of certain of the code regulations. They questioned, for instance, the legality of requiring that provision should be made in every day care service to provide comfort during meals. To the consultant this meant having children seated at tables of proper height and size and enjoying their meals in a relaxed atmosphere. Some judges failed to see the importance of having play materials not only appropriate, sufficient in number, safe and clean, but also "easily accessible to the children at all times." On the other hand they became indignant and even outraged when it was shown that children were inadequately fed, that their milk was diluted or that all their faces had been washed with a single dirty wash cloth. It seemed that standards of safety and hygiene were still more acceptable and more readily recognized as appropriate to regulation than those having to do with the subtler nuances of group living, such as having the program appropriate to the age and stage of development of the child. Nevertheless it was usually found that an operator who neglected one major area of concern was more often than not, equally negligent in others. Consequently, in presenting a case to the court, it was possible to select and emphasize those violations with which members of the legal profession were more sympathetic. The winning of each court case greatly strengthened the respect of the total community for the code itself and for the standard-raising effort of the Department. It also helped to diminish the number of deliberate code violators who sought a profitable financial heyday for themselves at the expense of the children.

Repeatedly in determining the innocence or guilt of an operator, the judge admonished the Health Department representatives for having been too patient and for having waited too long before having brought a case to court. In declaring an operator's guilt, the judges often warned him that if he ever again went into the field of day care in the City of New York, a maximum fine and a jail sentence would be imposed. So both the reasonableness and the legality of the code were upheld over and over again.

It became irrefutably clear that the day care law had been wisely conceived and carefully drawn. Its legislative intent and authority were also clear. Comprehensive yet specific, up-to-date and flexible, it assured equal rights to all children under six years of age in daytime group care in New York City.

A basic and fundamental question still remained. Was the code to be used merely as a measuring rod to determine which agencies were in compliance and therefore to be granted a permit and those that failed to measure up in order to deny their permit and close them down? If this was the purpose of the code, approximately half of the operating agencies would have been peremptorily closed in 1943 and half the young children in day care would have been relegated back to the streets to become latchkey children once again.

Or could the code serve as a leaven to encourage, stimulate, educate, support, awaken, push and prod when necessary all those who were ready, able and willing to respond both to the letter and the spirit of the code, by providing sound programs of ever-increasing quality and excellence for the children's benefit, protection and enjoyment?

Fortunately the second alternative was chosen, as a full scale, bootstrap operation got under way. Time was of the essence! Yet sufficient time had to be allowed for people to become thoroughly familiar with the code itself, to understand it in relation to their own agency and to remedy existing violations, if any. Day-by-day, step-by-step challenges had to be met, obstacles overcome, decisions made. The leaven began to work. As community resources were tapped on all sides, responses were on the whole gratifying. The day care unit front line consultant staff, though hard pressed, made itself constantly available. With a conscious effort they attempted as far as possible to see and understand each program as a totality before becoming involved in any of its numerous and often perplexing parts and pieces. A full perspective meant seeing an agency whole, in its full range of activities, recognizing its strengths and potentialities as well as its major and minor weaknesses. It meant recognizing and rooting out dishonest and improper practices whenever and wherever they appeared. It meant above all, keeping the main focus always on the needs and requirements of the children themselves. The rate of progress varied greatly in the kaleidoscopic pattern of day care throughout the city, but that there was a growing forward movement no one could deny. The code as a basic tool could become a guarantor of children's rights!

CHAPTER IV

CODE EVALUATION AND REVISION
A Continuing Process

No matter how carefully planned or comprehensive code regulations might be, their intermittent review, reevaluation and revision were essential. As the strengths and weaknesses of the New York City health code were tested through actual use, appropriate modifications needed to be made from time to time. As the conditions of city living changed, so too the laws affecting them had to change, if they were to remain meaningful.

The prewar laws had focussed entirely on physical aspects, whether of premises or of the child. It was emphasis on the frame that mattered, not the life within that frame.

Following World War II came a greater awareness of the fact that concern for the physical aspects, the tangibles only, was an incomplete and therefore invalid approach. Although children might be kept alive when provided with food, clothing and shelter, they required more than this if the mind and spirit were to thrive.

The preamble to the United Nations Declaration of Human Rights as adopted unanimously by the General Assembly in 1959 read: "Mankind owes the child the best it has to give." As understanding and knowledge were gained, more had to be given. To provide the best, requires unceasing effort to assure that children's rights to safety, protection, guidance and opportunities for the maximum fulfilment of their potentialities were met. Plump, clean, well-mannered children might be as thwarted, hurt and damaged inside as if they were hungry or diseased.

As was true in the 1943 rewriting of the code regulations regarding day care, subsequent attempts at code revision had to be clearly justified and rooted in the cultural hopes and aspirations of the people. With the yeast of the 1943 law at work, the ferment produced a momentum of vital importance. Only through self-awareness and a desire for self-improvement on the part of the day care operators could the impetus and vitality of the movement be sustained. The challenge lay in an awareness of the urgent need to serve more children and to serve them better. Minor changes made in Section 198 between 1943 and 1959 and numerous administrative agreements about procedures were worked out from time to time, but it was not until 1957 that a thorough full-scale review and revision of the entire Sanitary Code was undertaken, including Section 198 in its entirety. On the recommendation of Dr. Baumgartner, then the Commissioner of Health, the Board of Health approved having the entire code expertly scrutinized from beginning to end, to bring it up to date and make it streamlined, eliminating duplications, contradictions and outmoded sections. The study was undertaken by Mr. Frank Grad and a small team of experts from the Legal Research Division of Columbia University's Law Department. Over a three year period they worked closely and intensively with the staffs of the various bureaus and divisions of the Health Department. Section by section, any outmoded, unclear or duplicating regulations were eliminated. New sections were added in line with new thinking, new research finding, new practices and improved administrative procedures. Current and relevant state and national regulations were studied and compared. The end was a much improved code, completely reorganized from beginning to end.

The name as well as the format and some of the content of the code were changed. The Sanitary Code became the "Health Code." Section 198 of the old code became Articles 45 and 47 of Title II of the new code.[1]

The term "Day Care Service" replaced "Day Care Agency" as a more inclusive and adequately descriptive term. Article 53 of Title II was added, to introduce and begin to regulate a new service to be called "Family Day Care," another pioneering step in the story of day care in New York City.

Family Day Care Article 53 dealt primarily with children requiring daytime care but ineligible for admission, for whatever reason, to a regular day care service. It made provision for children under two years of age, for certain handicapped children and for others, who for a variety of reasons, would benefit more from an intimate home setting

---

1. Copies of Articles 45, 47 and 53 of Title II appear in the Addenda.

than from a larger group setting. Not more than two babies under two years of age were to be allowed in a Family Day Care Home. The total number of such children already placed for daytime care with unrelated families was unknown. Only one organization in the city offered such a service, the Jewish Child Care Association. Yet all social agency workers agreed that without doubt large numbers of children were being placed in such homes without supervision, guidance or safeguards of any kind.

As regulation number 53 of the code went into effect, the Health Department sought funds for a research project to investigate and study the extent and practice of Family Day Care in four of the Health Districts in New York City and to evaluate the soundness of the Family Day Care regulations as written. A three year study, financed by the Children's Bureau, finally got under way in 1963. Unfortunately, the results were inconclusive, but clearly and emphatically indicated the need for further study.

Beginning in 1957 numerous staff meetings and discussions on code revision were held by the Day Care Unit with Mr. Grad and his staff. Together they analyzed the soundness and effectiveness of existing principles and practices and probed possible ways of updating, clarifying and improving them. Administrative procedures already tested and worked out in practice were recommended for inclusion in the revised code.

After thorough discussion and deliberation, recommendations for change were submitted to the Board of Health with detailed explanation and full justification. After their official approval they went into effect as of October 1959, marking another milestone in the forward movement of day care. Although public hearings were not held on the recommended code changes, a series of preliminary drafts was prepared and widely circulated to concerned local, state and national organizations, associations and public departments, as well as to recognized leaders in the early childhood field. They were requested to study each draft and to respond with comments and recommendations. As their criticisms were received, each was given thoughtful consideration. When appropriate, they were incorporated in a subsequent draft and recirculated. Meetings and conferences were held with representatives of concerned groups by Mr. Grad, members of the Board of Health and other Health Department officials. All viewpoints were heard and most differences satisfactorily resolved.

A few protesting groups were convinced that code regulations were proper and necessary for others, but that they themselves were entitled to exemption. It seemed hard for them to understand the role of a public agency in its concern for the protection, health and well-being of all the children of all the people. To be effective, laws had to apply equally to all.

Code Changes

Following are some of the important changes in the day care regulations brought about by the 1959 revision:

1. Admission to a day care service was now to be limited to "Children between two and six years of age," instead of to "children under six" as heretofore. This was in accord with current thinking that infants and toddlers under two did not benefit from long hours of participation in group living. It was felt that they required more individualized care and mothering in an intimate and friendly home atmosphere. The problem of infant care was still unresolved.

2. There were changes in the requirement regarding the minimum allowance of floor space per child in a day care service. This had been a matter of controversy since the 1943 code went into effect. The original 20 square foot allowance per child had been interpreted by the Health Department as referring to the amount of open space available to each child, unencumbered by such fixed objects as pianos, shelves, lockers, etc.

   Some operators interpreted the regulations as meaning 20 square feet of wall-to-wall space, therefore allowing serious overcrowding (which increased their income). Since other public departments had traditionally measured space on a wall-to-wall basis, the matter needed clarification. The controversy was settled by a code revision requiring 30 square feet of wall-to-wall space for every child in attendance, as a minimum. This was still less than the minimum 35 square foot allowance considered adequate by such state and national standard-setting organizations as the Child Welfare League of America and the New York State Education Department. The compromise on 30 square feet of space per child, although regrettable, seemed reasonable in view of the extreme limitations of available space in New York City.

   On the other hand it might well have been argued that young children, already living in a cramped and crowded home environment, should be entitled to more "stretch space" during their daytime hours. Fortunately many day care operators, concerned with the critical need of young children for active play in open areas, were successful in finding premises with space that exceeded even the 35 square foot allowance.

   The 1959 code revision also indicated that the Health Department might "in its discretion" specify on the permit a somewhat higher maximum number of children for attendance during the summer months upon consideration of the availability of additional outdoor space. This was feasible because children tended to be outdoors more than indoors during July and August in New York City.

3. A new system of issuing permits was adopted. Upon receiving an application, the Health Department might, in its discretion, issue a temporary preliminary six-month permit. This allowed a program to operate under the legal jurisdiction of the Health Department prior to the issuance of its regular two year permit. This afforded the Day Care Unit staff the opportunity to observe the actual operation of a program before recommending the granting or denial of a permit. It also afforded the operator time to remedy any minor violations and to make effective use of the consultant's help.

4. Transportation of children from their homes to their day care service was also dealt with. Mounting traffic congestion and the lengthening distances to be covered made regulation necessary. The convenience to busy and often harassed parents of having their children picked up and delivered, door to door, often outweighed the undesirability of having children spend tedious, unprofitable and often long and trying hours in daily transportation. Too often the driver was the only adult in the car.

Every vehicle used for transporting children was now required to have on its windshield an unexpired certificate of inspection and approval issued by the Public Service Commission. No child was to travel more than one hour daily between his home and the day care service. Even this, for young children, seemed excessively long and often beyond their tolerance. Realizing this, many Day Care operators admitted only children who lived within a limited geographic area in order to restrict travel time, which should preferably have been not over half an hour each way.

Consultants encouraged operators to plan their routes so as to avoid possible accidents, use the shortest possible routes and approach each home from the nearest curb. Plans were also made to provide both staff and parents with adequate knowledge of their children's whereabouts at all times.

More and more day care operators provided volunteers or paid adults to ride regularly with the children in addition to the driver, a practice much to be desired. It helped to handle fatigue and children's occasional motion sickness. It guaranteed that an adult would always be present with the children in the event of an emergency and made it possible for the driver to escort each child to his own door and make sure that his parents were at home.

5. Detailed requirements for the certification of teachers and directors in the field of early childhood education were clearly spelled out in accordance with administrative agreements already reached between the city and the State Education Department.

   The object was to assure a staff of professionally qualified directors and teachers in every day care service.

   By January 1959, 1160 directors and teachers (79 percent of the total) in some 500 licensed programs had become fully qualified according to state standards. Twenty percent were actively working toward completion of their certification, according to officially approved plans. Only 1 percent had not yet met either of these requirements.

6. According to the 1943 code regulations, children with frequent epileptic seizures or an objectionable physical or mental condition had not been allowed admittance to a day care agency. In the 1959 revision this regulation was deleted entirely. Handicapped children were now to be admitted to programs for normal children so long as their needs could be adequately met and their presence would in no way jeopardize the safety and well-being of the other children. The physician, in examining a child before admission, would assume responsibility for recommending the admission or nonadmission of a handicapped child. He would also recommend any necessary treatment or modification of activities for any child to be admitted, with plans for his health supervision.

   Daytime groups of handicapped children now also came under the licensing supervision of the Department of Health. This included children who were blind, deaf, crippled, mentally or emotionally ill, suffering from speech defects, or multiply handicapped. This was another important milestone in improving conditions for children, for they had so often previously been considered social outcasts, kept hidden from public view. Now they were to be publicly recognized, accepted and helped.

   Licensing also affected those groups of handicapped preschool children living in any state institution within the boundaries of New York City. When the children receiving 24 hour care away from home were joined by six or more children for daytime care, they came under code regulations, with the agreement of the State Department of Social Welfare. Since there was a noticeable trend at the time in favor of keeping young handicapped children in their homes and with their families whenever possible, increasing numbers of such children went to the specialized institutions for training and peer contacts during the daytime hours only. More and more such groups then became licensed.

7. The revised regulations of 1959 established a number of improve-

ments in the physical premises and facilities used for children. These included new and improved lighting to be free from flickering, glare and uneven diffusion; drinking water to be not only near classrooms and playrooms but also to be within easy reach of the children; outdoor as well as indoor areas were to be safe, clean and readily accessible to the children, adequate in size and suitable to their needs.

8. A day care service was newly defined as applying to groups of six or more children under six rather than to four or more as previously.

Opposition to code regulations and defiance toward meeting them had by this time diminished noticeably. Only one relatively small group of commercial operators, after reluctantly meeting minimum requirements, but with a considerable show of resistance, managed to remain in "business." This group, first organized in 1943, ostensibly to stop the Department of Health from its day care licensing effort now resumed its negative activity to the revision of the code. The members again interpreted the Day Care Unit's efforts at standard raising as interference with their private industry of day care. Calling themselves the Metropolitan Association of Private Day Schools, they brought legal action against the Commission of Health, declaring five sections of the revised code regulations unconstitutional and attempting to restrain their enforcement. They claimed that the regulations were inconsistent with the laws of the State of New York and that they encroached upon the powers and functions of the State Education Department.

In a decision rendered by the Honorable Judge James S. Brown, of the Kings County Supreme Court, the charges of the Metropolitan Association of Private Day Schools were declared groundless. The judge stated that the Health Code as enacted did not "conflict, encroach upon or abrogate the regulations of the State Board of Education, but rather ran parallel and led to an enforcement of them." The judge also stated, in further interpretation of his decision:

Section 538 of the New York City Charter endows the Board of Health with a broad discretion in the selection of measures by which public health may be protected within the field of its jurisdiction. The Health Code of the City of New York has the force and effect of law within the city's boundaries.

The physical and psychological needs of the children cannot be separated. The purpose of the Health Code was to embody therein the most modern concepts and policies of health practice in nursery schools and kindergartens designed to protect and promote the physical as well as the psychological needs of children.

The mere fact that an enactment of a statute results in reduced income

48

and inflicts other pecuniary injury does not establish a denial of constitutional due process or equal protection under the law.

There can be no doubt that they (the code requirements) are calculated to protect the health and welfare of the children of our city in accordance with modern concepts and policies of public health practice.[2]

The complaint was dismissed and once again the soundness and effectiveness of the day care regulations were vindicated by the courts. The 1959 revision was thereby strengthened. It was clear that power as vested in the Board of Health by the New York City Charter, authorized it to add, alter, amend or repeal any part of the Health Code relating to the security of life and health. Its powers were not limited to matters of physical health alone. Its authority to regulate with respect to the health, safety, welfare and care of children within the City of New York was incontrovertible. The plaintiffs had failed to establish that the regulations of the revised code were arbitrary, discriminatory or unreasonable. It was established that, without doubt, they were calculated to protect the health and welfare of the children. Several community groups, including the Early Childhood Education Council of New York City, were granted leave by the court to appear as *amicus curiae* in support of the Department of Health.

In other cities too, it seemed, groups of private, commercially minded day care or nursery school operators had from time to time vehemently protested community efforts to establish mandatory day care standards. The New York City experience was not an isolated one.

---

2. Reported in the New York Law Journal of October 9, 1963.

CHAPTER V

SUMMER DAY CAMPS
And Year-Round After-School Play Groups

Early in the Day Care Unit's work, it had been found that the rapidly growing summer day camp movement and the year-round after-school recreation movement involved increasing numbers of young children who technically came under code regulation. This had not been anticipated when the initial code revision had been formulated in 1943. Growing pressures, brought on by the congestion of city living as well as the rising costs of 24-hour camping outside the city, had greatly stimulated a summer day camp movement within the city. The total lack of supervision or regulation of these groups by any responsible agency, except for extremely minimal health standards, had made it possible for any person or group, regardless of motive, to enter the field. As suitable play space for children dwindled (both indoors and out), public parks, museums and swimming pools came into more frequent use. As more and more large-scale low- and middle-income housing projects were built, each contained a concentration of young children who had nowhere to go and nothing to do in their out-of-school and summer vacation time and were without supervision. Numerous efforts to serve these children produced a wide range and variety of programs, from best to worst. Some were entirely motivated by profit making with no concern for the children's interests or well-being. The space provided for their recreation was sometimes a vacant lot, a small playground, a restricted lawn area, a remote beach, a school playground, or dark and unsanitary basement rooms, often poorly equipped and offering little of value to the children. The need for well organized, well equipped and responsibly supervised recreational programs became obvious, but difficulties and limitations were severe. Many voluntary philanthropic agencies opened summer day camps and year-round after-school recreation projects. They were insufficient in number and were faced with serious dilemmas, including both financial and space problems. These were usually most acute where the needs were greatest.

Even the use of public parks and other public facilities presented aggravating and sometimes seemingly insoluble difficulties. Park maintenance was often poor, preferred sites could not be regularly assigned as headquarters for exclusive use by a particular group of children since public parks had necessarily to be open to the entire public. Toilets, drinking water fountains, washing facilities, wading and swimming pools were often out of order or overcrowded. Shelter from sun or rain was often unavailable. There was no storage arrangement for supplies, no refrigeration for food, no provision for emergency care in the event of an accident or illness.

The Department of Health could not ignore the growing tide of concern which brought the manifold and pressing problems of day camping to its doorstep. A major step was taken in July 1951 by the establishment of a Day Camp Unit in the Day Care Division. The legal jurisdiction of the code was restricted to those groups serving children under six years of age for whom a license was required, but evaluation and consultant services were made available to any camp director who requested them. Complaints were also followed up. All this exerted a considerable influence on the day camps, although resistance was often encountered.

The setting up of the Day Camp Unit had been made possible by two preliminary grants, one from the New York Fund for Children and one from the Field Foundation. A small specialized staff of consultants, initially headed by Minerva Golden (Jorn) [1] became the nucleus of an intensive on-going effort to study the extent and nature of the entire day camp movement in New York City and to seek methods and procedures for its improvement. So it was that another significant and pioneering task, affecting the lives of some 100,000 children, was undertaken.

With an initial staff of three consultants, representing the fields of health, social group work and education, a comprehensive survey of summer day camps and recreation groups was undertaken. This study revealed for the first time the tremendous scope of the day camp move-

---

1. Followed by Lillian Margolin, June Labovitz and Ellen Herz. In 1969 Mrs. Jorn was appointed Coordinator of the Health Department's Infant Group Day Care Program and as liaison to the Department of Social Services.

ment within the five boroughs and revealed those specific aspects of camping in most urgent and critical need of improvement. It showed the wide range of quality of program as well as in motive, size, auspices, adequacy of premises, facilities, equipment and staff. It confirmed the fact that some 100,000 New York City children of all ages were enrolled in about 600 day camps each summer and that the numbers were growing. Although some camps were limited to six or eight children, others were found to enroll as many as a thousand children at one time.

To assist and advise the Department of Health in its work with the day camps, Commissioner Baumgartner appointed a Day Camp Advisory Committee in the fall of 1951. Its membership was drawn from community organizations, religious groups, professional and citizen groups and governmental agencies having an interest in children's recreational programs. This committee gave valuable help in identifying problems in the field, in locating and identifying the camps themselves and in interpreting the work of the Day Camp Unit to their respective organizations and to the public in general. They gave guidance to the Health Department in approaching the total problem of improving day camp standards throughout the city.

A further contribution was made by the work of a subcommittee (later called the "Standards Committee"). This group attempted to develop sound minimum standards for all day camps, including the groups of children of all ages. A proposed day camp code was promulgated, arousing both interest and controversy. Opposing ideas were aired. A series of three semiofficial hearings were held by the Health Department to interpret and clarify the intent of the code proposals and to stimulate the free expression of opinion by the public. Considerable and intense opposition to the idea of mandatory day camp licensing by the Health Department was evidenced in the hearings. The growing protest toward governmental "interference" in the work of private organizations, religious and otherwise, was manifested. It seemed the time was not ripe for what was considered by many to be an arbitrary "intrusion" by government into the day camp field. Fortunately other groups, such as the Play Schools Association and the American Camping Association were already making efforts to improve day camp and recreational standards.

The Day Camp Unit decided to continue to give guidance and consultative service to any camps requesting it while also requiring mandatory licensing under the day care regulations of all groups of children under six years of age. In this way help was offered in the evaluation of any day camp service, as well as in the advance planning of new programs. Invaluable cooperation was given by other Health Department personnel such as school physicians, nutritionists, sanitarians and health educators.

A number of articles, pamphlets and reports on day camping were published and widely distributed. Among these were:

"For the Well-being of Children in City Day Camps," written by the staff of the Day Camp Unit of the N.Y.C. Department of Health and published in October 1951 in "The Child" by the Children's Bureau, Federal Security Agency, Social Security Agency, Washington, D.C. (6 page reprint)

"Standards for Summer Group Programs for Children, with Special Emphasis on Day Camps for Children Over Eight Years of Age," jointly published in May 1951 by the Welfare Council of New York City with the cooperation of the Day Camp Unit of the N.Y.C. Department of Health. This report included a 1950 preliminary report on summer group programs for children with particular emphasis on standards for the physical care and safety of the children. (10 page pamphlet)

"Trends in Day Camping in New York City" by Cornelia Goldsmith and Lillian Margolin was published in June 1952 in Volume 7, No. 6 of the Group Workers' Bulletin of the Social Hygiene Division of the New York Tuberculosis and Health Association of New York City. (7 pages)

"Pointers for Parents Choosing a Day Camp for Children," printed by the Health Department in 1952, was made widely available to parents throughout the city. This brought an indirect but telling influence on camp directors who found parents increasingly aware of the basic requirements of a good camp and ready to question poor practices. (2 page leaflet)

"1950 Survey of Summer Groups and Day Camps in New York City" by the Day Camp Unit of the New York City Department of Health. Published in 1952. (7 pages)

"A Summary Report on Day Camps in N.Y.C. (7/1/51 to 10/1/53)," published by the Day Camp Unit of the N.Y.C. Health Department in 1954. It includes the 1953 Survey of Day Camp and Summer Group Programs. (61 pages)

"A Day Camp Director Speaks," published in 1958, a more comprehensive booklet aimed toward helping the camp director improve his services. (69 pages)

"Pointers for Parents about Day Camps for Children," published jointly by the Bureau of Nutrition and the Day Care Unit, 1958. (3 page leaflet)

"Can We Protect the Health of Day Campers?", a lead article in the Spring 1953 Quarterly Bulletin of the New York City Department of Health, written by Dr. Laurence Farmer and Lillian Margolin.

Only a quarter of a century earlier, not more than a handful of day camps had existed in the city. During the decade from 1933 to 1943, there had been such a dramatic and rapid growth that by 1950 there were 600 in operation. The community realized, with a start, that it was caught in a growing movement, often offering programs of questionable value to children, yet obviously there to stay. Complaints in increasing numbers reached the Health Department about unsafe, unsanitary and otherwise undesirable conditions in day camps. Visits by the Day Camp staff found many of the complaints to be justified. With the establishment of the Day Camp Unit, another long, hard pioneering task was undertaken.

CHAPTER VI

COPING WITH EXPLOITATION
Deliberate or Unintentional

In so large and complex a city, with its heterogeneous and mobile population and its rapid growth during the mid-twentieth century, it was to have been expected that some day care directors would enter the field for purposes of self-aggrandizement. This could be achieved only by depriving the children of such rights as sufficient space, safe premises, appropriate and sufficient staff members, suitable food, toys and equipment. Day care was not a field from which small fortunes could be amassed, normal operating costs of a good program were too high. Good business management usually provided sufficient income to cover the costs of adequate salaries, maintenance, etc., but not much more for groups of 30 or more children. For smaller groups the financial struggle to make ends meet was a constant one. Fortunately most boards as well as most directors were well-intentioned and struggled to improve their services. Only a relatively small minority was found to be unethical or devious, seeking to exploit children for their own profit. Among these a few revealed conditions so critical as to make immediate action imperative. In such instances when court action was too time consuming to safeguard the children from immediately hazardous conditions in which they were inescapably caught, only the Society for the Prevention of Cruelty to Children had the authority, under acute emergency circumstances, to remove the children bodily from the premises, notify their parents of the circumstances and place them in a temporary shelter to await a satisfactory plan for their care. Even under apparently reliable auspices, children were sometimes found to be neglected or endangered and the public deceived.

The motives and abilities of those offering services to young children covered an incredibly wide range. The Day Care Unit consultants, eager to help operators to improve their programs in every way possible, were initially quite unprepared to recognize and cope with those contriving deliberately to circumvent the day care regulations of the Department of Health for their own financial gain but detrimental to the children's welfare. As the eyes and minds of the consultants became sensitized to the dim and shadowy light of malpractice, clues to deceptive practices and procedures became more readily recognizable. When they had reason to surmise that things were not as they seemed, visits were made more frequently and without previous appointment. When the discrepancies became sufficiently apparent to be discussed, the operator would be told that unannounced and more frequent visits would be made until all violations had been overcome, reliability established and mutual confidence restored. Visits were then made at differing hours of the day and on different days of the week, making false record keeping, concealment of children and other deceptive practices difficult, if not impossible.

One nursery school director, with a strong profit-making motive, enrolled one more group of children than his space allowed. By an ingenious plan he sought to conceal the overcrowding. He used the school station wagon as an extra facility, to house one group of children on a rigidly scheduled rotating basis. In this way each of the four groups in turn was relegated for a specified period of time each day to journeying through the streets in a chauffeur-driven car, while three groups legitimately occupied the school premises. As each itinerant group returned to the school at a precisely scheduled time, it was replaced by another group, regardless of weather or circumstances. That mealtimes, resttimes and playtimes all had to be staggered was not to be observed by a casual visitor. When the consultant's visits were announced in advance, it was possible to keep one group out of the building all day and to falsify the attendance records accordingly. When she began to make unannounced visits the deception became apparent. The over-aggressive owner of this school had employed a technically "qualified" but subservient director who was presumably in charge but who was fearful of losing her job if she spoke up against a practice she could not condone. This school charged high fees, was in a high-income residential neighborhood, continued to require close supervision at all times.

As mentioned in the previous chapter, citizen complaints and false advertising became major clues to locating wrongdoers and agencies operating without a license. The following letter of complaint was typical of many received by the Day Care Unit:

Dear Sirs,

At this house where we live also is a woman named Mrs. K. She is taking care of a whole lot of young children of working mothers. She has no license. Ten years ago this same woman, under another name, had her lucrative business at another address. Your department reprimanded her. Now she doesn't even dare to give fresh air to those children for fear of their being seen and being reported to you again.

I beg you to call on her and forbid her to take care of children. She is much too old and too frail to give them proper care.

Respectfully yours,
Mrs. M.L.

A prompt field visit by the Day Care Consultant verified the complaint. A sickly elderly woman over 70 was caring for 15 infants and toddlers in her small apartment, under most deplorable conditions. The parents were notified to remove their children and advised to place them only in licensed agencies. They were then referred to the Information and Counselling Service of the Department of Welfare for further guidance. Quite often elderly women whose children had grown and left home and whose husbands had died, found themselves with a large empty house, a limited income and no job competencies. Their experience years before in raising their own children seemed to them entirely adequate preparation for operating a nursery school in their own homes. To them, renting rooms to boarders seemed unladylike and demeaning, selling the house too uprooting. Usually, as the code was interpreted to them and it became clear that they would have to employ a qualified teacher to take charge of the program, the incentive and the enthusiasm dwindled, as both their financial profit and their community status would be diminished.

At times deliberate deception went on even under religious auspices. A group of tenants in an apartment house complained that a church was operating an unlicensed and badly overcrowded day nursery in their building. The minister was contacted. He feigned complete ignorance of the code regulations, although the Day Care Unit records showed that a copy of the code had been sent to him some months previously. To prove his good faith the minister promptly made application for a license for 50 children. According to the regulations, the available space allowed for only half that number. At a subsequent office conference with the minister and the members of his day nursery board, full and fervent cooperation was assured. Every code regulation would be met in full. The minister declared vehemently that, "Nothing, not even the Board of Health, will come before our service to humanity through this day nursery." Coincidentally, an inquiry related to this situation reached the Day Care Unit office at just this time. It came from the District Attorney's office and was in reference to this same minister who had been well known to the D.A.'s office over a period of many years. It seemed he had previously spent a year in jail, had been required to pay a $500 court fine for having committed grand larceny and before that had been convicted of operating a house of ill fame. Christine R. Kefauver, then Legal Counsel to the Department of Health, in recommending denial of license to the minister, stated that "a permit is not a right but a privilege" and that "barring arbitrary or unreasonable actions on the part of the grantor of the license, he may refuse a permit where the bad character of the applicant justifies it. In this case, where the man has a criminal record, the Department (of Health) was completely justified in refusing to entrust the physical and moral welfare of little children to the care of such a person."

On the front lawn of a simple frame house in a residential area, a tremendous sign had been erected announcing that this was a school for all children of all ages, whether normal or handicapped, whether enrolled by the day, the month or the year, whether requiring class instruction or individual tutoring and with transportation offered to all parts of the city's five boroughs. Apparently no child would be excluded, no matter how far he might have to travel or what might be the nature of his problem. Upon entering the school, the Day Care consultant was immediately impressed by the unbelievable array of framed diplomas and degrees that hung on the walls of the office through which one entered the school. All named one or the other of the codirectors, who were presumably man and wife. According to the framed documents one was an M.D. and the other a Ph.D. The poorly equipped classrooms with their rows of fixed desks were meagerly attended. As an inept teacher sat at her desk at the front of the room, the children behaved like puppets being put through a familiar act. The program seemed disorganized and meaningless. Everything seemed unreal—like a stage play. A young crippled child sat idly and most uncomfortably throughout the morning on the hard wooden seat of an adult size desk with her feet dangling. Something was obviously seriously wrong. Why were these children here?

The school library, adjacent to one of the classrooms, gave a startling clue. The shelves on three walls were filled with large sets of obsolete and obviously unused high school textbooks. The fourth wall was filled from floor to ceiling with up-to-date gynecological medical books and journals. And from this library, another door led directly into a physician's fully equipped medical examining and operating room. The Commissioner of Health ordered an immediate investigation of the premises to begin the morning after the consultant's visit. The investigation made the previous day's visit seem like a mirage. The medical books had been entirely replaced by colorful children's books and the medical office completely transformed into an attractive teacher's lounge. Further investigation was obviously indicated. All the diplomas and degrees hanging on the office walls proved to be fraudulent. The codirector who had claimed to be an M.D. was found to have been a pharmacist whose pharmacy license had been previously revoked by the State Board of Pharmacy. Procedures to close the school were immediately initiated with the active cooperation of the State Education Department. The codirectors of the school were however not to be so easily thwarted. They purchased a small stone church building in the neighborhood and persuaded a Rabbi to take charge and to make application in his own name to the Department of Health for a license to operate a new Day Care Agency. The meager program continued as before, inadequately staffed, disorganized, and poorly equipped. The children drifted about aimlessly. Both the Rabbi and the codirectors were then taken to court by the Day Care Unit. After innumerable postponements and delays, the court finally upheld the Health Department's recommendation for denial of license and the school was finally and irrevocably closed.

During World War II, when food rationing was still in effect, a distressed government rationing officer called the Day Care Unit about an event which had occurred on the previous day. He reported that a strange, over-emotional woman, claiming to be the owner and operator of a large private school, had requested him to replace her food ration ticket, which she said had been lost. Her obvious personality disorder and unkempt appearance had made the officer suspicious and he had refused to issue her another ration book. All night he had worried about the possibility that he might have made a wrong decision and that the hundreds of children in that school might be left without food. "Is there such a school," he asked, "and is the owner a reliable person?" The school and the owner were only too well known to the Day Care Unit. It operated four different nursery schools which came under the jurisdiction of the Unit, as well as a large boarding school and home and a camp in an adjoining state. All were under close surveillance. Many complaints from both teachers and parents had been received. Numerous serious charges against the school by parents had resulted in court action, but it seemed that such cases were always dismissed. The woman in charge of the advertising department of a large metropolitan newspaper had previously called the Day Care Unit to inquire what action was being taken against this school. She too had met the owner and after a visit to the school had refused to accept any more advertising for the school. This school, too, accepted any children who applied at the highest fee obtainable. This included normal children as well as those with severe emotional problems, mongoloids, those with cerebral palsy and those who were mentally retarded. All were admitted with alacrity and with promises that the school would prepare them for admission to the public schools. Anxious parents who had trouble finding any facility that would accept their children, or who were unable to accept a true diagnosis of their child's difficulty, flocked to this school. Many consultant visits and office conferences had already taken place and data was being gathered. Nevertheless, as the result of the ration officer's call, an immediate unannounced visit was made by a day care consultant. She arrived at the school just before noon. As she approached the entrance, a grocery boy pushing a well-loaded cart entered the gate. Entering with him, the consultant casually lifted the cover of the cart revealing quantities of meat, butter and other shortage items that could presumably not be purchased without a ration card. Commenting that the children in this school were obviously not suffering from any food shortage, the boy smiled broadly, winked slyly and replied "Any school could do the same by admitting the butcher's children to the school without fee." To close this school was an extremely time-consuming task. It required the cooperation of the State Education Department which found the quality of the educational program so far below minimum standards, the premises so unhygienic, the food so inadequate, the teachers so inept, that it was officially declared "not a school" and ordered closed. To terminate its activities the doors of the school had finally to be padlocked by the Police Department upon the order of the Commissioner of Health, as a risk to the public health. Congratulations poured into the Day Care Unit office, from individuals and organizations after the closing of this school. For years it had been a blemish on the body politic.

Wherever children were considered as commodities, to be merchandised to order for the convenience of each parent customer, educational goals were either nonexistent or lost, the school having totally forsaken its declared purpose. Two young men, recently released from the armed services, requested an immediate office conference with a

Day Care consultant. As a means of livelihood they were planning to form a partnership in order to operate a day care agency. They had come to New York from Florida where they had heard that "there was real money to be made in this business in New York City." They knew nothing about children and cared less. Eagerly they sought advice as to which section of the city would be most lucrative, where parents would be able to pay the highest fees. As the code regulations were reviewed and interpreted, their interest ebbed away. "But surely," they said, "there must still be some cities that are free of such awkward obstructions as mandatory standards and regulations in regard to day care services?" Unfortunately their choice was still wide. They left the city disappointed and quite disillusioned but apparently still hopeful of finding greener pastures, where they might still make their fortune "off young children." Many ingenious plans for group "baby-sitting services" came from a wide variety of sources such as heads of department stores offering children's clothing, toys or furniture, film houses, bowling alley operators, toy manufacturers and exhibitors, and operators of beauty shops, barbershops and laundromats. To relieve parents from the care of their children so as to free them to purchase their products or services was usually their sole purpose. The children themselves were of minimal concern. They seldom warranted proper supervision, adequate space and an appropriate setting. When operators were told that they would have to comply with Section 198 of the Sanitary Code of the Department of Health, including an up-to-date record on the premises of each child's medical record and health history before admission, they usually abandoned the project. Other means of relieving parents of the care of their children, which would benefit both children and parents, would have to be found. One manager of a national chain of launderettes decided there was money to be made for his organization by incorporating a child care service in his laundry, cleaning and shoe-shining shops. He decided to try out his idea in his New York City shop first. There he selected a dark, unused corner of the shop, installed a low partition with a turnstile entrance, equipped it with a round table and chairs, a television set high on the rear wall, a few desultory toys and a practical nurse in a white uniform to be in charge. Numerous parent and citizen complaints were received immediately. A day care consultant made an unannounced visit. A few straggling children, including infants in their carriages as well as school-age youngsters, had been admitted and tagged with their names and the hour of their admission. Children of any age could be "dropped off" at any time and picked up at any time so long as they paid the required hourly fee, which was just below what a parent would pay to a "baby-sitter" in her own home. The nurse looked indifferent and bored as she tagged the few children who came and collected the fees from the parents of the few who left. The local manager showed little interest in the project, stating that it was not paying off. The nurse would soon have to be replaced by a less costly employee. He responded in the affirmative when asked whether he had young children of his own, but added unhesitatingly that he would never want to have his children in this group. He seemed greatly relieved when told by the consultant that the program was operating in violation of the Health Code and would have to be discontinued at once. The children had been "more trouble than they were worth" he said.

A diaper service advertised blatantly that it was making arrangements to accommodate up to 1,000 infants and children during the coming Christmas holiday season. Every child left with them would be entitled to 1½ hours of "free parking." Each mother would receive a numbered tag to match the numbered tag which would be placed on her child's arm band, to make identification easy. The "baby-sitters" were to be 30 attractive models selected from an institute for models. According to the advertisement, each model would have received an "extensive training course in the art of 'baby-sitting'." Fortunately, insufficient numbers of mothers responded and the plan was quietly abandoned.

A young hospital attendant, entirely untrained, had worked in a hospital baby ward. She found the work too strenuous and demanding, the pay too low, and she resented having to work only under the supervision of qualified nurses. She gave up her job and set up a replica of a baby ward in her own home where she could be her own "boss." Here she found the work much easier, the pay much better and the freedom from supervision entirely delightful. Outside her apartment, in a crowded and impoverished part of the city, she hung her shingle:

ATTENTION . . . . ATTENTION

Children kept by the day or week.
Infants our specialty.
Special attention to newborn and
underweight babies.
Now you may go to work or
take a vacation and know that
your darling is in the best of hands.

62

Our services are at the very lowest prices.
Take the opportunity to go out
and earn money today.

All this was in the name of "The Empire Darling Service." In spite of the urgent need for such services in the neighborhood and the good intentions of the operator, the project had to be terminated.

A rash of complaint letters and phone calls were received about a particular private nursery school from the very day it opened, in spite of numerous and thorough-going preliminary conferences. The complaints came from both parents and teachers and were primarily focussed on the untrustworthiness of the director, a personable, technically qualified but unreliable person. She knew the professional "lingo" and used it freely, but primarily to impress. The school was a show place, with serious defects behind the gay and colorful "scenery." Her aim was to establish a chain of nursery schools across the country, but always serving families in upper income neighborhoods. Door to door transportation was offered to any part of the five boroughs, at an extra fee. Three- and four-year-olds might travel an hour each way daily in order to attend a two or three hour program. The school accepted children for two, three, four, five or six days per week, for either morning, afternoon or all day sessions. Anything that parents requested, demanded or found convenient was promised, if it were paid for. Children were being shuttled in and out of the school constantly, as though it were Grand Central Station. Any teacher who openly criticized the meager and confused program was immediately fired, labelled as incompetent, her salary was withheld and she was threatened with court action. Any parent who complained about the school's failure to carry out agreements made to her was placated and cajoled with new promises. When a Day Care consultant identified specific and irrefutable code violations, those particular ones were promptly eliminated while equally serious new violations were deliberately permitted to occur. Whenever the consultant offered criticism, the director shouted "prejudice." False advertising, broken promises, recurring code violations, the false front, were aimed at hiding the mediocrity of the program. The complexity of the total organizational structure, made it necessary to keep close and constant, though unwelcome, surveillance of this school, year in and year out. Hopefully, parents would become increasingly aware of how to evaluate a quality program and would demand something better for their children.

In New York City, as in all the restless and growing big cities in the United States, the very young, the very old and the helpless seemed to be ready targets for exploitation by the ignorant and the misinformed as well as by the malicious. Safeguards had to be firmly established and upheld. The more lucrative and easy the rewards, the more numerous became the attempts at exploitation, whether deliberate or unintentional. Two attractive, intelligent young women came in to the Day Care Unit office enthusiastic about what they thought was a new and original idea. They admitted from the beginning that they were primarily eager to make a lot of money quickly and easily. Their plan would also help harassed parents of infants who could not leave their babies for an evening of recreation at a theater, concert, movie or dance. They planned to open a night-time group "baby-sitting service" for infants under 2½ years of age. They would rent a store in the heart of the theater district in Manhattan to accommodate from 40 to 50 infants. Each child would be kept in a special, separate and enclosed cubicle to avoid contagion. The hours of care would be from nine o'clock to midnight. Fees would be 24¢ per hour, with an extra charge of 15¢ for each diaper change, 15¢ for each formula feeding and 35¢ for each meal feeding. They estimated their monthly expenditure at $1,200 and their monthly income at $2,400. Their enthusiasm dwindled when the health hazards of such a plan were brought to their attention. Although keenly disappointed to learn that their project would be disallowed as detrimental to the children and as contrary to law, they accepted the verdict with good grace and went out to seek their fortune elsewhere.

It seemed to be a common belief that anyone at all could take care of other people's children, so long as it was in the good cause of helping the mother. People seemed to be under the impression that the reason for placing a child in any day caring facility was primarily to make it possible for the mother to go to work, or to provide her with relief from the relentless burden of child care, or to give her an opportunity for some well-deserved relaxation and recreation. The lack of readily available grandparents or other relatives, the disappearance of household help, the mobility of families and the rising cost of living all accentuated the mother's legitimate and urgent need for relief. Yet her role alone did not present the total picture.

While it was necessarily the adult who made the rules and regulations in every household and the adult who was responsible for carrying out such plans, it was the children who too often became disadvantaged captives to the plans. Mothers who needed desperately to go to work to get off the relief rolls or who wished (for whatever reason) to take their places in the growing army of women in the labor force, saw any all-day child care program as of primary importance to them. Yet it was as necessary for the center to be right for the child as it was for the job to be right for the mother. She considered the many factors regarding her job with the greatest of care. What was to be the salary? What were to be the hours? Was the location convenient? Did she have the appropriate job competencies? What would be her fringe benefits? Her take-home pay? Was transportation available? Would she be required to join a union? Was it the best job available?

But for the young child about to have his first regular group experience with his peers and away from home, it was even more important to ask whether he was ready to separate from his mother and to take his place in a group program. Were the demands of group living too overwhelming? Would the adult in charge be able to give him the individual attention that would help him meet the vigorous and untried challenges of his new environment? Was he ready for the weaning from home and family—always a close tie, no matter how disadvantaged his family might be? Was he able to express himself, by word or action, so as to be understood? Would he be valued as a unique and worthwhile person in his own right? Were the hours too long for him to tolerate? While the woman chose her work, the child had to accept his placement, with no alternative. Yet the child was to spend *his entire waking day* for five, or sometimes six, days of every week in the child care center. And this was during *the most impressionable and vulnerable years of his entire lifetime.* The child had need for more than food, shelter and safety. He had hunger for acceptance, for companionship, for finding his place in the sun, for opportunities to learn, to ask questions, to gain confidence, to have fun and to extend his horizons. How carefully then should a center be chosen in terms of the readiness and personality of each particular child! Parents should select with care, visit in advance of the child's placement and carefully observe the program in action. Possible alternatives should be considered. For some children, a homemaker as a mother surrogate, or a family day care service, might be preferable to long hours of group care. In making such decisions, the guidance of a well-informed social worker, familiar with community resources and with the needs of young children and their families could be of inestimable help. The total situation deserved the most careful consideration as to the needs of both mother and child. Neither should be sacrificed to the other. When this was done, exploitation whether deliberate or intentional went out the window.

CHAPTER VII

THE CONSULTANT'S ROLE
An Essential Factor

Ordinarily a "consultant" is a person referred to for his expert advice or guidance in some specialized field, whose help is sought by the recipient. The Day Care Consultant's task became more complicated and difficult because his role required that he give not only skilled professional guidance and evaluation but that he also assume responsibility for the interpretation and enforcement of mandatory legal standards. Under these circumstances he had a difficult, dual role to play. Whether or not his help was sought or even welcomed, he was obligated to offer it and even when necessary to demand compliance with the legal regulations. To handle this sensitive, double task required unusual insight and tact as well as courage and wisdom. Although the majority of day care operators cooperated with varying degrees of enthusiasm, some resented what they called "interference" with their private affairs by a public employee. Many, having received no previous evaluation or supervision of any kind, had operated for decades comfortably unaware of any need for improvement. This was particularly true of some commercial operators and of the independent long established day nurseries, each deeply convinced that theirs was the best service in the city. The idea of any criticism whatsoever, was an error they felt was not to be tolerated.

Just as the success of a day care program depended on the skill, integrity and dedication of its director and staff, so the ultimate success of a day care standard raising and licensing unit depended without doubt on the caliber, skill and dedication of its consultant staff. This was equally true regardless of the particular profession from which the consultant might have been drawn, whether pediatrics, early childhood education, psychiatry, psychology, nursing, guidance, pediatrics, nutrition, sanitation, mental health or social work. Every day care consultant became a front-line pioneer responsible for carrying out a most delicate and often formidable frontiersman's task with a strong public relations component. The several aspects of his role were sometimes hard to reconcile and to interpret. A fundamental honesty of approach, a genuine liking for people (adults as well as children), an awareness of community needs and resources, an objectivity and consistency, combined with a reasonable flexibility but above all a maturity of judgment were basic. The consultant's work demanded both a friendly, nonthreatening approach and the judicious use of peremptory legal authority. While maintaining positive human relations whenever possible, he needed also to handle his modicum of authority without arbitrariness or attitude of superiority. Fortunately it was possible for the consultant staff to allow a reasonable extension of time to an operator who was making a sincere effort toward the completion of code requirements. This allowance of time contributed toward the removal of pressures and often helped even the most intransigent to change their attitudes and move confidently ahead.

Day after day the consultant was involved with an incredible variety of people including both professionals and nonprofessionals, from cooks to bus drivers, from architects to students, from teachers to maintenance workers, from parents to volunteers, from community workers to government workers. They dealt with centers providing services of exceptional excellence to others so destitute of quality as to provide only meaningless or even harmful experiences to the children. What a many-faceted role the consultant had to play!

The critical importance of having a dedicated, mature and skilled front-line consultant staff can hardly be overemphasized. They needed to have the ability not only to observe closely and objectively, but to recognize strengths as well as weaknesses and to see the whole before becoming involved in any specific or peripheral detail. They needed to have a broad, comprehensive perspective in order to be able to help each agency to assess its own potentialities and to determine its own goals and priorities. The consultant often had to make clear to an operator, by word and action, that he had neither the wish nor the authority to impose his personal philosophy or will upon him. His primary responsibility was to assess the operation, interpret the code regulations, assure their full and sustained compliance and be available for further help and guidance as requested or needed. Mandatory authority was used only as a last resort or when children were found to be at risk.

Some examples:

1. The head teacher of a group of blind children was observed by the consultant to have such an overriding absorption in their handicapping conditions as to make every other consideration inconsequential. The teacher recognizing only the children's blindness had conscientiously taken every course offered on eye anomalies at the university —but felt no need to know anything at all about child growth and development. For several months the consultant worked intensively with this teacher in an effort to help her recognize the fact that blind children were *primarily children* and only secondarily blind. The program continued sterile and stilted. In an endless, repetitive refrain the children were told to take their hands out of their eye sockets and to stop their desultory movements such as head or foot banging. Emphasis was entirely on what they should not do because they were blind. At this point even recommended courses in early childhood education were not enough to counter the teacher's obsession and inflexible focus on the child's blemish rather than on his personality development. It was only after the consultant finally recommended that the teacher be replaced by a well qualified and sensitive early childhood teacher (even though unspecialized and inexperienced in blindness) that the children came alive and the program became a true delight to them. The necessary medical and nursing specialists and a psychiatric social worker continued to give the needed expert guidance to the teacher as well as to each child's family.

2. Some traditional day nursery boards, having operated proudly without change for many decades, were valiantly opposed to relinquishing their attitudes of benevolent charity in serving only those children whose parents they personally considered morally worthy and desperately poor. Board membership had become an inherited responsibility, passed on from generation to generation in wealthy families. Each took pride in giving generously of time, effort, and money. What right had the city government, they asked, to interfere with such voluntary alms giving?

   To help in overcoming these outmoded concepts and practices, the Day Nursery Association, first under the leadership of Hilma Satterlee and later of Winifred Allen (Moore) cooperated with the Day Care Unit by conducting a series of institutes for day nursery board members. Here board structure, function and responsibility were fully discussed and newly considered. Gradually a recommended plan for the rotation of board members on a carefully selected basis brought in younger persons who were familiar and sympathetic with new trends and practices in the day nursery field. The day care consultants attended many board meetings to help overcome both the hidden and the open hostilities toward code compliance and to help bridge the gap between old values and new.

Gradually one day nursery board after another replaced its trusted but servile matrons with qualified directors and group teachers. Gradually their intake-procedures changed to include broader categories of need. Gradually too, the content of each day's activities for the children was enriched and made more meaningful. The extremely long day of 10 to 12 hours was shortened whenever possible. The group care of infants was discontinued.

One board transferred its concern for infants to supporting a community agency in a program of family day care of babies in carefully selected and well supervised homes. And gradually board members began to take pride in their identification with change rather than in defending the status quo of custodial care. Typifying this change of attitude were changes in name of a day nursery, such as replacing "The Bread Donor's Day Nursery" with "The League for Child Care."

3. Among the recognized institutions of higher learning in New York City was one which challenged the ingenuity and patience of the day care consultants in an unprecedented way. The wives of graduate-school faculty members opened a parent-cooperative nursery school in an abandoned greenhouse on the university campus. With the employment of a partially qualified teacher-director they were in business, without having made application for a license.

The premise having been found inadequate for flowers was even less adequate for children. However, all correspondence, all efforts to make field visits, all requests for an office conference were ignored. Every possible approach proved to be of no avail. The prestigious university, it seemed, felt itself above and beyond the jurisdiction of the Department of Health.

After several months of futile effort had passed without any response to letters or phone calls, an official letter signed by the Commissioner of Health was sent directly to the president of the university by special delivery, with a return receipt requested by the Health Department. The letter, enclosing a copy of the Sanitary Code (Section #198), frankly described the situation in the nursery school and the lack of response of the teacher-director and the board. The sluice-gates opened wide and a prompt appointment was requested by top echelon representatives of the university with the Commissioner of Health and the appropriate consultants from the Day Care Unit. Communication was established. The innumerable violations were overcome and a license granted. Finally it came to pass that a unique and excellent nursery school, of which everyone could be proud, was housed in a charmingly modernized greenhouse. Later, when the university needed this premise for the erection of a large university building it had to move to other quarters, retaining its original name "The Greenhouse Nursery School."

4. Since the long-day child care centers and day nurseries served children of low income, troubled or broken families or working mothers and the private nursery schools served primarily those who could pay substantial fees, increasing numbers of young middle-income parents fell between the two. Although they valued what a good nursery had to offer their children, they were ineligible for admission to either the day nurseries or the child care centers for they were not impoverished. Yet they could not afford the high fees of the private nursery schools.

With great enthusiasm, nonprofit parent-cooperative nursery schools sprang into high gear to fill the gap. To reduce costs the mothers volunteered their time and skills with ardent zeal. A half-day program, close to their homes, usually met their needs. Once a site was selected, the fathers helped in the construction of equipment and play materials and handled the repairs and painting during their evening hours. The mothers helped with the housekeeping, secretarial, transportation and kitchen duties and some worked as assistant teachers or relief teachers.

It became the consultant's task to help harness and use the vigor, intelligence and enthusiasm of these impatient young parents while helping them to work through their numerous and often unrecognized problems. As was to have been expected, the consultants usually found such groups lacking in organizational skills, without agreement on essential administrative, personnel or budget policies or on their educational goals. Each mother assumed that in a cooperative every other mother would cooperate with her. They were often unaware of the need to meet basic code requirements and of the need for some experienced professional leadership.

The educational director of a successful parent-cooperative needed the insight and skill of working both with the participating parents and with the children. Such schools, when well founded offered unique benefits to the child and to his family. Perhaps the most difficult aspect of the consultant's job in relation to parent-cooperative nursery schools was to use a checkrein on the actual opening until unanimity of purpose had been achieved, areas of responsibility defined, budget clarified, health, fire and safety standards met, and personnel and grievance machinery established. Working out a set of preliminary by-laws was a great help in reaching mutual agreement. When sufficient time was allowed, many cooperatives worked through their problems to successful operation. Unfortunately others too quickly lost their initial enthusiasm, relinquished control to the most aggressive members, found that they lacked sufficient funds and fell into competing cliques. These contingencies the consultant needed to anticipate and make every effort to prevent.

In addition to the personality characteristics of a consultant what should be his training and experience? What should be his motivation? In most of the related fields, such as pediatrics and public health nursing, criteria were already established by the various professions. Nevertheless, even for those professionals whose previous experience with children had been based on individual, one-to-one contacts only as in an office, clinic or hospital, additional observation of and direct experience with groups of young children seemed to be clearly indicated. Only so could even the most highly trained and competent specialist understand the nature of group living and its impact on the young child in his new role as a social entity among his peers. The supervision of a group of young children was found to be quite a different matter than interviewing or examining one individual child at a time in a psychiatrist's or a pediatrician's office.

When the Day Care Unit was first established in 1943, criteria for early childhood education consultants had not yet been officially determined by the New York Civil Service Commission. No such title as Early Childhood Education Consultant existed as yet. It was not until 1949, after the Unit had been accepted on the city's public fund budget, that the Civil Service Commission announced its first open, competitive examination for the position of consultant in early childhood education. This was cause for rejoicing for it verified the acceptance of the Unit as part of the city structure. From then on the Day Care consultant positions could be filled only by individuals who met the Civil Service requirements and passed their Civil Service examinations. In 1950 the first such examination was given, and by 1951 the first so-called "permanent appointments" were made. After passing written, oral and physical examinations, appointments were finalized only after an additional six month period of actual trial on the job had proved successful. Three years later (in 1954) the first examination for Senior Consultant in Early Childhood Education (Chief of the Division) was announced and the appointment officially made as of June 1955. After 12 years had passed, the challenge of the work was undiminished. Although these were days of uncertainty for staff members, all of whom took the examination, nearly all came through with flying colors.

The eligibility requirements for applicants for the position of Consultant in Early Childhood Education, then established by the Civil Service Commission, were as follows:

Candidates must have each of the following or its equivalent,

a) A Masters Degree with a major in Nursery Education.

b) At least 30 semester hours in approved educational courses, 12 semester hours of which must have been in supervised practice teaching in a nursery school, a kindergarten or primary grades and

c) At least three years as an educational consultant in nursery education in an agency adhering to acceptable standards, or as the director of an approved nursery school.

Duties were defined as follows:

To survey, study and evaluate individual nursery schools in order to help them improve the educational service for children in regard to program and administration; recommend appropriate equipment and adequate supervision; establish and interpret standards of acceptable educational care and coordinate this with other services rendered in day care agencies; establish accurate and up-to-date record systems; participate in conferences and community planning in relation to sound standards for the group care of young children; act as consultant to the professional staff as well as to other public and private agencies; perform related work.

Duties for the Senior Consultant in Early Childhood Education who functioned as Chief of the Division were defined as follows:

Under direction to formulate and carry out administrative policies and procedures for the Division of Day Care and Foster Homes; to direct, supervise and coordinate the work of the staff; to cooperate with other agencies in establishing and improving standards of care for children away from home; to act as technical consultant to Health Department personnel, as well as to the staffs and boards of day care agencies, shelters and institutions for children, day camps and play groups; to enforce the regulations of the Sanitary Code with respect to day care agencies, foster homes and shelters; to recommend code changes to the Board of Health where needed; to plan and conduct in-service training programs; to be responsible for research studies or surveys; to perform related work.

No matter how broad and far-reaching the scope of his work, and no matter how numerous or complex the problems of a day care service, it was the consultant's first responsibility to familiarize himself with all aspects of the operation. His overall evaluation and diagnosis often helped to bring disparate parts together and to clarify their interrelationships. It could throw new light on as yet unidentified problems and give a fresh perspective to those so immediately involved that they lost their objectivity. An offer of constructive help or encouragement to an agency often marked the dividing line between a sense of confusion or failure and a readiness to take the necessary steps toward ultimate success.

It was also the consultant's responsibility to help day care operators to clarify both their immediate and their long-range goals and to recognize the relevancy between them. No matter how eager they might be to achieve immediate results, basic gains, once well established and understood, meant far more in the long run than any hasty or superficial gains. Glib temporary solutions, tricky short cuts, and expedient devices were seldom, if ever, of lasting benefit either to the children or to the adults.

In addition to helping with the practical aspects of budgeting, staffing, equipping and planning a sound program for the children the consultants were also concerned with the more subtle aspects of helping to revitalize and regenerate over-routinized and mechanized programs. With an imaginative approach, a keen listening ear, a seeing eye and a patient willingness to explore all possible solutions, consultants were often successful in helping to bring about changes in an operator's attitude toward the children and toward his work. This sometimes took months and even years of patient effort, but the results were gratifying to operator and consultant alike. And the children reaped rich benefits.

Consultants, in their contacts with such a wide variety of operators and agencies in various stages of development, had the rare opportunity of encouraging contacts between those coping with similar problems who might be helpful to each other. Reciprocal visiting provided opportunities to observe and discuss each other's programs. This often resulted in the cross-fertilization of ideas and opened new vistas. Such sharing was sometimes more effective than any amount of theorizing and advising by the consultant.

The day care consultants were, of course, expected to keep abreast of new trends, innovative experiments and research findings in the field of child growth and development at local, state, national and international levels. This meant being "au courant" with a growing mass of professional literature, with research studies and with legislation affecting young children. It meant also the participation in both long and short-range planning with governmental, community and citizen groups and organizations, as well as professional and lay groups with concern for the group living of young children.

It became increasingly clear that the most valuable and rewarding contributions that a consultant could make were those offered at the earliest possible stages of planning. It was then that errors could be most effectively and economically prevented. It was then that the basic tenets of the code could best be interpreted and promulgated. A thoughtful preliminary study and review of site selection might reveal zoning regulations that would disallow the operation of a day care agency. Early review of an architect's preliminary sketches of a proposed new building might help greatly to minimize operational and administrative costs later on. Having sufficient storage areas accessible to each classroom made it possible to purchase toys and equipment at wholesale rather than retail cost. Placing the isolation room for a sick child adjacent to the director's or the nurse's office avoided the necessity of withdrawing a teacher from her group in order to supervise the sick child until his parents could come to take him home. Having a play-yard directly accessible to a classroom made supervision easier and provided greater flexibility in programming. Having a low, flat-bottomed sink with a mixing faucet in each playroom enhanced water play, easel painting and work with clay, and gave children a sense of independence about washing their own paint brushes, getting their own drinks of water and washing their doll clothes and doll dishes.

As lack of space in the city often necessitated the multiple use of space in day care services, playrooms often had to be transformed into both dining areas and sleeping areas. To achieve this, tables, chairs and cots had to be lightweight and stackable. By installing tubular, aluminum furniture, the children could handle the stacking and removal themselves instead of necessitating the employment of a maintenance man to do this work. A convenient outdoor fireproof storage shed with wide double doors, located between two playground areas, prolonged the life of costly movable equipment such as wagons, tricycles, ladders, luggage carriers, large hollow wooden blocks, cleated climbing boards, saw horses, etc. Whenever possible sound-proofing or sound-retarding of the activity rooms was found to be an asset, particularly in long day programs. A centrally located kitchen with separate delivery entrance, adequate and readily available refrigeration, sterilization and food storage facilities diminished the work of kitchen and maintenance staff and brought numerous other operational economies. Where funds were available, a director's conference room, a separate teacher's lounge, a parent's workshop and a sufficiently large community meeting room contributed greatly to the effective functioning of the school and to the neighborhood itself.

Another important and too often overlooked area was the need for a quiet, easily accessible wing or alcove adjacent to each classroom to which a child might feel free to withdraw from the stimulation of constant group interaction, when seeking moments of relaxation, meditation or concentration. Early consideration also needed to be given to having floors draft free, readily cleanable and nonslippery. The outdoor playground needed to be well-drained, offering both sun and shade with opportunities for digging, climbing, planting, running, jumping and swinging. Safety from traffic hazards had to be assured, usually by a sturdy wall or small-meshed metal fence.

It was soon found that each consultant had much to learn from those in the other professions. Constant and simultaneous exchanges kept things on the move, kept them balanced and very much alive. Here was a sound basis for fruitful cooperation as each professional found his special skills not only highly valued by other consultants but also frequently challenged. As everyone struggled to reach a common goal of excellence, each traveled by a different route. In this process, each became something more than he had ever been before. The original decision of the Day Care Advisory Committee to have a multiprofessional consultant staff carry on the work of the Unit was predicated on this assumption. This coordination maximized the use of each one's special skills and minimized duplication of effort, while greatly expanding the scope of the work itself. This proved to be true.

The modicum of staff assigned to undertake such an overwhelming job made it necessary to consider with great care how to make the best possible use of a team approach. With insufficient staff to provide a team to each agency, another plan was evolved. Each consultant was assigned a caseload of day care agencies for which he took primary responsibility. With these he familiarized himself as fully as possible, making the field visits, conducting office conferences, handling all licensing and relicensing procedures, responding to inquiries, answering correspondence, making reports and evaluations, and keeping the file complete and up to date. However, when this consultant found the need for help or guidance in an area outside his skill or experience, he was at liberty to request the cooperation of a consultant from another field to work with him in whatever way seemed indicated. In this way each consultant had his own caseload, assuring continuity of contact, while at the same time each was on call to the others as needed, on a temporary basis. This provided an effective yet flexible team approach giving continuity of contact through the primary consultant while at the same time offering the skills, knowledge and resources of the other professionals as needed. This brought economy in the use of staff time while also utilizing all the expertise within the unit.

Field visits and office conferences were held as often as was deemed necessary in the considered judgment of the primary consultant. New applicants and those with unusually complex or troubled situations required a far more intensive series of field visits and office conferences. On the average, once an agency was well launched and licensed, a regular field visit was made about every six months. Preceding each recommendation for license or the biennial renewal of license, an entire (announced) full day's visit was made. This included observation of the children's activities, indoors and out, at play, at rest and at meals, as well as a detailed checking of health and attendance records. A thorough review conference was then usually held with the director and board representatives, preceding the actual granting or renewal of license.

An effort was made to give each consultant a variety of types of agencies to work with, as well as including in his assignment agencies in various stages of their development. To keep horizons widening and the challenges lively, each consultant was afforded the opportunity to work with new applicants as well as those having operated unchanged for many years, with a church group, a private commercial group, a parent cooperative, a child care center, a group of handicapped children and a demonstration or research center. This diversity helped to keep foremost in the minds of the consultants both the uniqueness of each enterprise and the basic concerns underlying them all. The team approach helped to keep ideas limber and to prevent, to a considerable degree, the competitiveness all too frequently found between professionals from different fields, vying with each other for the major role. When the loyalty of each to his profession became subservient to the loyalty of all to a common human cause, each was enabled to use his special skills to the maximum without competing for dominance. The well-being of young children was such a compelling human cause.

The struggle to secure and maintain sufficient numbers of well qualified consultants to keep up with the growing numbers of day care agencies in operation, became a serious one. As caseloads mounted to sixty or more agencies, the quality and effectiveness of the consultant's task necessarily declined. In order to merely cover the ground at such times, the creative, comprehensive approach had to give way to more cursory, superficial and hasty work. The sap went out of the tree. At such times the job could just as well have been handled by a staff of indifferent file clerks. Fortunately, however, at such times also, the active support of community agencies was forthcoming, after which consultant vacancies were filled, and little by little new positions established. On April 23, 1953, for example, a resolution sent by the Child

Welfare Division of the Welfare and Health Council of New York City to the Mayor, the Board of Estimate and the Director of the City Budget, brought effective action:

> Whereas the Day Care Unit of the Department of Health has provided an essential service to the City of New York in connection with the licensing of day care agencies under Section 198 of the Sanitary Code, giving guidance, direction and setting standards for this field; and

> Whereas this service has stimulated the work of social agencies, private schools, parent cooperatives and commercial organizations to provide services of high quality, while at the same time preventing the continuance of harmful and exploiting services; and

> Whereas knowledge of this licensing authority has given assurance to parents in using these day care organizations for their children, and

> Whereas the projected substantial reduction in the already overloaded field staff of this unit can result only in so crippling the work of the Unit that its usefulness and effectiveness in fulfilling its legal responsibilities would be seriously threatened;

> BE IT RESOLVED that the Day Care Committee of the Welfare and Health Council urge His Honor the Mayor, and the members of the Board of Estimate of the City of New York to continue this Unit at its present size, regarded as minimal in view of the number of licensed agencies (440 at this date) and the volume of related work including investigation of complaints about the neglect and abuse of young children. A smaller staff could discharge neither the legal function nor the intention of Section 198 of the Sanitary Code.

The integration and coordination of the entire staff was brought about not only by their team efforts and the challenge of the work itself but also by the continual inservice training that went on through frequent staff meetings, open dialogue, workshop discussions, conferences and meetings, providing many kinds of opportunities for idea interchanging and elbow-rubbing. Recognizing that no two consultants could be considered identical, the greatest asset of each was in the fullest possible use of his own skill, experience and best judgment. To assure fairness and objectivity, however, it was necessary for the staff to develop a certain consistency of attitude and approach. The code itself provided the basic criteria for judging every program fairly. It was agreed that no one would attempt to impose his personal philosophy on any operator.

Every consultant thus became, of necessity, a keen observer, a good listener, a thoughtful evaluator, an informed guide and a wise counselor. He needed to be able to accept people (himself and others) as he found them, and to proceed from there. As a professional he needed to use his insights and skills to strengthen others as well as himself, whether they were children or adults. His primary goal was the discovery and use of the human potential for the fullest possible benefit to the young child. Only so could the two-way process of teaching and learning become mutual, continuous and effective.

CHAPTER VIII

WHAT HAD GONE BEFORE
Historic Roots of Day Care in New York

Beginnings are seldom as precipitous as they seem. Every changing milieu brings new challenges—awakening, impeding or altering latent trends. Each generation, rejecting to greater or lesser degree the aims and values of its predecessors, rediscovers or reinvents for itself those human goals and values appropriate to its time. Change comes about also because it is man's nature, from earliest childhood and throughout life, to push at the green growing edge of the familiar to investigate and explore what lies beyond. Having pioneered until land, air and water areas had become identified and charted, the drive toward further searching inevitably led him into such new ventures as outer space and deeper knowledge of himself, his fellow human beings and his society. His querying moved from "the what" to "the how" and "the why" of things and events. Each step into the unknown left its imprint on those that followed. Liminal ideas, ignored or unacceptable at one time might be enthusiastically heralded at another. Some measure of readiness there had to be, or the idea returned to dormancy.

To gain perspective in day care, as in any field, it is well to look back from time to time at relevant but changing attitudes and events occurring during its recent past. Often happenings that had created tremendous national controversy and upheaval, once accepted, were taken entirely for granted only a century later. One such event was the attainment of universal, free, compulsory education throughout the United States during the course of the nineteenth century. The fulfillment of this ideal, against vigorous opposition, meant turning entirely away from total dependence on private systems of education based on religious, class and economic distinctions. To provide a common school system of free universal education, supported wholly by public taxation, was a great achievement. . . . It had been accomplished, in the main, throughout all the states by the end of the nineteenth century. Thomas Jefferson had proposed a complete system of public schools for the state of Virginia in 1799, but failed to win the support of his legislature. Beginning with six- or seven-year-old children, the eight year elementary school put primary emphasis on the three Rs, attempting only very gradually to broaden its curriculum. When New York created its state board of regents (1784), under the title "The University of the State of New York," a state superintendent of schools was appointed soon after (1812), the first in the United States. New York, at that time, was known to be the most advanced state educationally.

Even so, education was still considered to be a formal, academic process acquired through concentration on rote learning of factual information best achieved under strict discipline. Children, on the whole, were expected to behave like well-mannered miniature adults, to be seen and not heard.

The Day Nursery

The earliest efforts to bring together groups of preschool children, including infants and toddlers, were those of the Day Nurseries. Here shelter was given to the young children of impoverished women, forced to work during the industrial revolution in order to support their families. Following a pattern originated in Paris in 1844, the first New York City crèche or day nursery was opened in 1852. It was known as the Nursery for the Children of Poor Women, operating in a wooden cottage on St. Mark's Place under the auspices of the Nursery and Child's Hospital.[1]

The day nursery movement spread rapidly across the country without guidelines or supervision of any kind. After the Civil War a number of day nurseries were opened to provide care for the infants and toddlers of war widows. The goals were to "feed the starving, clothe the naked and lighten the soul of half-orphaned mothers who

---

1. In the Museum of the City of New York is a collection of photographs by Edward W. C. Arnold. One of these dated 1827 is labelled "First Infant School" and shows from 200 to 400 small children, all under five, learning their lessons in a church basement "by the aid of a few ladies of respectability." Under the monitorial system (the scholars taught one another to a great extent), decorous babies sat in a row, learning sums out loud in chorus.

'mbert's Lithography.   **VIEW FROM THE ROSTRUM**   *A. Robertson &c.*

Monitor. Nine & Six?   *Scholars Fifteen! &c.*

VIEW FROM THE GALLERY.

The Children Marching & Reciting aloud,"Twice two's Four &c"

81

were forced to seek employment." [2] The six day nurseries established in the United States by 1880 had increased to 90 by 1892, of which 18 were in New York City. A few of these continued to operate, without interruption, for a hundred years. In 1892 the first national conference of day nurseries was held, preliminary to the formation of the National Day Nursery Association. By 1921 there were 110 known day nurseries in New York City alone, out of a total of 600 in the entire United States. Some 40,000 of New York's children of the poor were served in this way. Through charitable means they provided for their care by offering "to feed them, wash them a little, keep them from injuring themselves and return them whole and reasonably happy to their parents." [3] Groups of wealthy, well-intentioned men and women volunteered to form the operating boards. Incorporated under state law as charitable institutions, the board members made contributions, raised funds, employed and instructed the matrons and other caretakers, made home visits to determine eligibility of the children according to the degree of poverty of the family and its morality, and set the fees accordingly.

Day nursery premises varied from large sturdy buildings to unsuitable, dark, shabby rooms in impoverished neighborhoods. Their gloom was often accentuated by the customary dark brown color of walls and woodwork. When parents complained occasionally about the poor care their children received or offered criticism of any kind, they were considered ungrateful and their children often dropped from the rolls. The matron usually lived on the premises where she often became the queen of the castle, living in comfort and even luxury, in sharp contrast to the meager living of the children. Each board member's contribution to the nursery was acknowledged by a large, engraved brass plate conspicuously hung on the children's dormitory wall or fastened to an infant's crib. Cleanliness, orderliness, physical care and a rigid scheduling received major emphasis during the course of each day. Through such day nursery programs, often for 12 or more hours a day, the group care of infants and young children first became visible in the United States.

The 1924 Annual Report of the Association of Day Nurseries contained an article entitled "Day Nurseries in New York City" by E. H. Lewinsky-Corwin, Ph.D., presenting a summary of principal findings of

2. From a typed report in the library of the Child Welfare League of America in a "Historical Sketch of the Day Nursery Movement" New York City, 1940. Page 7. Author unknown.
3. From the Day Nursery Association files in the library of the Child Welfare League of America, New York City.

a study of day nurseries made at that time by the New York Academy of Medicine. A few excerpts give a close-up of the situation:

> The nursery day, in the main, coincides with the mother's day in industry, since she takes the child to the nursery on her way to work and calls for it on her way home. The nurseries having the longest day have the largest daily attendance. One half of the nurseries are open Saturday mornings and a few all day Saturday.

> Many day nurseries are poorly adapted for the work they are trying to do because of the totally inadequate quarters and personnel. . . . There is need for more than perfunctory supervision of day nurseries on the part of the Department of Health. . . . Questions of ventilation, light and other facilities, as well as of staff, do not enter into the prerequisite for a Health Department permit.

> The only requirement of the Health Department for the day nursery premises is related to cubic air space, safety from fire hazards and a certificate of occupancy from the Bureau of Buildings.[4]

> A few nurseries seem to have evolved the theory that education should be the aim of the day nursery and are emphasizing this phase of the work. . . . The standards of day nurseries differ so widely that it seems difficult to speak of them as a group.

> Utilization of the day nursery to the extent of three-quarters of the capacity certified by the Health Department indicates that the aggregate facilities of the city are sufficient; there is however an inadequacy of accommodations for infants under two years of age.

> Only 57 percent of the day nurseries belong to the Association of Day Nurseries which requires minimum standards to be complied with before a nursery can become a member. However, the association has no executive powers. The results accomplished in raising standards are achieved through educational methods alone. The budget of the association is so small that no effective work through frequent inspections can be done.

> The immediate needs in the day nursery field in New York City are:
> a) a well thought out consideration of the scope of day nursery activity in connection with the whole field of social endeavor in order to determine its proper function and

> b) more emphasis on the opportunities of the day nursery in the field of preventive medicine, particularly among preschool children.

The above report by Dr. Lewinsky-Corwin made it obvious that there was growing awareness of the potential for preventive social

---

4. In 1924 the 50 cubic foot allowance of space per child in a day nursery was barely sufficient for an infant's crib (2' by 4' by 6½').

service as well as for education and health benefits to be derived in the group care of infants and young children. It should be remembered that the day nursery had been originated before the fields of social work, pediatrics, child psychiatry and early childhood education had been fully recognized. The child labor laws had not yet come into effect and social security was nonexistent. Although some day nurseries were making contributions to child health in the areas of nutrition, hygiene and regular medical supervision, progress was slow. Yet there were those who were thinking ahead, probing the uncertain future to find better ways of serving young children and their families.

The Kindergarten Movement

While the day nurseries were making headway (in numbers if not significantly in quality of program) another movement concerned with young children, but under the aegis of education, became the focus of attention. It brought evidence of important changes in philosophy and attitude, both overseas and in the United States. The kindergarten movement was based on the idea that preschool children could actually learn through play. As early as 1837, Friedrich Froebel had founded an institution in Germany which he called "the kindergarten," (the Garden of Children). He conceived of kindergarten education as the happy guidance of the preschool child's development through a sequence of carefully planned play activities. He believed that the educational reform most needed involved the early years of childhood, those before regular school age. He believed that humanity as a whole was revealed in each individual child in a unique and mystical way. Education, he thought, should provide for the free personality development of the child through kindly guidance rather than through firm control and severe restriction. Conceiving of man as a social animal, he was convinced that social cooperation should be cultivated from infancy in all children. To him the schoolroom represented society in miniature, with play and self-activity as essential components.

Froebel developed a series of materials and activities to accompany his mystical, philosophical concepts, which he called "gifts" and "occupations." In an orphanage in Switzerland he worked out games, songs, marches and play forms, in what he considered a proper sequence, to guide the young child's development, stage by stage. Only 25 years after his death, which occurred in 1852, kindergartens had been established in all leading cities in the United States. They had become acceptable units of elementary education in many public as well as private schools. Kindergartens became an official part of the New York City public school system in 1883 when a Kindergarten Department was first established by the Board of Education. Four- and five-year-olds were not *required* to attend. Permissive legislation, passed in Albany, allowed communities to provide kindergartens for children whose parents wished to send them without their coming under the compulsory education laws. By 1894, 191 kindergarten children were enrolled in seven New York City public schools. Another forward step occurred in 1945 when the Bureau of Early Childhood Education replaced the Kindergarten Department in the New York City Board of Education. By this time early childhood education was recognized as encompassing not only the kindergartens and nursery schools, but the primary grades as well. For education, like growth, was after all a continuous process rather than a series of separate episodes.

With the growing public acceptance of kindergartens, confidence in the traditional teacher-dominated, routine, mass education of the public schools and the indifferent custodial care offered by the day nurseries came more and more under question. As the young child, who had previously waited to reach school-age in order to be recognized as educable, became the "key child" to his own future. Fundamental changes in the total concept of education began to come about.

1. Individual differences began to be not only recognized, but valued. Personality differences, as well as varied patterns and rates of growth, began to be acknowledged and given credence.

2. The young child was found to be eager to learn rather than resistant to learning. His natural curiosity and enthusiasm needed to be nurtured and enjoyed rather than pushed and pressured. When his environment of things, events and people provided appropriate stimulation, nourishment and encouragement for mind, body and emotions at each stage of growth, he learned.

3. The child was found to be educable from the time of his birth and throughout his entire life. Everything that happened to him, whether at home, at school or elsewhere, every experience affected and influenced him.

4. The child's inner thoughts and feelings, not only their external manifestations, were to be given consideration.

5. As the school began to realize that it had no premium on learning, even though this was its major function, it became essential for home, school and community to cooperate if the child was to develop as a whole person and to attain his fullest potential.

6. Every child's relationships with his peers, as well as with his family and community members had meaning. Attitudes and relationships

affected his ability to learn and affected his I.Q. (Intelligence Quotient).

With the expansion of kindergartens, the need for increasing numbers of kindergarten teachers became apparent. The first New York City training school for elementary school teachers had opened in 1840 (the fourth in the nation); it was not until half a century later (in 1889) that the first kindergarten teacher training school was opened as a two year "Normal School." By 1966 a record number of five-year-old kindergarten children were enrolled in the New York City public school system—92,564—with an additional waiting list of 4,226. By this time, the two year "Normal Schools" had become four year, state accredited, degree granting teacher education colleges. By this time also, there were more degree granting, teacher education colleges offering a major in the field of early childhood education. This gave further evidence of the changing public attitude toward the educability of young children, of play as a legitimate means of learning and of the professionalization of the early childhood education field.

The Nursery School Movement

Another strong influence on the group living of young children was the nursery school movement. The chaotic period during and following World War I had produced a ferment of ideas, changing attitudes and the promulgation of new professions, especially in the humanities. The educational system came under sharp attack. The shock of the war had brought profound dissatisfaction with existing practices and theories on the part of many, as having made the war possible.

In Deptford, London, Rachel and Margaret McMillan had already established the first nursery school for children from two to five years of age (1909). Although instituted primarily to meet social and economic needs, nursery schools from their inception were considered to be instruments of education. Therefore they were called "schools," in contrast to the day nurseries which provided "custodial care" only. The nursery school movement also spread rapidly, gaining support in both England and the United States during a period when ideas and ideals were very much in flux. Replacing the old concept of "child training" with the new concept of "child development" made motivation in the learning process important. Could it be that to encourage and stimulate interest in learning was more effective than to use adult authority merely to command it? The lack of governmental interference or regulation of any kind in the preschool field left the way open to surface and to try out new ideas. The relationship between an educa-

86

tional system and the social order became increasingly clear. The philosophies of Sigmund Freud, John Dewey, Arnold Gesell and many others rallied followers dedicated to experimentalism in the early childhood field. A many-sided, profound interest in the early years was stimulated across the country, creating a new and sympathetic approach to the inner world of childhood and its patterns of behavior. In the plethora of new ideas and methods about child rearing that followed, one common denominator was to be found: the desire to observe, understand and individualize the child with fresh eyes. Only so could the schools be improved and the educational lockstep of the school system be broken.

Nursery school educators, not having been involved in the rigid system of public education, were the most free to innovate. Other previously overlooked and neglected areas of childhood also began to be recognized and gradually dealt with, i.e. the physically and mentally handicapped child, the slow learner, the gifted, the defective, the delinquent, the emotionally disturbed and the disadvantaged. Little by little they too were seen as developing human beings, no matter how thwarted, rather than preordained unfortunate, static organisms, bringing shame and guilt to their parents and unrecognized by society. With the forward looking impetus of a multidisciplinary approach, education began to extend its concern to encompass all children. In so doing it pointed irrevocably to the need for elasticity in approach rather than rigidity, to many approaches rather than to a single model.

Immediately after World War I a number of experimental "progressive schools" came to life in various parts of the country. In New York City a number of these have made lasting contributions to educational thought and have continued to operate since that time. They should be mentioned here. Each had a unique approach, a particular emphasis, that became the core of its program. All agreed that education encompassed the preschool years.

The City and Country School

In 1914 Carolyn Pratt opened her Play School (later called the City and Country School) in Greenwich Village. Although originally focussed on providing an enriched life for young slum children, it soon became an experiment in creative education for all children, regardless of economic status. Without forsaking the three R's, the program was expanded to include the arts, the neighborhood environment and the adult activities essential to meeting the needs of an industrial society. Although books, pictures and other resource materials were used, major emphasis was put on the educational value of direct, firsthand experiences both inside and outside the classroom. Actual seeing, hearing, tasting, smelling, touching and feeling laid the foundation for verbalizing, theorizing, symbolizing and categorizing. The acute senses of the young child were called into play in investigating and extending his world and with help, to seek answers to his boundless questions. The children went on neighborhood trips to such places as wholesale markets, food stores, the harbor, piers, bridges, parks, zoos, fire houses and police stations, a post office, an ocean-going ship, the Staten Island Ferry, etc. Back in their classrooms they were encouraged to reenact their experiences in their own terms. Selecting from a wide variety of materials, both raw and contrived, they rebuilt, relived and requestioned their adventure. With the help of skillful teachers and with access to appropriate books and other resource materials, curiosities were satisfied leading on to further curiosities, enhancing the entire learning process and giving it a new dimension. Carolyn Pratt saw children as embryonic engineers, sculptors, roadbuilders, aviators, musicians, writers, architects and industrialists, all eager to express their ideas, improve their skills and add to their knowledge.

The Walden School

Margaret Naumburg founded the Children's School (later called the Walden School) in 1915. Following the educational approach of John Dewey and using the implications of psychoanalysis, this undertaking sought to find new clues and new, more genuine understandings of the "whole child" and by new methods to release his full potential. This required an analytically oriented staff and parent body, aware of the dominant role played by the emotions in the intellectual and physical life of every person. It required a willingness to try out new theories as to the meaning and scope of education. Accepting the concept of "learning by doing" (the activity program) it was found that the capacity to learn was seriously diminished by a child's feelings of insecurity, shame, guilt, frustration or fear. The environment of home and school needed to offer the child protection and support. During his early years, the child's primitive drives and impulses, it was felt, should be understood and released rather than merely suppressed or arbitrarily controlled. It was more important for the child to express his own honest ideas and feelings than to provide the adults with the answers they expected or demanded.

Walden became an exciting, creative and lively child-centered school, where initiative, particularly in the arts, flourished. Those involved and others, were convinced of the importance of its contribution to education, having demonstrated the soundness of its approach when psychoanalysis was still young, yet a powerful stimulus to new thinking. The roots of American tradition were not as deep as in Europe. Progressive American parents prided themselves on having their children outdo them by their spontaneity, creativity and independence. The general public was not able to distinguish between well-planned permissiveness and unhampered self-indulgence. Nevertheless, Walden ideals had a profound, if indirect, effect on educational thinking.

The Harriet Johnson Nursery School

The Harriet Johnson Nursery School opened in 1919 for children between 14 months and 4 years of age. It was the educational and research laboratory of the Bureau of Educational Experiments, organized in 1916 by Caroline Pratt, Lucy Sprague Mitchell and Harriet M. Johnson. Within a decade, the Bureau had added to its numerous undertakings a writer's laboratory, producing both children's books and books about children, and also an experimental program for the education of teachers of young children. Books for parents as well as for children and teachers followed in rapid succession. After Lucy Sprague Mitchell's "Here and Now Story Book," wide windows were opened through literature, on the adventurous world of reality. The outcome of these various, interrelated efforts resulted ultimately (in 1950) in the development of an institution called the Bank Street College of Education, accredited by the New York State Education Department to grant the degree of Master of Science in Education. The Children's School became an integral part of the college, to be used for early childhood education, for demonstration purposes, for research and for teacher training. Winning national recognition, it has continued its growth and influence throughout the twentieth century, particularly in the fields of research and teacher-training.

The Little Red School House

Under the leadership of Elizabeth Irwin, the Little Red School House opened in the fall of 1921 on East 16th St. for 100 children. Its aim was to build an elementary school from kindergarten through sixth grade which would provide the children with opportunities for full personality development and "as adequate a preparation for junior high school in subject matter and skills as is at present provided in the regular elementary schools." [5] Instead of being achieved by a routine process of instruction, it was to be accomplished by a well planned and expanding "series of experiences which will awaken interest in the children and develop a facility for meeting individual and social situations." A major challenge met boldly and effectively by the Little Red School House staff was the provision of an enriched activity program while duplicating the usual public school group size (32 to 35 children) and at the public school per capita cost.

By 1942 the Little Red School House had grown to an enrollment of 350 children from 4 through 14 years of age in 11 groups, plus a class for children needing special attention, by providing an activity program with fundamental understanding of each individual child and by building sound and wholesome habits of thinking and acting in an atmosphere of childlike concerns and enthusiasms. Although the "curriculum bears little resemblance to that of the traditional school . . . children upon graduating take their places readily in high school and (children) above the second elementary grade transfer easily to other schools."

The financial challenge had been met by economies that kept the furnishings simple but adequate, and by making "full use of everything the city has to offer in the way of playgrounds, parks, swimming pools and other recreational facilities," as well as by the tuition fees of the children. So it was proven that limited funds and large classes were not necessarily a deterrent to individualized teaching nor to an enriched developmental program.

The WPA Nurseries

During a period of deep economic depression, between the two world wars, many families were forced onto home relief rolls. The federal government, through the Works Progress Administration, opened thousands of nursery schools across the country for the children of such families. Although established primarily to provide work for unemployed adults, far more was achieved. Standards of group care of young children were improved by sensitizing the teachers, other workers (including parents), and the community to the nature and needs of the children. Nourishing meals were provided, health and safety precautions taken, sufficient and appropriate materials devised

---

5. Pages 2 and 3, Chapter I of the "Little Red School House," by Agnes de Lima and the staff of the Little Red School House, with introduction by John Dewey. Published by the Macmillan Co., N.Y. 1942.

and provided and child-sized equipment and furniture made available. Lively orientation and in-service training programs for staff members were launched. Parent education programs were initiated and the work was interpreted with enthusiasm to the community.

Although initially set up by the government to meet crucial welfare needs of adults, the WPA nursery schools were identified primarily as an educational service to both children and adults. Customarily they were under the jurisdiction of state departments of education and under local educational authorities as well. However the New York City Board of Education took no part in their administration or supervision. In 1938, when there were 14 WPA nursery schools in New York City, only one was located in a public school building. Others were in settlement houses or wherever else free space was available. Several local teacher training institutions gave short, intensive orientation courses to prepare the workers for their tasks. By this time there were over 1,500 WPA nursery schools in operation across the country (see also the October 1942 Commissioners' Report to Mayor La Guardia as quoted in Chapter II of this book).

A National Directory of Nursery Schools

The first and only attempt to publish a fully comprehensive national directory of all types of nursery schools and child care centers was compiled in 1951. The task was undertaken by Clark E. Moustakas and Minnie Berson of the Merrill-Palmer School staff in Detroit, Michigan. It identified 3,539 nonpublic, preschool programs in operation under seven different categories. Of the 503 such programs operating in New York State, 372 were in the City of New York. The following summarized data, drawn from the directory, shows their variety and the numbers under each category. Public school kindergartens were not included in the directory. At that time there were 1,416 public school kindergarten classes enrolling 35,400 five-year-old children in the city of New York.

National Directory findings, as of 1951:

Private nursery schools 137
Cooperative nursery schools 32
Child care centers (long day) 70
Philanthropic nursery schools 44
Church nurseries 55
Laboratory nursery schools 9
Summer preschool groups 25

Total 372

Out of the total number of child care centers and nursery schools in the United States (3,539 at that time), over 10 percent were in New York City.

The Montessori Movement

Dr. Maria Montessori began her work with young, mentally retarded slum children in Rome, Italy in 1907. As the first woman doctor in Italy, she had developed remarkably successful teaching techniques and materials for working with these children at the psychiatric clinic of the University of Rome. Familiar with the contributions of Froebel and others, she too developed a new method of teaching through a variety of didactic materials, designed as a series, to provide sensory training and intellectual competence to children in an orderly progression. The materials themselves, as well as the specific methods recommended for their use, encouraged children to proceed at their own individual rates rather than for all to follow the teacher's direction at the same time and in the same way. Madame Montessori recognized individual differences in the development of skills, comprehension, judgment and self-control. The materials themselves were self-corrective. As with a picture puzzle, they could be used properly only if each item was put into its special and proper place. Through the prescribed use of a wide variety of carefully devised and beautifully designed materials, it became obvious to the child that there was only one correct way to properly achieve success. His challenge lay in finding that way and mastering it. Such carefully planned and controlled activities were believed to help the child not only to gain skills and intellectual competence but also to learn to live within proper limits. This was considered essential to the child's orderly development. Madame Montessori emphasized the importance of using the child's motor-sensory apparatus as a major help toward learning. Through seeing, hearing, touching and feeling, and through the use of his muscles, intellectual learning was stimulated and confirmed. This was found to be as true for the normal child as for the mentally retarded.

Interest in the Montessori method of education was evidenced by the many Montessori nursery schools that were opened across the country. Their popularity reached a peak between 1910 and 1914, launching a controversy among parents as well as teachers. The highly structured and controlled environment, the self-limiting aspects of the materials, the rigid form and sequence of the curriculum and the lack of opportunity for direct contact with raw materials seemed to many to minimize and even exclude opportunities for the development of the child's creative and imaginative talents to develop. Were the spontaneity and natural experimental and exploratory investigations so natural to young children and considered so important to their learning, being overlooked? Were the development of social interchange and the use of individual initiative being hampered? Most educators believed that young children needed structure and control to function well. Might they also learn by trying out their growing skill and prowess through different ways and other media and often of their own selection? A lag was observable until after Madame Montessori's death in 1952 when the advances of the new scientific era brought a nationwide reemphasis on intellectual achievement. With it came a resurgence of interest in Montessori schools with a renewal of the controversy about her goals and methods.

The Progressive Education Movement

In the great movement toward social reform following the depression years, the progressive education movement emerged in strong protest against the narrow formalism of traditional education. As dissatisfied parents and teachers joined the crusade, a gradual but considerable change began to come about. As already described, a number of independent experimental schools were established in New York City. The range of education began to be extended to include both the younger so-called "preschool" child and the older child beyond the elementary school.

The major focus of the progressive education movement was not on any particular system of education, but rather on a profound search for the ultimate purpose, meaning and scope of education at all ages and levels and for the process or processes by which it might best be achieved. Old, limiting and limited goals and methods were discarded as unacceptable in favor of those based on new and deeper understanding of the child himself—of how he grew and learned and had his being. New approaches, in line with greatly expanding goals, sharpened the observation and study of the child himself, activating research and encouraging innovation. Old, fixed, traditional concepts of education were more and more challenged. The whole gamut of human growth and development was being reassessed through new eyes, in new terms and with new insights. "The Child-Centered School," "Learning by Doing," "Educating the Whole Child," became slogans of progressive education.

Although Frances W. Parker had attacked rote learning and had tried to make children's school experiences more meaningful to them as early as 1870, and many other outstanding leaders had supported the idea of change before World War II, it was John Dewey who became the recognized spokesman of the progressive education movement with the aid of William Heard Kilpatrick, the interpreter of Dewey's philosophy. During the 20 years after its founding, in 1919, the Progressive Education Association had gained a membership of 10,000. Its quarterly journal, "Progressive Education," launched in 1924, became a national clearing-house for the movement. Unfortunately, with its growing influence came increasing criticism as well as schisms between its protagonists. Charges of overpermissiveness, of irresponsible radicalism, of un-Americanism and the neglect of historical, factual and systematized knowledge were levelled against the organization. Conflict within and the attacks from without forced it to disband in 1955. Publication of the journal was discontinued in 1957. The swing of the pendulum back to conservatism in political and social thinking exaggerated the weaknesses and misunderstood the motives of the progressive education movement, slowing its momentum and putting it on the defensive. It could not, however, eradicate its profound and lasting influence on the character, scope and direction of education in the United States for decades to come.

The Development of National Organizations
Concerned with Young Children

The National Day Nursery Association, already described earlier in this chapter, was organized in 1892.

The National Kindergarten Association, founded in 1909 and headquartered in New York City, concerned itself solely with the extension of public kindergartens throughout the United States, leaving the question of standards to the school systems involved.

The Association for Childhood Education International, founded in 1892, was concerned with the education and well-being of children between the ages of two and twelve, but primarily with those of public elementary school ages. Although essentially a professional teacher's organization, its membership was broad, including parents, community workers and members of other professions as well as teachers. Its purpose was to promote desirable conditions, programs and practices in the field of education. A journal "Childhood Education," as well as other bulletins, books and leaflets were published offering information about findings, materials and procedures relating to children. A nonprofit organization with a membership of over 102,000 by 1966, it included persons from other countries as well as from all the states.

Through national and regional conferences, local branches and through its publications, it sought to "stimulate thinking rather than advocate fixed practice; explored emerging ideas; probed various points of view; presented conflicting opinion, supported wherever possible with research." [6]

The National Association for Nursery Education (later called The National Association for the Education of Young Children). In 1925, the surge of nurseries had brought about a national meeting of leaders in the field in Washington, D.C., resulting in the first national conference on nursery education. It was held in New York City in the spring of 1927, bringing together some 225 people from 24 states as well as from Hawaii, England and the District of Columbia. In addition to the nursery school and kindergarten teachers and directors who attended, there were physicians, social workers, school principals and supervisors, psychiatrists and research workers. Interest was keen as they compared notes and discussed the various aspects of nursery school operation, from programming to parent education, housing, equipping, health and nutrition, budgeting and teacher preparation. A "follow-up committee on nursery schools" was organized, with a sub-committee delegated to prepare an official statement on "The Minimum Essentials for Nursery Education." The resulting pamphlet was published and repeatedly republished and widely used as a guide for the establishment of nursery schools. During a second nursery education conference, held in Chicago in 1929, the National Association for Nursery Education was officially organized. By 1964 it had attained a membership of 10,000 and by 1970, 18,000. Membership remained open to all those interested in young children, including students, parents, volunteers and members of other professions. From then on, national conferences were held regularly in rotation, to different parts of the country—first biennially and beginning in 1964, annually. Cooperation with other organizations having concern with the well-being of young children was encouraged to further the "adoption of a broad national policy of child conservation and the development of effective programs." [7] Although recommended and/or minimum nursery school standards were formulated by NANE, no single philosophy or set pattern of nursery school practice and procedure was advocated. It was

6. From an editorial in the November 1969 issue of "Childhood Education," Journal of the Association for Childhood Education International, 3615 Wisconsin Ave., N.W., Washington, D.C. 20016.

7. From an article by Hazel Gabbard entitled "How the N.A.N.E. Began—1925 to 1945," in *Young Children*, November 1964.

recognized that further study, experimentation, research and innovation were essential to further progress in the field. Perhaps the accommodation of each program to meet the particular and perhaps somewhat unique needs of its children, their families and the community from which they came, would necessitate variety in the style and development of sound programs. No single model could possibly be appropriate to all groups in all neighborhoods, no matter how competent and dedicated their efforts, although certain basic principles might be essential to all.

The early publication of a "Nursery Education Newsletter" soon became the *Journal of Nursery Education,* the official mouthpiece of NANE. Other leaflets, pamphlets and books followed. In October 1964, when NANE became NAEYC (the National Association for the Education of Young Children), the *Journal of Nursery Education* became the journal of *Young Children.* These changes gave recognition to the fact that the infancy and primary years, as well as the nursery and kindergarten years in a child's life were included in a continuum called "the young child" or by the term "early childhood education."

Numerous other national groups, focusing on different approaches to the betterment of community, family and child life also had their beginnings in New York City during the late nineteenth and the early twentieth century. This brought a considerable and highly stimulating cross-fertilization of ideas. Among these organizations were the Settlement Houses (later to become the United Neighborhood Houses) beginning in 1887, The Children's Aid Society (1853), The Child Study Association (1888), The Public Education Association (1895), The Educational Alliance (1889), The Family Service Association of America (1911), The All Day Neighborhood Schools (1936), The Child Welfare League of America (1915), The Play School Association (1917), the American Ortho-psychiatric Association (1923).

Two additional local organizations concerned with the health, welfare and education of children in New York City carried a wide influence. These were the Citizens' Committee for Children of New York City (1943) and the Day Care Council (1948). Another group calling itself the Intercity Committee for the Day Care of Children, brought representatives of east coast cities together (1958) subsequently forming the National Day Care and Child Development Council, headquartered in Washington, D.C. eight years later. Expansion and change had become the order of the day in regard to services for young children.

Public interest and concern for the health, education and welfare of young children, particularly those who were economically disadvantaged, were quickened by President John F. Kennedy's plan for an all-out war against poverty in the United States. With this effort, the expectations of those interested in young children, from whatever vantage point, rose to unprecedented heights. Subsequent action by President Lyndon B. Johnson and the Congress, in setting up the federal Office of Economic Opportunity with its national Head Start Program (1965) for impoverished preschool children, brought tremendous response and enthusiasm. As innovative programs got under way, first for the summer only and then on a year-round basis, great gains were visualized. The inclusion and involvement of parents, community members, volunteers, professionals from many fields and paraprofessionals as well, brought new and old challenges and controversies to the local level, in what seemed the urgency of a national emergency. Political involvement, federal budgeting and the innovative nature of the program accentuated the resulting power struggles. Inevitable confrontations came about with the established order, as well as between many groups. Throughout the myriads of controversies surrounding the Head Start program, it retained its vitality, provided necessary opportunities for elbow rubbing between the many and varied protagonists, and above all it seemed to make the close interrelationship between child, family and community irrefutable.

Each of the educational movements so cursorily described in this chapter brought strong alignment with the forces of change; each made important and unique contributions to the lives of children. Each brought healthy opposition from its critics whose security was often threatened by any departure from the familiar, established order of things. The full impact of the educational revolution still lay ahead, while viable new ideas continued to circulate. Hopefully, education would never again become totally isolated from the best interests of the children it sought to serve. As John Dewey had written, "children are people. They grow into tomorrow only as they live today."

CHAPTER IX

VARIED AND CHANGING PATTERNS
As They Affected Children

As the winds of change blew ever stronger in New York City and across the country, it was inevitable that children and their families would feel the swirling gusts. Those working with or for young children struggled to understand and assess the varied and changing patterns in the programs and services that were emerging. Where were they leading?

Not too many years before, the idea of "the whole child" had been featured. Having taken him apart in the nineteenth century, his component parts of body, mind and spirit were being put together again in the twentieth. What a miracle to discover that the whole child was then found to be far greater than the sum of his parts. From every aspect, he was found to be a learner from the time of his birth—or was it from the time of conception? Infancy was becoming a recognized part of the early childhood sequence. The continuity of growth and development throughout these years was assuming new importance. This meant that the entire nature of the learning process had to be reassessed.

What was to be the role of child workers, whether teachers, social workers, nurses, pediatricians, parents or others? Were they to be primarily environmentalists, disciplinarians, technicians, humanitarians, observers, researchers, or caretakers and would a galaxy of such specialists be needed? Or would some mysterious blend help the young child even more? Could the children's rights be defended and their capacities fully developed if the adults in contact with them were not simultaneously developing their capacities? While teaching and parenting of the school-age child seemed often to have become static, recognition of the educability of the so-called "preschool" child had become a phenomenon of the times. The implications were tremendous and far-reaching. The concept of learning began to include not only the acquisition of knowledge and skill, but perhaps even more important, the development of attitudes, concepts and motivations.

Unfortunately the discovery of the young child's capacity to learn brought many parents, teachers and others, to exert pressure in an effort to force children to learn more and more at younger and younger ages, regardless of their readiness. To further "child care" as separate from "child education" tended to disunite him. Just as some malnourished children needed more vitamins or protein in their diets than others, so some needed more educational or cultural stimulation or more TLC (tender, loving care) than others. All needed nourishment, in appropriate blends. It was readily observable that no child could leave any of his basic needs outside the home or the day care door as he entered, as he might leave behind a pair of rubbers on a rainy day. He marched in with them, as inseparable from him as his own skin, as essential a part of him as his appetite or his curiosity. Once the appropriate ingredients of a good day were available to him, his health, education and care became indistinguishable. Their proper mix best met his basic needs.

Although segregation of young children for reasons of race, color, creed or national origin seemed on its way out, segregation for reasons of economic status seemed again on its way in. Other prejudices than those towards poverty were also shown in the tangential pulls for autonomy between the professions of health, education and welfare. Each tended to claim jurisdictional authority in its own name. Edges between them were sharpened rather than blurred or blended. Separateness was often intensified as each profession became increasingly convinced of the importance of the early years of childhood. Nevertheless, widening public interest, as well as deepening professional concerns, were evidenced by the stirrings of national groups in the field of day care.

1. A first national statistical survey of "Child Care Arrangements of Full-Time Working Mothers" had been conducted by the United States Bureau of the Census in 1958, at the request of the Children's Bureau in Washington, D.C. It was published in 1959 as Children's Bureau Publication No. 378. In the foreword of this report by Henry C. Lajewski, Mrs. Katherine B. Oettinger, then Chief of the Children's Bureau, wrote:

Clearly the trend in our culture for the employment of mothers is part of a change so large, so strong and so rapid that we must take it into account in our planning for children. Our task is to try to preclude any ill effects it might have on the children whose mothers are in the labor force to learn more about how different circumstances and conditions affect children and to use what we learn in their behalf.

How are we going to meet the problems of the working mother and her children? Just as we have met problems before—through individuals and groups working separately and together for better community service—struggling and stumbling and trying again, to keep abreast with the rapid changes occurring in our culture.

This survey, revealing startling figures, was limited to the children of full-time working mothers. It presented evidence of such critical and widespread areas of neglect and of need, that communities began to look more closely at the adequacy of their child care services.

2. In 1959 the Child Welfare League of America undertook a three-year research and action project in the field of day care for children, using "day care" in a broad sense—to cover *all* daytime child care arrangements when the mother herself did not provide this care. Florence A. Ruderman, Director of the project wrote in the League's journal "Child Welfare" (June 1963):

(The Child Welfare League) wanted to view daytime child care as part of the contemporary scene—a feature of our rapidly evolving society—and not as a problem restricted to particular groups, predefined conditions or special facilities.

This study included "not only formal facilities but also informal arrangements; not only working mothers, but also nonworking mothers, in all classes or groups of the population."

The study found in some seven dissimilar communities in different geographic areas, "not only the numbers of children who need substitute care during the day, but also the family patterns and the social attitudes or values which give rise to these needs, and in part determine how they are met."

The aim of the project is to advance our knowledge of contemporary social patterns and to help stimulate and improve day care services for children.

In 1960 the Child Welfare League published its "Standards for Day Care Service," prepared by a national committee of "experts" drawn from all related fields, child development, education, mental health, psychology, medicine, psychiatry, sociology, genetics and anthropology.

In the introduction to these standards, Joseph H. Reid, the executive director wrote, "Concepts of day care services for children are changing rapidly. This momentum of change reflects phenomenal cultural, economic, sociological and scientific developments throughout our world. Therefore no formulation of standards for day care services can be thought of as final. It is essential that there be periodic review, reevaluation, and rewriting of standards as new knowledge and experience are gained."

3. Under the leadership of Elinor Guggenheimer and Sadie Ginsberg, the National Committee for the Day Care of Children (initially called the Inter-City Committee for the Day Care of Children) [1] was incorporated in New York City in June 1960. The purpose of this young and active organization is to interpret as widely as possible the needs of children for day care; to promote good standards for day care; to encourage study and research in the field of day care; to encourage cooperative effort throughout the country towards the establishment of adequate day care services for children; to stimulate the exchange of information, ideas and experiences in the field of day care.[2]

The NCDCC defined day care as "a service which provided essential care and protection to children outside their homes *for a major part of the day,* on a regular basis.

"Good day care assures opportunities for physical, emotional and intellectual growth to the maximum of the child's capacity, through group programs for preschool and school-age children as well as through family day care."

4. The 1960 Golden Anniversary White House Conference on Children and Youth was held in Washington, D.C., with 7,000 participants. This conference, to a far greater degree than any previous White House Conference, focussed on the mounting national interest and concern about the day care of young children across the country.

Selected quotations relating to the day care of children were excerpted by the National Committee for the Day Care of Children. Extracted from a multiplicity of conference publications as well as from the hundreds of resolutions that came out of the conference, the following were a few of the recommendations:

That, to achieve optimum services for children there be better communication and more comprehensive coordinated planning and action

1. Later called The Day Care and Child Development Council of America, 1426 H St., N.W., Washington, D.C. 20008.

2. Quoted from the Newsletter of the National Committee for the Day Care of Children, Vol III, No. 2. Jan. 1963, 44 E. 23rd St., N.Y. 10, N.Y

among all agencies, groups and individuals concerned with the growth and development of children—specifically between:

Federal, state and local units of government;
Public and voluntary agencies;
Public and private lay and professional organizations;
Corporate bodies, including management and labor.

Regarding mobility of families—

That all public and private agencies on every level accept joint responsibility for coping with the impact of family mobility.

That to maintain the important relationship of infant and mother, children under three remain in their own homes unless there were pressing social or economic reasons for their care away from home.

That every group be supervised by *at least* one person qualified in early childhood education.

That personnel working with young children have the opportunity for college training and appropriate in-service training.

That salaries of nursery school teachers be raised, as a means of attracting capable and well-trained men and women to this field.

That it be mandatory for State Departments of Education to establish standards for certification of all nursery school and kindergarten teachers.

That State Departments of Health, Education and Welfare and Mental Health cooperate to secure effective legislation establishing and strengthening standards, inspection and licensing requirements for personnel and facilities of both public and voluntary programs for the care, safety and education of young children in groups away from home.

That research be undertaken . . . (regarding) the readiness of young children for group experiences and the development of criteria other than chronological age in educating the child in the group.

5. As an immediate follow-up to the White House Conference, the first nationwide Conference on Day Care was held in Washington, D.C. on November 17 and 18, 1960. It was cosponsored by the Children's Bureau and the Women's Bureau of the U.S. Department of Labor. The initiative, energy and leadership of Elinor Guggenheimer became a key force in bringing day care to national attention. With great enthusiasm she stimulated and alerted local groups and organizations to the day care needs in their communities. The purpose of this Conference was stated as follows:

Through the working participation of 500 representatives of voluntary and public agencies, citizen and professional organizations, labor and management—

To encourage development of day care services for children *who need them.*

To examine the extent and variety of day care needs and resources.

To identify roadblocks in providing day care services which are adequate in quantity, quality and distribution.

To promote good standards for safeguarding the children served.

To foster wider understanding of the pressing needs for day care services.

To stimulate broader community responsibility for day care services.

To develop recommendations for citizen and professional action at local, state and national levels.

6. In May 1962 the APHA (American Public Health Association) set up its first Day Care Committee.[3] Its first step was to assess the health needs (broadly interpreted) of children in daytime care and the extent to which such needs were met. To find this out, the national committee circulated a comprehensive questionnaire to all State Commissioners of Public Health. Responses showed tremendous variation in every respect and often total indifference to the needs of preschool children.

A second step was taken in response to a request from the Children's Bureau to prepare a Health Guide for Day Care. It was to be a comprehensive guide, applicable to all types of day care services, regardless of their basic organizational goals or funding, and whether public, voluntary or proprietary. The importance of high standards for all types and facilities was considered basic to the thinking of this group. Health was broadly conceived as including physical, mental and emotional health.

7. The first federal funds appropriated by Congress for day care since World War II were signed into law by President Kennedy on July 25, 1962. Although it was not until over a year later, August 7, 1963, that the funds were finally allocated ($4 million for the entire country) the dire need for day care services for children had become sharply visible, especially for mothers who were working. Day care activity across the country received a tremendous stimulus. Many states proceeded with immediate plans to establish statewide day care standards and to implement them. Others followed. Too often, how-

3. Anne DeHuff Peters, M.D. was chairman of this committee which was ultimately responsible for the publication of "Early Child Care—The New Perspectives" by the Atherton Press, New York, 1968.

ever, standards were established at minimal levels with experience and know-how lacking in the leadership.

Thirty-nine states assumed some measure of mandatory responsibility for the standard setting and licensing of day care services, sometimes broadly conceived, sometimes narrow, with concern limited to the children of working mothers, sometimes at a high level—sometimes extremely minimal.

At the close of 1963, 45 states had taken responsibility for the licensing of day care services. In 33 states the Department of Welfare had assumed responsibility for licensing, in six states the Department of Health, and in three the Department of Education. In three additional states, licensing was the joint responsibility of the Departments of Health and Education. What a kaleidoscope of patterns! What an upsurge of interest.

In 1963, there were 3⅓ million working mothers with children under six years of age. Yet there were only 185,000 licensed day care facilities throughout the nation. Mrs. Oettinger, chief of the Children's Bureau in Washington, D.C., in commenting on the new federal law said, "Today we have more latchkey children in our nation than even at the height of World War II."

As of July 1, 1963, State Welfare Departments, cooperating with state health and education authorities, assured maximum use of their agencies to children in day care. All facilities in receipt of federal funds were to meet the state's licensing requirements.

Here was a significant new trend toward federal subsidy in support of day care, conditioned upon the cooperative endeavors of State Departments of Health, Education and Welfare.

Unfortunately the federal Departments of Health, Education and Welfare in Washington, D.C. had themselves not yet found the way to achieve full and close coordination of their three-way responsibility in the field of day care. The Children's Bureau in the Department of Welfare had taken the lead, but with primary and almost exclusive concern for those children whose families were legally entitled to welfare subsidy. Education and health were lagging far behind. How then were the needs of all the young children of all the people to be more fully met?

8. In a 1961 Policy Statement by the Council of Chief State School Officers in Washington, D.C., on "Responsibilities of State Departments of Education for Nursery School and Kindergarten" presented another approach:

104

The nursery school and kindergarten represent an extension of education below the primary grades. The growth of schools for children under six, and the widespread acceptance of parents that children should begin their education before compulsory school age, placed high priority on this area for educational planning and leadership.

As early as 1950 the Council of Chief State School Officers recognized the responsibility of state departments of education for nursery school and kindergarten programs. In an earlier publication, (Our System of Education), the Council had recommended that the scope of elementary and secondary education be extended and that *an appropriate tax-supported public education program* should be free and available to each person who had reached the age of three years. This platform provided a blueprint for the future. This too stimulated advances in establishing early childhood education programs.

Other important educational bodies charting the trends and developments in education also endorsed nursery schools and kindergartens as the beginning units of elementary education.

Among these groups are the National Education Association, the Educational Policies Commission, the Association for Childhood Education International, The National Society for the Study of Education, the United States Office of Education, as well as the White House Conference of 1950 and 1960.

Increasingly state educational agencies are confronted with urgent needs in early childhood education which call for immediate and long-range planning. . . . Education in the first years is recognized as significant in laying the foundation for the education which follows, and the formative years are known to be the period of most rapid learning in life; in view of these facts, educational leadership for these programs is essential. The guidelines in this statement are focussed, therefore, on state responsibility for improving the quality of nursery school and kindergarten education organized under *public or nonpublic auspices or a combination of both.*[4]

The pooling of practices and experiences of state departments of education in this field will be of service to all states in evaluating present programs for young children and in determining how these services can be improved and extended.

9. Numerous other national groups were clearly on record in affirming their support of a sound program in education for all children under six, usually beginning at three.

Among these were the American Association of School Administrators, the American Association of University Women, the Asso-

---

4. Italics are the author's.

ciation for Supervision and Curriculum Development, the National Association for Nursery Education,[5] the National Citizens Commission for Better Schools, the National Congress of Parents and Teachers, the National Council of State Consultants in Elementary Education, and the National Kindergarten Association.

Statewide, standard-raising and mandatory licensing of preschool programs were a new phenomenon. The idea spread rapidly, especially since the bill for day care had been passed by Congress. Many communities felt that minimum standards were the answer—since they aroused the least controversy, created the least hardship and expense for the operators. Here, educators missed the boat—for the well-being of the children themselves was not the primary goal. Had standards of quality been established, all programs might have been on the forward march. With an allowance of time for making necessary improvements, with guidance and help, no program would have been allowed to settle back and drift on what was known to be unsatisfactory "minimum standards" with their downgrading of effort on behalf of children. Nevertheless, it was a time of new thinking, new approaches to new problems. Much progress was being made. Research was adding tremendously to many aspects of child growth and development. It had been proven beyond a doubt that the old concept of fixed intelligence was no longer valid, human intelligence was not static. This presented a challenge to everyone working with children of any age, but particularly to those working in the uncharted field of the young child. Research was also offering enlightenment about children with handicapping conditions, whether physical, mental or emotional, and whether or not due to cultural deprivation, inheritance or genetic factors.

The signs of the times were clear. Day care was at a crossroads. Varied and changing patterns were all around. There was movement everywhere, even though uneven, spotty. There were tremendous problems at all levels, local, state and federal. In most instances the gap between what was known and what was done for children was wide indeed. How to narrow the gap, how to synchronize the efforts—this was the challenge!

Were the universities and government agencies playing their full leadership roles? Were parents truly involved? What were the goals of the educators in the midst of the turmoil? Was teacher training ac-

---

5. Later called NAEYC (National Association for the Education of Young Children).

commodating to the widened and deepened scope of early child care? As more children were born, as medical science was making it possible to keep more children alive and healthy, as city living became more complex and congested, the only solution seemed to be to synchronize efforts and energies, to select early childhood as a priority of concern, to extend knowledge and skill and concern in this area to the utmost. Standard setting, licensing, research, teacher training, parent involvement, community coordination were all high-sounding phrases, yet they were also the road signs to be followed if young children were to get a square deal, or any deal at all.

The Head Start Program begun in the summer of 1965, became popular beyond all expectations and moved quickly to become a year-round program for disadvantaged preschool children. (See Chapter VIII, page 97.) A wave of new thinking about young children and their families, followed. The popularity of the Head Start Program was a clear sign of the growing importance of the preschool years in the eyes of the public. It also brought the question of where the licensing authority should lie again under scrutiny.

Several thousand years ago there had lived a Greek philosopher named Heraclitus, called "The Obscure." He believed that nothing was permanent except change, for even opposites, when most divergent were connected. He was able to find hidden attunement between variables. Perhaps this was what was later meant, in the twentieth century, by what was then called "integration." Could the efforts on behalf of children and their families be seen whole, could they be joined to assure progress from the past to the present and from the present on into the future?

CHAPTER X

CHANGING PERSPECTIVES
A Decade Later

The year is now 1972. Nearly a decade has passed since the preceding chapters were written. These were years of acute restlessness and extreme anxiety about man's life and purpose on the earth. Evidences of conflict appeared everywhere. Great scientific developments and a growing awareness of impending ecological disaster changed his perspective. Rapid and drastic social and economic changes also affected the people of every continent. Many called it a time of worldwide revolution, both in thought and action.

Simultaneously a world-encircling population explosion threatened to overtax the world's food supplies, bringing vast additional problems and fears in its wake. Only a century and a half earlier, the world's population had reached its first billion. It was estimated that by 1975 it would reach 4 billion. All people, everywhere, including young children, were affected in numerous ways. In the United States, presumably the most affluent and powerful of all nations, it was found that thousands of children went to bed hungry at night. Uncounted numbers lived in pockets of severe poverty in the ghettos and slums of large cities and in many remote rural areas.

In New York City, as in all large and tightly packed centers of population, life was geared to an ever-increasing degree of complexity, overcrowding and sophistication. As acute problems affected more and more people, and as the awareness of their implications grew, reactions became increasingly intense and acute, bringing controversy and challenge, and often an overwhelming sense of defeat and hopelessness. Each of the many different minority groups, whether ethnic, social, political or religious, became mobilized, articulate and often hostile, even to each other. Each sought, by its own means, to express its growing sense of dissatisfaction and resentment toward "the establishment," "the system," or "the power structure." Each demanded greater recognition and support. Impatience with the remoteness and complexity of government brought frustrations often so deep as to lead to violent behavior. Discouraged by the rising costs of living, the mounting taxes and unemployment rolls, and the apparently meaningless and fruitless Viet Nam war, more and more groups and individuals became negatively activized and often radicalized.

The voices previously raised in defense of young children were now often muted or pushed aside by the overriding concerns of adults to solve their own immediate and critical problems. Ideological battles were fought on many fronts and by every possible means: the press, television, radio, strikes and street rallies, protest marches, college campus disorders, riots and even bombings. Confrontations seemed to widen the gaps, whether between the generations, between the sexes, between minority and majority political groups, between different ethnic groups, between the rich and the poor, the traditionalists and the innovators, the powerful and the powerless. Distress signals in great variety emanated not only from the pockets of poverty in Harlem, Bedford Stuyvesant, the Lower East Side and the South Bronx, but from the unrecognized and the disadvantaged everywhere. Tensions and misunderstandings grew into enmities. Drug addiction, robberies and street crimes increased to such a degree as to give many the feeling that their homes and streets were unsafe. The sense of crisis, mistrust and imminent danger made the whole world seem awry. It was as though the fabric of democracy was being tested, with pulls on every thread. The shift of population out of the city to the suburbs, for those who could afford it, only increased the general sense of desolation and discontent.

Young children were repeatedly caught in the cross fires between opposing forces. Adult conflicts had a direct impact on all aspects of childbearing and childrearing. Parents reported that their young children seemed to need less sleep, that they were more highly keyed and were learning more at a faster rate and at an earlier age. There was much discussion as to whether violence on the screen encouraged violent behavior in the children. As in the earlier days of progressive education, permissiveness on the part of parents was thought by many to be responsible for the revolt of the young against the authority of their parents and teachers. Parents demanded greater educational opportunities for their children as a right rather than a privilege. Each

109

group interpreted "quality education" and "comprehensive education" in their own terms. Parents wanted to become more directly involved in the decision-making processes in matters affecting them and their children.

The ready availability of birth control information, the newly liberalized abortion laws, changing attitudes toward marriage and family life, rising divorce rates, increasing numbers of children being born to younger and younger women (whether wed or unwed) and the influence of the Women's Liberation movement, all helped to bring more and more energetic and dissatisfied women into the labor force. Growing demands for day care services for all who wanted or needed them, including infants, became more and more vocal and defiant. Ultimately, it was hoped by many that the broad dissemination of birth control information and the legalizing of abortion clinics would check the population growth and assure that only wanted children would be born. Yet, during this transitional period, child neglect and child abuse cases continued to mount.

Among the sleeping giants that were reawakened in the 1960's was the Women's Liberation movement. It was the aftermath of the long dormant Women's Suffrage movement. After the Revolutionary War, when the United States Constitution was drafted, the question of women's rights aroused great controversy. But it was not until the nineteenth amendment to the Constitution was ratified in 1920 that women were granted even the right to vote. The Women's Liberation movement of the 1960's now demanded that all rights of women be equal to those of men. This meant the freedom to bear or not to bear children, freedom to work or not to work, whether inside or outside the home, equal pay for equal work and equal opportunities to be employed. It meant the provision of publicly subsidized day care services being made available to all who wished to use them, on a twenty-four hour basis if necessary. The realization that women comprised 51 percent of the total population of the United States gave added impetus and political weight to their demands. At this time the first two women were elected to Congress from New York City—Mrs. Shirley Chisholm and Mrs. Bella Abzug, both strong advocates of women's rights and of public day care.

The pressures and counterpressures exerted by local groups began to bring some measurable results in New York City. A big step was taken, after much controversy, when the entire public elementary school system was decentralized into 31 local school districts throughout the five boroughs. Each district was to be governed by a locally elected board, bringing the schools and their manifold problems closer to the people.

Another significant step was taken by Mayor John V. Lindsay in his second term of office. He reorganized the existing city departments into a more limited number of super-agencies. The aim was to clarify, simplify and coordinate public responsibilities and procedures, again also to attempt to bring government closer to the people. One of the new super-agencies was the Department of Human Resources. It was set up in 1966 and on July 1, 1970 came under the leadership of Mr. Jule Sugarman, former director of the national Head Start Program in Washington, D.C. All Head Start, day care, and child development programs in New York City, and particularly all those in receipt of public funds, were to come under his jurisdiction.

An Early Childhood Development Task Force had been appointed by the mayor, under the chairmanship of Mrs. Trude Lash, executive director of the Citizens Committee for Children of New York City. With the help of a number of subcommittees and much conflicting testimony, recommendations and guidelines were developed for clarifying issues and establishing directives for day care programs. After frequent and often tumultous sessions, the task force presented its report to the mayor, indicating that "there were over-lapping functions, duplication of effort and lack of communication among the various city agencies which licensed and administered child care programs." Consequently, the mayor, by Executive Order #38,[1] created an Agency for Child Development in the Human Resources Administration as of July 1, 1971. Mrs. Georgia L. McMurray was appointed as the first New York City Commissioner of Child Development, with the appointment soon after of Miss Elizabeth A. Vernon as Assistant Commissioner for Program Development.[2] The task to be undertaken was a formidable and momentous one:

> To assume responsibility for developing, planning, administering, operating, contracting, coordinating, supporting, monitoring and evaluating programs for day care and child development services.
>
> To promote and prepare for the consolidation of as many day care and

1. Executive Order #38, July 1, 1971, office of the mayor, creation of an Agency for Child Development.

2. Miss Vernon had succeeded Cornelia Goldsmith in 1963 as Head of the Division of Day Care in the New York City Department of Health and had also been the director of Head Start in New York City during 1966 and 1967. Miguel O. Martinez became Deputy Commissioner, with Robert K. Davis and Hannibal Herring as Assistant Commissioners.

child development programs and functions as possible into the agency.

To establish, with the approval of the Administrator of the Human Resources Administration a Child Development Commission which shall include democratically selected parent representatives of community groups and such other advisory or policy making groups as may be required by federal or state law.

Among a number of deeply concerned groups, voluntarily contributing to the development of sound day care guidelines was an ad hoc subcommittee of NAEYC (The National Association for the Education of Young Children). This committee, calling itself "The Early Childhood Committee," comprised of 15 experienced and highly qualified professional educators, prepared a statement on "The Fundamental Learning Needs of Today's Young Children." [3] In summary their recommendations were:

All early childhood group programs should meet the fundamental needs of a child in order to foster his receptivity to learning and his growth, both as a unique, whole person and as a group member. To achieve this, every child requires

Comprehensive health supervision and adequate nutrition.

A safe, comfortable yet stimulating environment.

Appropriate opportunities for rest, relaxation, recreation and exercise.

Opportunities to learn from first hand experiences and to master skills without pressure.

Group experiences which help him become a happy, social, self-confident person.

Flexible structuring of activities to give him a sense of independence, security, challenge and developing self-control.

The sure knowledge that he is accepted and cared for by people he can trust and who understand how to help him develop and learn.

Establishing and developing quality early childhood programs can be accomplished only when all groups mutually concerned with the young child search for new ways of working together. This can be done by pooling all assets and deciding to focus on the good of the child and his family.

Adequate funds and practical budgets are essential in every child-caring situation. They require careful preliminary and on-going planning. Early childhood programs in any form, cannot be considered a cheap service. Group size is necessarily small and the ratio of adults to children neces-

---

3. Published in "Young Children" the Journal of NAEYC, Volume XXV, No. 6, September 1970 (pages 326 to 336).

sarily high. The hours are often longer than those involving older children. During their most vulnerable and dependent years, many young children spend almost their entire waking life in a group program.

Agencies such as Departments of Health and Social Services and local school boards need to become deeply and specifically involved in planning, organizing and implementing the establishment of sound early childhood programs. The supervising and licensing agencies would vary depending on the specific needs of the community. Each is unique with a variety of structural social components.

It seems that, today, people are willing to pay for what they value, whether it be remedying past mistakes, venturing into new scientific areas, fighting social inequities, or giving a definite priority to the strengthening and development of our future potential—our human young! All those working for or with our young children should be dedicated and committed to them if man's precarious future is to become a positive and productive one.

Federally, too, changes were coming about in relation to the Head Start Program of OEO (Office of Economic Opportunity). At the conclusion of the 1965 summer Head Start program, President Lyndon B. Johnson announced that Head Start would continue on a year-round basis, with a follow-through program for Head Start children in the public schools. The overall goals would continue "to insure that no young poverty child shall lack the environmental stimulation and opportunity which will make it possible for him to fulfill the complete range of his developmental capacities." [4] Thus the program continued on its precarious way, dedicated to the all-out attack on poverty, with growing emphasis on diagnostic, remedial and developmental efforts focussed on health, social, nutritional and psychological services and enriching preschool learning experiences. Each child was to be provided with at least one full meal a day. Parents were to be invited to participate in every phase of the program. Many already worked as teacher aides and in other nonprofessional capacities. Special courses for parents were held on such subjects as home economics, food budgeting, food purchasing, child care and home management.

In 1966, under Title I of the Elementary and Secondary Education Act (ESEA), the federal Office of Education made funds available for preschool programs for children of low-income families, when sponsored by school boards or boards of education. This brought, in addition

---

4. From Bulletin published in January 1966—written by Richard E. Orton, Staff Director, Project Head Start, Office of Economic Opportunity, Public Affairs, Washington, D.C. 20506.

to community and political involvement, also public school involvement. Expectations rose to high levels as it became apparent that comprehensive reforms under federal auspices and with federal funding were underway. Program quality was uneven, but a variety of research and demonstration projects produced imaginative, experimental approaches and innovative programs. It was hoped that the child development centers, with their new insights into how young children learn, into the needs of families and the special characteristics of their communities, would help further improve and expand the program.

The broad scope and the constant changes implicit in the development of the Head Start program made it difficult for many to understand and accept, just as 20 years earlier this had happened in the experience of the Day Care Unit. The increasing depth and breadth of its goals threatened the defenders of custom and tradition. To replace the age-old charity concept of offering minimal custodial care to the poor with the idea of comprehensive, quality programs as a child's right was hard for many to support. It was equally difficult for many to understand and accept the idea that a primary source of vitality and promise for the future in the child care field lay in its diversity and flexibility, in its ability to accommodate to the varying needs of children, their families and their communities. All this seemed a sharp reversal of deeply rooted, earler trends focused on adjusting and accommodating the child to arbitrary standards of behavior and achievement both at home and at school. Nevertheless, by 1967, more than 3,000 Head Start programs, involving some 1,500,000 children were in operation across the country.

The complexities inherent in any attempt at coordinating the many, various federal agencies concerned with some aspects of early child care became evident in the publication of "Federal Interagency Day Care Requirements" pursuant to Sec. 522 (d) of the Economic Opportunity Act, as approved by the United States Department of Health, Education, and Welfare, the United States Office of Economic Opportunity, and the United States Department of Labor on September 23, 1968. In the preface, signed by Jule M. Sugarman, then Chairman of the Federal Panel on Early Childhood, he stated that:

> The Requirements will be supplemented from time to time by Interagency Recommendations issued through the Federal Panel on Early Childhood. This interdepartmental panel consists of representatives of the Department of Agriculture; the Department of Housing and Urban Development; the Department of Labor, including the Women's Bureau

and the Manpower Administration; the Office of Economic Opportunity; and the Department of Health, Education, and Welfare, including the Assistant Secretary for Health and Scientific Affairs; the Health Services and Mental Health Administration, the National Institute of Health, the Office of Education, the Social and Rehabilitation Service, the Children's Bureau, and the Assistance Payments Administration.

The Panel is responsible for revising standards from time to time and for issuing interpretations of the Standards whenever required.

Harmonizing and coordinating the points of view of all these national groups could hardly be accomplished over night.

In 1969 the announcement of sweeping changes in the organization of federal programs for children came from both the White House and the Secretary of the Department of Health, Education, and Welfare (HEW). Head Start was moved into this department where an Office of Child Development (known as OCD) had been created. In this office, emphasis was placed on the experimental Parent and Child Center Program, including children under three years of age. Consultant teams of experts were sent out to give technical assistance where needed. Training opportunities were set up through the universities and the junior colleges. Programs of research studies and program evaluation were undertaken. Every federally supported program was still to be required to provide "maximum feasible participation of the poor in both planning and action." Parents were to be offered appropriate counselling, legal services, job and open housing opportunities. Civil rights were to be protected. Obviously, the way of so ambitious and complicated a program could not be expected to be smooth. The new office was designed as the administration's attempt to end the fragmentation of responsibilities at federal levels. Dr. Edward F. Zigler, appointed in April 1970 by President Nixon as the first director of the federal Office of Child Development and Chief of the Children's Bureau, was given three specific charges:

1. To administer child development programs of high quality.
2. To coordinate federal services for children and to provide leadership to states and localities.
3. To be an advocate and an innovator for children.[5]

Dr. Zigler, previously a professor of psychiatry and child psychology at Yale University, had been one of the early architects of the Head

_____

5. See article by Dr. Zigler on "A National Priority: Raising the Quality of Children's Lives" in the September-October issue of "Children" 1970, Volume 17, No. 5, an Interdisciplinary Journal for the Professions Serving Children.

Start program and was fully cognizant of the difficulties and problems he would face. Under his leadership national committees were set up to develop guidelines for program development and evaluation, career ladders for personnel functioning in child care activities, and for establishing and researching a variety of meaningful and appropriate models offering communities choices as to their preferences. Further study, observation, research and evaluation of each model was to be undertaken. All models would presumably:

1. Stimulate positive and innovative changes in educational methods, to help young children and their parents to improve their lot.
2. Achieve greater interdisciplinary cooperation among professionals in related fields and between professionals and nonprofessionals.
3. Increase parental and community involvement in the decision-making processes and in the carrying out of the program itself.
4. Provide medical, dental, nutritional and psychological services as well as educational and social services.
5. Further research, experimentation and evaluation of programs.
6. Emphasize a child-focussed and child-oriented approach.
7. Reduce class size and extend the adult-child ratio to one teacher plus one or two aides for every group of not more than 15 or 20 children.
8. Help the preschool child of a disadvantaged family to take his place among the more advantaged children of middle and upper income families when he enters public school.
9. Encourage public school teachers and administrators to adjust their programs to more fully and more flexibly meet the needs of all children.

As these promising goals were articulated, they brought new hope and renewed effort. Was a bridge beginning to be built between the ardent supporters and the outspoken critics of quality child care programs?

Head Start ideas were also beginning, almost imperceptibly, to influence other programs. A number of pilot projects had made their way into school and communities, such as: "Follow Through"; the "Four C's" (Community Coordinated Child Care); "Vista," the home-based branch of the Peace Corps; "Urban Redevelopment"; "Model Cities"; the "Job Corps"; "Family Day Care"; "Infant Care"; New York State's "Experimental Pre-Kindergarten Program," and others. Young children and their families were directly involved in them all. Recognizing that family and community needs, as well as those of business and industry had to be considered in making plans for child care services, it was the needs of the child himself that had to be given top priority. It was he who actually *lived* the program—it was he who had the most at stake. Benefits to mothers and employers might be added advantages, but the primary focus was necessarily on the child himself.

In some programs set up ostensibly for poverty children, other children whose parents could pay a fee were also admitted. With a sliding scale of fees, based on parent's ability to pay, doors could be opened to all, on a voluntary basis. In this way, the unfortunate pattern of segregating the poor could be eliminated and an invaluable experience in democratic living made possible for the children. Perhaps the work of the United Nations in maintaining peace in the world could best be buttressed by those who had early first hand experiences in a genuinely democratic group of his peers.

Encouraging changes were occurring in the teacher's colleges and in the rapidly growing two-year community colleges. Reevaluating their curricula, many offered revised courses on an open admission basis to paraprofessionals as well as professionals working with young children. A degree was no longer to be considered the sole measure of a person's fitness, competence and skill for work with young children. Here another frontier with new and greatly expanded horizons in the preparation of teachers and other child workers, was opening up. The remnants of an arbitrary authority attitude by a teacher at her desk or on a symbolic pedestal had been removed to allow a more meaningful reciprocal relationship with the children and a partnership relationship with parents and other adults. Men were coming gradually into the day care picture, contributing particularly to fatherless children from single parent families.

A greatly increased interest in federal legislation affecting children was evidenced during this period. Of the 11 million women already in the labor force, 5 million were known to have preschool children. Of these, it was estimated, less than a third were enrolled in any kind of daytime program, whether good, bad or indifferent. Only by legislative action at the federal level could appropriate action be taken to provide all states with the needed funds, guidelines and the skilled leadership that would assure protection and true benefits to all the children so critically in need of them.

In 1970, through amendments to the ESEA (Elementary and Secondary Education Act) Public Law Number 91-230 was extended to remain operative through 1973 and expanded to include disadvantaged and handicapped children. Through consolidation of the ESEA with the NDEA (National Defense Education Act) limited and specified funds were also made available for adult counseling and guidance in child

117

care, for exemplary and innovative child care programs and for comprehensive and continuing planning and evaluation. Guidelines and criteria prohibiting segregation by race were reaffirmed. Although the complicated procedures, limited funds and community rivalries discouraged many, the field of day care was again stimulated and helped to make gains.

In the fall of 1971, Congressional activity regarding child care legislation reached a crescendo. Numerous hearings on different child care bills were held in Washington, D.C. before a number of different committees. There was much controversy as drastically different points of view and approaches were argued and defended. After much procedural maneuvering, a comprehensive, landmark child care bill (Number S 2007) sponsored by Senator Walter F. Mondale from Minnesota, was actually passed by both houses of Congress. However, it was vetoed by President Nixon, for administrative and financial reasons, who preferred to consider day care as part of a welfare reform bill. Only two years earlier, in his 1969 message to Congress, the President had said:

> So critical is the matter of early growth that we must make a national commitment to providing all American children an opportunity for healthful and stimulating development during the first years of life.

Although the Mondale and Nelson bill was defeated by the President's veto in January 1972 it had received wide support in both houses of the legislature as well as from a broad spectrum of organizations representing not only professional and citizen groups, but labor, religious and political groups, as well as Women's Liberation members. Such an unprecedented degree of support assured renewal of effort at the next legislative session.

As excitement and encouragement came to more and more people they became committed to the concept of comprehensive, quality day care for all young children. The idea had taken wing and was gathering sufficient strength and sense of direction to combat the thwartings and crosscurrents of controversy. With farsighted, dedicated and statesmanlike leadership it would bring new hope and accomplishment to young children, their parents and ultimately to all citizens who believed in man's future. The young child himself, without public voice or vote, gave unremitting evidence of his immeasurable potential talent. As more and more people became committed to his value and well-being, it became apparent that, even in troubled and revolutionary times, he might yet be looked after well and perhaps even soon.

And so it was that the New York City Department of Health conducted the first comprehensive, all inclusive, city-wide standard raising and licensing program in the entire country. Through an imaginative and pioneering approach, ways were found to merge public and private efforts on behalf of young children and their families. By synchronizing the work of a multiprofessional staff of consultants another pioneering step was taken, bringing together the knowledge and skills of early childhood educators, social workers, pediatricians, public health nurses, parent educators, nutritionists, sanitarians and (regrettably for a short time only) a child psychiatrist. The total dimension of day care was expanded when the inseparability of the young child from his own family was recognized. This realization brought with it the necessity for a warm, close partnership between the day care center and each child's own home. Government thus played a profoundly humanitarian role with an objective yet creative approach, bringing both consistency and innovation into the scheme of things. No profession was to be "pedestalized," yet the contribution of each was to be respected and used. Participants in the operation of a day care center, drawn from all levels of training and experience, required mature and knowledgeable leadership with a well planned, stimulating in-service training program for the entire staff. No one person or profession had all the answers. It was not the children alone who were to grow and develop to their fullest potential, but the adults as well. It was the rich mix of professional and parental expertise that would continuously enhance and coordinate the entire program.

In-service training sessions were basic also to the work of the consultant staff of the Day Care Unit. Seminars, discussions, staff meetings, lectures, the presentation of controversial issues, brought self-questioning and cross fertilization of ideas, stimulating a continuous search for new and better solutions to unresolved problems.

It seems now as though government (whether local, state or federal) is hard pressed to find appropriate new ways to use its resources and authority. Undoubtedly in day care, this means new legislation, new approaches to the evaluation process, new clues for the measurement of quality and new procedures for the coordination of effort between public and private sectors, between home, school and community, between professionals, and between services to the poor and the nonpoor. All this is to be accomplished in the face of powerful pushes for the immediate availability of infant care programs, for drop-in services for children (at any hour on any day), for evening and all-night programs, for community control, for greatly expanded day care facilities, and for federal funds to make it all possible.

New federal legislation is in preparation; federal guidelines are being developed, career ladders are being formulated while a new era in child care is awaited. Who then are to be the true advocates of the coming generation? And how will they be orchestrated?

ACKNOWLEDGMENTS

Without the concern and vision of Leona Baumgartner (Langmuir), Adele Rosenwald Levy, Helen Harris, Alice Keliher and Amy Hostler, the work described in these pages would not have been possible.

Without the ceaseless efforts of the dedicated members of the Day Care Unit staff, countless hurdles would not have been overcome and continuing progress in the face of criticism would not have been made. Among the many who contributed richly, only a few of the early members can be mentioned here: Yetta Bokhaut (Deutsch), Hila Thompson, Milton Levine, Lil Brissman (Graham), Anita Ress (Sievers), Vera Zorn, Minerva Golden (Jorn), Mabel Davis, Hugh Chaplin, Ruth Sachenhaus (Bloch), Esther Vernoff (Migdal) and nutritionist Dorothy Williams.

Without the encouragement and support of growing numbers of people in many different areas of endeavor, caring deeply about improving the quality of life for young children, this book would not have been written.

But above all else, it was the clear, primary and unquestioned focus on the children themselves that released and extended enthusiastic interest in work with and for young children.

SUGGESTED READING

Aldrich, C. Anderson & Anderson, Mary M. *Babies are Human Beings.* New York: Macmillan Co., 1938.

—————. *Feeding Our Old-Fashioned Children.* New York: Macmillan Co., 1941.

Allen, Winifred & Campbell, Doris. *The Creative Nursery Center.* New York: Family Service Association of America, 1948.

Almy, Millie. *Ways to Study Children.* New York: Teachers College Press, Columbia University, 1959.

Almy, Millie, Chittenden, Edward & Miller, Paula. *Young Children's Thinking.* New York: Teachers College Press, Columbia University, 1966.

Anthony, Katherine. *Mothers Who Must Earn.* New York: Russell Sage Foundation, 1914.

Alschuler, Rose H. (ed.). *Children's Centers.* New York: (Issued by National Commission for Young Children) William Morrow & Co., 1942.

—————. *Two to Six* (rev. ed.). New York: (Issued by National Commission for Young Children) William Morrow & Co., 1937.

American Public Health Association. *Health Supervision of Young Children.* New York: American Public Health Association, 1955.

Auerbach, Aline & Roche, Sandra. *Creating a Preschool Center.* New York: John Wiley & Sons, Inc., 1971.

Baruch, Dorothy W. *Parents and Children Go to School.* Oakland, N.J.: Scott, Foresman & Co., 1939.

Baumgartner, Leona. *One Hundred Years of Health.* Bulletin of the New York Academy of Medicine, June 1969.

Baumgartner, Leona, Goldsmith, Cornelia & Bokhaut, Yetta. *The Day Care of Little Children in a Big City.* New York: Child Welfare League of America, 1946.

Bereiter, Carl & Engleman, Siegfried. *Teaching Disadvantaged Children.* Englewood Cliffs, N.J.: Prentice-Hall, 1966.

Bettelheim, Bruno. *Love is Not Enough.* Glencoe, Ill.: Free Press, 1950.

Biber, Barbara. *Young Deprived Children and Their Educational Needs.* Washington, D.C.: Association for Childhood Education International, 1967.

——————. *Challenges Ahead for Early Childhood Education.* Washington, D.C.: National Association for the Education of Young Children, 1969.

Bloom, Benjamin S. *Stability and Change in Human Characteristics.* New York: John Wiley & Sons, Inc., 1964.

Bloom, Benjamin, Davis, Allison & Hess, Robert. *Compensatory Education for Cultural Deprivation.* New York: Holt, Rinehart & Winston, 1965.

Blow, Susan E. *The Songs and Music of Friedrich Froebel's Mother Play.* New York: D. Appleton & Co., 1898.

Bowlby, John. *Maternal Care and Mental Health.* Geneva, Switzerland: World Health Organization, 1951.

——————. *Deprivation of Maternal Care—A Reassessment of Its Affects.* Geneva, Switzerland: World Health Organization, 1962.

Breckenridge, Marion E. & Vincent, E. Lee. *Child Development.* Philadelphia, Pa.: Saunders & Co., 1960.

Brim, Jr., O. G. *Education for Child Rearing.* New York: Russell Sage Foundation, 1959.

Bruner, Jerome S. *The Process of Education.* New York: Random House, 1963.

Butts, D. R. Freeman & Russell, William F. *Search for Freedom—The Story of American Education.* New York: Teachers College Press, Columbia University, 1960.

Chandler, Carolyn, Lourie, Reginald A. & Peters, Anne D. *Early Child Care—The New Perspectives.* New York: Atherton Press, 1968.

Cole, Luella. *A History of Education, Socrates to Montessori.* New York: Rhinehart & Co., 1950.

Coombs, Philip H. *What is Educational Planning?* Paris, France: International Institute of Educational Planning, UNESCO, 1970.

Council of Chief State School Officers. *Nursery and Kindergarten Responsibilities of State Departments of Education.* Washington, D.C., 1961.

Cremin, Laurence A. *The Transformation of the School: Progressivism in American Education 1876-1957.* New York: Alfred A. Knopf, 1962.

de Lima, Agnes. *Our Enemy the Child.* New York: The New Republic, Inc., 1925.

——————. *The Little Red School House.* New York: Macmillan Co., 1942.

De Schweinitz, Karl. *Growing Up (2d ed. rev.).* New York: Macmillan Co., 1935.

Dewey, John. *Democracy and Education.* New York: Macmillan Co., 1915.

——————. *Human Nature and Conduct.* New York: Macmillan Co., 1922.

——————. *The School and Society.* New York: Macmillan Co., 1899.

——————. *Freedom and Culture.* New York: Macmillan Co., 1939.

Dittmann, Laura L. *Children in Day Care with Focus on Health.* Washington, D.C.: U.S. Children's Bureau Publication No. 444, Superintendent of Documents.

——————. *A Guide for the Development of Parent and Child Centers*. Washington, D.C.: U.S. Office of Economic Opportunity, 1967.

Dixson, C. Madeleine. *High, Wide and Deep*. New York: Day, 1938.

Erikson, Erik H. *Childhood and Society*. New York: W. W. Norton & Co., Inc., 1950.

Fraiberg, Selma H. *The Magic Years, Understanding and Handling Problems of Early Childhood*. New York: Charles Scribners Sons, 1959.

Frank, Lawrence. *The Fundamental Needs of Children*. Columbus, Ohio: Charles E. Merrill, 1938.

Frank, Lawrence, Hartley, Ruth & Goldenson, Robert M. *Understanding Children's Play*. New York: Columbia University Press, 1952.

Franklin, Adele & Benedict, Agnes E. *Play Centers for School Children*. New York: William Morrow & Co., 1943.

Freud, Anna & Burlingham, Dorothy. *War and Children*. Medical War Books, 1943.

——————. *Infants Without Families*. New York: International Universities Press, 1949.

Froebel, Friedrich. *Education by Development* (translated by Jarvis). 1899.

Gans, Roma. *Reading is Fun*. New York: Teachers College Press, Columbia University, 1949.

Gans, Roma, Stendler, Celia Burns & Almy, Millie. *Teaching Young Children in Nursery School, Kindergarten and the Primary Grades*. Yonkers-on-Hudson, N.Y.: World Book Co.

Gardner, D. Bruce. *Development in Early Childhood—The Preschool Years*. New York: Harper & Row, 1964.

Gesell, Arnold L. & Ilg, Frances L. *Infant and Child in the Culture of Today*. New York: Harper Bros. 1943.

——————. *The First Five Years of Life*. New York: Harper Bros., 1940.

Gruenberg, Sidonie Matsner. *We, The Parents—Our Relationship to Our Children and to the World Today*. New York: Harper & Bros., 1939.

Heffernan, Helen & Todd, Vivian. *The Kindergarten Teacher*. Boston, Mass.: D.C. Heath & Co., 1960.

Hunt, J. McV. *Intelligence and Experience*. New York: Ronald Press, 1961.

Hymes, Jr., James L. *Teachers Listen, The Children Speak*. New York: Committee on Mental Health, State Charities Aid Association, 1949.

Isaacs, Susan. *The Nursery Years*. New York: Vanguard Press, 1930.

——————. *Intellectual Growth in Young Children*. New York: Harcourt, Brace & Co., 1930.

Johnson, Harriet. *School Begins at Two*. New York: The New Republic, Inc., 1936.

Keliher, Alice V. *Life and Growth*. New York: D. Appleton-Century Co., 1938.

Key, Ellen. *The Century of the Child*. New York: G. P. Putnam Sons, 1909.

Lady Allen of Hurtwood. *Planning for Play*. Cambridge, Mass.: MIT Press, 1968.

Lady Allen of Hurtwood, Fiekkay, M. S., Sigsgard, J. & Skard, A. G. (eds.).

Space for Play. Copenhagen, Denmark: OMEP, 1964.

Lambert, Clara. *Play—A Yardstick of Growth*. New York: Child Study Association of America, 1938.

Landreth, Catherine. *Education of the Young Child—A Nursery School Manual*. New York: John Wiley & Sons, Inc., 1942.

Lajewski, Henry C. *Child Care Arrangements of Full-Time Working Mothers*. Washington, D.C.: U.S. Children's Bureau Publication No. 378, Department of H.E.W.

Leeper, Sarah Hammond, Dales, Ruth, Skipper, Dora & Witherspoon, Ralph. *Good Schools for Young Children*. New York: Macmillan Co., 1968.

Lemkau, Paul D. *Mental Hygiene in Public Health*. New York: McGraw-Hill, 1955.

Leonard, George B. *Education and Ecstasy*. New York: Delacorte Press, 1968.

Levy, John & Monroe, Ruth. *The Happy Family*. New York: Alfred A. Knopf, 1938.

Lewis, Claudia. *Children of the Cumberland*. New York: John Wiley & Sons, Inc., 1946.

Mayer, Martin. *The Schools*. New York: Harper & Row, Inc., 1961.

Mearns, Hugh. *Creative Youth*. New York: Doubleday Page & Co., 1925.

Mead, Margaret. *A Creative Life for Your Child*. Washington, D.C.: U.S. Children's Bureau, Dept. of H.E.W., Headliner Series No. 1, 1962.

McMillan, Margaret. *The Nursery School*. New York: Dutton, 1919.

Montessori, Maria. *The Montessori Method*. New York: Frederick A. Stokes Co., 1912.

Moustakas, Clark E. & Berson, Minnie. *A Directory of Nursery Schools and Child Care Centers in the United States*. Detroit, Mich.: Merrill-Palmer School, 1951.

Murphy, Lois Barclay. *Social Behavior and Child Personality*. New York: Columbia University Press, 1937.

——————. *The Widening World of Childhood*. New York: Basic Books, 1962.

Myrdal, Alva. *The Power of Education*. New York: Harper & Row, 1962.

New York State Education Department. *Child Development Guides for Teachers of Three-, Four- and Five-Year-Old Children*. Albany, N.Y., 1957.

Olson, Willard C. *Child Development*. New York: D.C. Heath & Co., 1949.

Owen, Grace (ed.). *Nursery School Education*. New York: Dutton, 1920.

Piaget, Jean. *The Language and Thought of the Child*. New York: Harcourt Brace & Co., 1926.

——————. *Judgment and Reasoning of the Child* (translated by Marjorie Warden). London: Paul, Trench Trubner & Co. Ltd., 1928.

——————. *The Origin of Intelligence in Children*. New York: The International Universities Press, 1952.

Poulsson, Emilie. *Love and Law in Child Training: A Book for Mothers*. Springfield, Mass.: Milton Bradley Co., 1899.

——————. *Finger Plays for Nursery and Kindergarten*. Boston, Mass.:

Lothrop, Lee & Shepard, 1921.

Pratt, Caroline. *I Learn From Children: An Adventure in Progressive Education.* New York: Simon & Schuster, 1948.

Pratt, Caroline & Stanton, Jessie. *Before Books.* 1926.

Provence, Sally & Lipton, Rose C. *Infants in Institutions.* New York: International Universities Press, 1962.

Rand, Winifred, Sweeney, Mary E. & Vincent, E. Lee. *Growth and Development of the Young Child.* Philadelphia, Pa.: Saunders, 1930.

Read, Grantley Dick. *Childbirth Without Fear—The Principles and Practices of Natural Childbirth.* London: Heinemann, 1933.

Read, Katherine H. *The Nursery School.* Philadelphia, Pa.: W. B. Saunders Co., 1950.

Redl, Fritz & Wineman, D. *The Aggressive Child.* Glencoe, Ill.: Glencoe Free Press, 1957.

Ribble, Margaret A. *The Rights of Infants.* New York: Columbia University Press, 1943.

Ridenour, Nina. *Mental Health in the United States: A Fifty Year History.* Cambridge, Mass.: Harvard University Press, 1961.

Riessman, Frank. *The Culturally Deprived Child.* New York: Harper & Row, 1962.

Rousseau, J. J. *Emile* (translated by Barbara Foxley). London: J. M. Dent & Sons Ltd., 1921.

Rudolph, Marguerita. *Living and Learning in Nursery School.* New York: Harper & Bros., 1954.

Rudolph, Marguerita & Cohen, Dorothy M. *Kindergarten: A Year of Learning.* New York: Appleton-Century-Crofts, 1964.

Rugg, Harold & Shumaker, Ann. *The Child-Centered School: An Appraisal of the New Education.* Yonkers-on-Hudson, N.Y.: World Book Co., 1928.

Russell, Bertrand. *Education and the Good Life.* New York: Boni & Liveright, 1926.

Sears, Robert R., Macaby, Elinor E., & Levin, Harry. *Patterns of Child Rearing.* Evansville, Ill.: Rowe, Peterson & Co., 1957.

Shoemaker, Rowena M. *All in Play.* New York: Play Schools Association, Inc., 1958.

Spencer, Herbert. *Education, Intellectual, Moral and Physical.* London: Williams & Norgate, 1861.

Spock, Benjamin. *The Common Sense Book of Baby and Child Care.* New York: Duell, Sloan & Pearce, Inc., 1946.

Strain, Frances Bruce. *Being Born.* New York: D. Appleton-Century Co., 1936.
—————. *New Patterns in Sex Teaching.* New York: D. Appleton-Century Co., 1934.

Tarnay, Elizabeth Doak. *What Does the Nursery School Teacher Teach?* Washington, D.C.: National Association for the Education of Young Children, 1965.

Taylor, Katherine Whiteside. *Parent Cooperative Nursery Schools.* New York:

Teachers College Press, Columbia University, 1954.

Terman, Lewis M. & Merrill, Maud A. *Measuring Intelligence.* Cambridge, Mass.: Riverside Press, Houghton Mifflin Co., 1937.

Trager, Helen C. & Yarrow, Martin R. *They Learn What They Live: Prejudice in Young Children.* New York: Harper & Bros., 1952.

U.S. Children's Bureau. *The Child from One to Six.* Washington, D.C.: U.S. Children's Bureau Publication No. 30, Dept. of Labor, 1935.

Updegraff, Ruth et al. *Practice in Pre-School Education.* New York: Mc-Graw-Hill Book Co., Inc., 1938.

Washburn, Ruth. *Children Have Their Reasons.* New York: Appleton-Century-Crofts, Inc., 1942.

Watson, John Broadus. *Behaviorism.* New York: W. W. Norton Co., 1925.

White House Conferences on Children and Youth. Washington, D.C.: Publication each decade of national reports, studies & findings.

1909 Under President Theodore Roosevelt

1919 Under President Woodrow Wilson

1930 Under President Herbert Hoover

1940 Under President Franklin Delano Roosevelt

1950 The Mid-Century Conference under President Harry Truman

1960 Under President Dwight Eisenhower

1970 Under President Richard Nixon

Wickes, Frances G. *The Inner World of Childhood.* New York: Appleton, 1927.

Woodcock, Louise P. *Life and Ways of the Two-Year-Old: A Teacher's Study.* New York: E. P. Dutton, Inc., 1941.

Journals and Newsletters

American Education. Journal of the U.S. Dept. of Health, Education, and Welfare, published 10 times a year by the U.S. Office of Education, 400 Maryland Ave., S.W., Washington, D.C. 20202.

Australian Pre-School Quarterly. Journal of Early Childhood Education (4 issues yearly), 36 Newry St., North Carlton, Victoria 3054.

Childhood Education. Journal of the Association for Childhood Education International, published monthly by ACEI, 3615 Wisconsin Ave., N.W., Washington, D.C. 20016.

Children Today. (formerly *Children*). Published by the U.S. Department of Health, Education, and Welfare, Office of Child Development, Washington, D.C.

Elementary Education. Quarterly journal for elementary educators, published by the American Association of Elementary Educators (EKNE of the (NEA), Washington, D.C.

Head Start Newsletter. Published by Project Head Start, Office of Child Development, Dept. of Health, Education, and Welfare, Washington, D.C.

International Journal of Early Childhood. Published by OMEP (World Organization for Early Childhood Education), U.S. Office: P.O. Box 142, Boston, Mass. 02113 U.S.A.

News. Published by the National Commission for Support of the Public Schools, 1424 16th St., N.W., Washington, D.C. 20036.

Report on Pre-School Education. Published every other Wednesday by the Education News Services, Capitol Publications, Suite G-12, 2430 Pennsylvania Ave., N.W., Washington, D.C. 20037.

Reporter. Published by the National Committee for Children and Youth, 1145 19th St., N.W., Washington, D.C. 20036.

Voice. Published monthly by the Day Care and Child Development Council of America, Woodward Bldg., Washington, D.C. 20005.

Young Children. Journal of the National Association for the Education of Young Children (formerly the *Journal of Nursery Education*), published bi-monthly by NAEYC, 1834 Connecticut Ave., N.W., Washington, D.C. 20009.

Curent Index to Journals in Education. C.I.J.E. is a monthly cataloging and indexing publication for journal and periodical literature in the field of education. It is available from C.C.M. Information Corp. (a subsidiary of Crowell, Collier, & Macmillan Co., Inc.), 866 Third Ave., Room 1126, New York, N.Y. 10022.

ADDENDA

T.. New York City Council

THE COUNCIL

Res. No. 112   June 14, 1938

Resolution Creating a Committee to Investigate, Determine and Report
on the Desirability of Establishing Nursery Schools in the City
of New York, and on Ways and Means of Establishing and Financing
the Same.

Whereas, Nursery Schools are socially desirable for the purpose of providing care and training of children below school age, under competent guidance
and supervision; and
Whereas, Many underprivileged children of pre-school age are now deprived
of such care and training by reason of insufficient and inadequate free public
facilities therefor, and the inability of their parents, because of depressed
economic conditions, to provide the same, and the fact that many mothers are
required to leave their children and homes during the day in order to supplement the family earnings; and
Whereas, Public spirited citizens, social agencies and educational authorities
are unanimous in recognizing the urgent need and advantage for the establishment
of nursery schools to cope with this problem; and
Whereas, Standards for nursery schools and for nursery school teachers are
now being prepared and formulated by the Department of Education of the State
of New York; and
Whereas, There exists a trained and competent personnel experienced in teaching in accredited public and private nursery schools, who can meet eligibility
requirement for appropriate examinations, if granted sufficient time therefor;
and
Whereas, The New York Chapter of the New York State Association for Nursery
Education is prepared and capable of providing initial data and statistics on
standards and educational research for various localities within the City of
New York; and
Whereas, Public nursery schools have heretofore been established in the City
of New York under the supervision of the Works Progress Administration; now
therefore be it
Resolved By the Council of The City of New York, that a committee of five
members of the City Council be named, appointed and constituted to investigate,
determine and report on the desirability of establishing such nursery schools
in the City of New York, and on ways and means for establishing and financing
the same.
Adopted by the Council on January 31, 1939

MINUTES OF THE BOARD MEETING OF THE ASSOCIATED EXPERIMENTAL SCHOOLS
January 4, 1939

Present: Miss Elizabeth Goldsmith, Miss Elisabeth Irwin, Mr. and Mrs. Fincke,
          Miss Margared Harrison, Miss Elizabeth Moos, Miss Barbara Biber, Miss
          Janet Howard, Miss Bertha Delahanty, Ralph Hill.

Chairman: Miss Irwin.

The minutes of the last meeting were read and approved.

Miss Irwin presented the following schedule of committee personnel to the group:

Officers: Mrs. William Hodson, Treasurer; Mrs. William Fincke, Secretary.

Board of Directors: Directors - Elizabeth Moos, Hessian Hills
                                  Caroline Pratt, City and Country
                                  Elizabeth Goldsmith, Walden School
                                  Elisabeth Irwin, Little Red School House
                                  William Fincke, Manumit School
                                  Barbara Biber, 69 Bank Street

                     Teachers - Janet Howard, Little Red School House
                                 Bertha Delahanty, City and Country
                                 Cornelia Goldsmith, Walden School
                                 Mildred Fincke, Manumit School
                                 Gertrude Hodson, Hessian Hills

             Members at Large - Lucy Sprague Mitchell
                                Ralph Hill
                                Margaret Harrison
                                Alice Keliher
                                Edouard Lindeman
                                Mrs. William Hodson

Executive Committee: Barbara Biber, 69 Bank Street
                     Adele Franklin, P. S. 33
                     Elisabeth Irwin, Little Red School House
                     Elizabeth Goldsmith, Walden School
                     Mildred Fincke, Manumit School
                     Gertrude Hodson, Hessian Hills

Education Committee: Elisabeth Irwin, Barbara Biber, Sybil May, Bill Fincke,
                     Tess Ross, Nell Goldsmith.

Publicity Committee: Margaret Harrison, Mildred Fincke, Elisabeth Moos,
                     Ralph Hill, Rhoda Harris.

        Considerable discussion took place about who should make up the members of the
Executive Committee, Miss Moos suggesting that there should be a member from each
school. Miss Irwin objecting to the unwieldiness of such a number for a monthly
meeting. Finally the executive committee was decided upon to be as follows:
        Miss Irwin, the head of the Executive Committee as well as the head of the Board
        Miss Moos or Mrs. Hodson from Hessian Hills
        Mildred Fincke from Manumit, as secretary
        Barbara Biber from the Nursery School
        Adele Franklin
        Elizabeth Goldsmith
According to the by-laws, four make a quorum. Miss Harrison was to come upon call.
This committee is to meet on the first Tuesday of every month, at 12:30 for lunch
at the Fifth Avenue Hotel, and to hold the afternoon open until at least 3:30.
It was agreed that every person would turn up unless ill, and not send a substitute.

131

Miss Biber made a report upon the decision of the Education Committee about the Worlds Fair project for this summer. The proposition was that a teacher from each of the A.E.S. schools should be chosen to work in a demonstration school at the Little Red School House this summer. There would be five groups of children in all, and at least two or more special teachers. New York University has expressed its willingness to make a contribution of $1500 to this project if each of the schools will give $100 a piece. A salary of $300 would then be available for each group teacher. The supervisor would be Clara Skiles Platt of New York University School of Education. Three days a week would be set aside for observation by New York University students, and two days for observation for visitors from the Worlds Fair. It is possible that to this program should be added afternoon discussion and question periods for the visitors who are interested, with admission fees paid by the visitors. The publicity for this would be managed by having a flyer in the New York University summer catalogue, and by recommendation at a booth at the Worlds Fair by the Child Study Association, which is much interested in the project. The majority of the A.E.S. schools expressed their willingness to make the $100 contribution and provide teachers. The two exceptions were Hessian Hills, which was unwilling to do it unless they could be sure that there would be special teachers, and the City and Country School, which said that its financial condition was such that it could not afford to pay $100. Miss Moos was asked to present the decision of the Education Committee that there should be special teachers to her staff as soon as possible, and to communicate with the Education Committee at once as to what their decision was. Miss Delahanty was requested to see if it would not be possible to get a special contribution from some parent of $100 for this purpose, as a failure to present a united front and to have City and Country represented was considered to be very serious.

Miss Goldsmith pointed out that as good as this idea was, the demonstration school in the end would not be truly representative of the philosophy or procedure of any one of the schools, but somewhat of a conglomeration of all of them.

The Education Committee requested that the staff of each of the A.E.S. schools send to the Education Committee, whose chairman is Miss Irwin, within fourteen days, their nominations for teachers to work in the demonstration school. With these teachers' names should come a description of their particular qualifications, the age groups they are best fitted to handle, their hopes, strengths, and weaknesses, in order that the Education Committee can make as wise and as democratic a choice as possible. These names and descriptions should be in Elisabeth Irwin's hands by January 15th.

There was some discussion about sending a letter to Albany about the refusal of the Board of Regents to give credit to student teachers who had done work in private schools. No conclusion was come to. This was in Miss Harrison's hands.

The next meeting of the Board of Directors is to be subject to call by the Executive Committee.

Respectfully submitted,

Mildred Gignour Fincke,
Secretary.

132

THE COMMISSIONER OF HEALTH
CITY OF NEW YORK

March 1, 1943

Dear Madam:

You are operating a day-care service for children under permit from the Health Department. I know that you will be interested to know that Section 198 of the Sanitary Code, under which regulations you now operate, were revised by the Board of Health at a meeting on February ninth. I am enclosing a copy of these new regulations. In the course of the revision of this Section, many individual agencies and all of the standard setting and coordinating groups interested in the promotion of good standards in child care in the City were consulted.

You will note that permits, contrary to previous practice, are now good for a period of only two years and if your agency was given its permit more than two years ago, it will be necessary for you to have a new permit. Later on in the year, you will receive an application blank to be filled out and returned to the Health Department. In the meantime we believe you will wish to study the new regulations.

The war-time emergency has focused our thinking on the care of children, and the "Survey Guide" which I am also sending you is intended to assist you in checking the quality of the health program in your own unit. This has been based on the best thinking of the leaders in the field of child care today and I hope you will find it helpful.

It is the concern of us all to make it possible for children to live and grow under happy healthy conditions and I appreciate the effort that you are making to maintain these good standards of care. The Bureau of Child Hygiene of the Department of Health stands ready at all times to assist you with problems which may arise in connection with your service.

Sincerely yours

Ernest L. Stebbins, M. D.
Commissioner

Encl. Section 198
Survey Guide for Evaluating Health
Services in Centers Providing Day-
Care for Children

CH-13-43

Dec. 1942

C I T Y   O F   N E W   Y O R K
DEPARTMENT OF HEALTH

S U R V E Y   G U I D E
f o r

EVALUATING HEALTH SERVICES
i n
CENTERS PROVIDING DAY-CARE FOR CHILDREN

Ernest L. Stebbins, M.D.
Commissioner

Leona Baumgartner, M.D.   Amelia H. Grant, R.N.
Director, Bureau of Child Hygiene   Director, Bureau of Nursing

134

TABLE OF CONTENTS

SUPPLEMENT TO THE SURVEY GUIDE

A survey of the existing literature on day care for children in the spring of 1942 revealed no tool which would adequately guide the field worker in evaluating the facilities, staff and programs of units providing such care. In New York City a section of the Sanitary Code provides that all agencies giving day care be licensed by the Department of Health. The rules and regulations under which these units operate seek to provide a safe and healthy environment for children, an adequate and suitably pre- pared staff to care for them, and appropriate facilities to promote healthful living. The need for evaluating present conditions was aug- mented because of the wartime situation and the Department of Health, therefore, decided to develop an evaluation form for conducting a survey of health services in day care units.

An advisory committee made up of members from the field of child care and preschool education was formed to guide a project designed to develop and to use experimentally in the field an evaluation form, soon called "the survey guide." Two public health nurses assisted by other professional staff acted as the active field staff. The development of an instrument for evaluation became the major object of an experimental project though it was agreed that the utility of this instrument should not be limited solely to evaluation by extra-mural investigators but that it should also be valuable for use in self-surveys by staffs of the day care units, for those who wish to establish new units, and in the education of those interested in the health care of young children. Following the initial draft of the "survey guide", field staff used it in the field and revisions were subsequently made.

This "survey guide" as herein presented is a result of the research activities outlined above and is presented with the hope that it will be useful to the many persons who are devoting much of their lives in bring- ing better care to young children. It is believed that continued use of it will forge an improved instrument and it is hoped that those who use it will adapt it to their own use and share with us the benefit of their experience.

Of the many who have assisted in making this "survey guide" possible, particular credit should be given to the project field staff: Yetta Bokhaut, Laura S. Story, Mary Brooks and Roy W. Bixler, Ed. D., and to the active advisory committee: Barbara Biber, Ph.D., Ernest G. Osborne, Ph. D., Myra Woodruff, Genevieve K. Bixler, Helen Manzer, Lillian A. Hudson, and Benjamin Spock, M. D., under the chairmanship of William H. Bristow, Ph. D.

125 Worth Street
New York, N. Y.
December 31, 1942.   Leona Baumgartner, M. D.

INTRODUCTION TO THE SURVEY GUIDE

Derivation and Interpretation of Criteria

The evaluative criteria contained in the Survey Guide are based on the activities, the physical facilities, and the environment deemed essential to the fulfillment of a satisfactory health program in agencies giving day care to children. Such a program should be designed to achieve the following purposes:

> To prevent and control disease
> To promote and develop healthful living

The term "essential" is not used in the sense of minimum essentials. The criteria have been developed on the assumption that anything as important as the health of children should be provided for in terms of maximum standards. Such standards embody American ideals concerning the worth of the child and the conservation of human resources.

These criteria are based on the belief that the health program of an agency giving day care to preschool children is an integral part of the agency's total program. The health implications inherent in the child's daily activities must be recognized by workers if a satisfactory health program is to be provided for the child.

How the Survey Guide May Be Used

As a device for evaluating health programs in existing agencies giving day care to preschool children

As an aid in the health supervision of such agencies

As an aid for the in-service training of personnel concerned with the health of preschool children

As a general guide in planning for the establishment of new agencies

Instructions for the Use of the Survey Guide

In evaluating the activities and the physical facilities the primary aim is to judge them in terms of their effectiveness in achieving the health purposes. The tendency to consider inadequate facilities or any limitation in the health service as qualifying the judgment should be guarded against. The quality of an activity should not be rated higher merely because it is being performed as well as possible under the circumstances. Credit is given for ingenuity in adjustment to such limitations in the evaluation of the program as a whole.

Use of Checklist

The checklists cover the activities, the physical facilities and the environment considered desirable for achieving the health purposes. Six symbols, which have no mathematical significance, are used in making the checklists. These symbols and their meaning are as follows:

✓ ✓ Activity, condition or characteristic is performed very satisfactorily, or is present to an outstanding degree

✓ Activity, condition or characteristic is performed satisfactorily, or is present to a satisfactory degree

- Activity, condition or characteristic is not performed satisfactorily, or is not present to a satisfactory degree

A Activity, condition or characteristic is absent

I Activity, condition or characteristic is irrelevent or inapplicable to the situation being observed

U Activity, condition or characteristic is not observed

Evaluations

At the end of each section an evaluation is made. It is recognized that a formal scheme for recording critical judgment cannot be perfectly adapted to every kind of situation observed. Therefore, space is provided for specific observations or comments to be used in recording concrete data that substantiates and makes the formal evaluation more meaningful. Low ratings must be explained when the reason is not explicit in the checklist. Any additional data not covered by the checklist which affects the evaluation should be included here.

The general evaluation of the program as a whole is made at the end of the guide. The questions should be answered explicitly, and reasons for the judgment given.

Four points of quality differentiation are used in recording the evaluations. The symbols used and their meaning are as follows:.

S. Satisfactory - good, not much need for improvement

P Passable - fair, not distinguished, improvement desirable

U Unsatisfactory- poor, acceptability questionable, improvement essential

A Absent - activity, condition or characteristic is absent

Techniques

The Survey Guide should not be marked while interviewing, but as soon as possible after the observation. Time should be taken before leaving the premises to look through the guide to determine whether all observations have been made. The evaluation of each program should be completed before going to another agency.

139

GENERAL INFORMATION ABOUT THE AGENCY

Date of Observation _____

Agency Observed _____

Location _____
        (Street and Number)   (Borough)

Membership in Coordinating or Standard Setting Agencies _____

    Name _____

       _____

Supervision by: New York City Department of Health _____
                New York City Board of Education _____
                New York State Dept. of Education _____
                New York State Dept. of Social Welfare _____

Type of Agency: Full Time Care _____ Part Time Care _____

Registration: Maximum Number of Children Permitted by License _____

         Under 1 Year _____ 2 Years through 4 years _____
         Under 2 Years _____ 5 Years and Over _____

Staff:

	Full Time	Part Time
Total Number _____	_____	_____
Director	_____	_____
Teachers	_____	_____
Assistant to Teacher.	_____	_____
Attendant	_____	_____
Social Worker.............	_____	_____
Practice Teacher..........	_____	_____
Volunteer.................	_____	_____
Nurse.....................	_____	_____
Physician.................	_____	_____
Janitor...................	_____	_____
Domestics.................	_____	_____
Others, Specify...........	_____	_____
_____	_____	_____
_____	_____	_____

Name of Observer _____

                          _____
                                Title

CRITERIA FOR THE ESSENTIAL ACTIVITIES

Prevention and Control of Disease

Bringing children together may increase the incidence and spread of communicable disease unless preventive and protective measures are observed. This health hazard is greater for children of preschool age than for older children, since a greater proportion of them have not had or been exposed to communicable diseases and they are less able to protect themselves and others from exposure. Then too, there is greater danger of complications which may affect the health of the child permanently.

Prevention and control are largely dependent upon immunization against specific diseases, avoiding direct or indirect contact with infected individuals and maintaining good health. However, the measures outlined in the Survey Guide do not guarantee freedom from communicable disease, nor do they preclude the necessity for close continuous observation of individual children and alertness to the presence of these diseases in the neighborhood or the families they serve.

Workers should be thoroughly acquainted with the provisions of the Sanitary Code as set up by the Board of Health. A copy of the rules and regulations governing communicable diseases should be kept in the agency, and when questions as to procedure to be followed or other difficulties arise they should consult the agency's physician or the Department of Health.

IMMUNIZATION

Checklist

_____Every child is immunized before admission against
_____smallpox, and
_____diphtheria

_____A supplementary injection against diphtheria is given after
three years.

_____Workers help parents acquire a proper understanding of
immunization.

Specific Observation or Other Comments

Evaluation

_____How adequate is the immunization program?

141

MORNING INSPECTION AND DAILY OBSERVATION OF THE CHILD

Checklist

_____ Morning inspection is made by a person familiar with the child and competent to recognize signs and symptoms of communicable disease or ill health.

_____ The child is inspected before coming in contact with the group.

_____ Morning inspection is utilized constructively by the staff and parents for an exchange of information concerning the child's behaviour in the last 24 hours.

_____ When signs or symptoms of ill health are noted the child is sent home with the parent _____, who is instructed in the immediate care of the child _____.

_____ Workers observe children continuously throughout the day for signs or symptoms of ill health that may occur after morning inspection.

Specific Observations or Other Comments:

Evaluation

_____ How adequate is the morning inspection and daily observation of the child?

ISOLATION

Checklist

_____ When contagion is discovered or suspected later in the day, the child is immediately isolated _____, or taken home _____.

_____ The parents _____, and the school physician or Health Department are notified _____, and the child is called for as soon as possible.

_____ The isolated child is given adequate adult supervision _____ and is provided with some form of amusement _____.

_____ The parents are instructed in the immediate care of the child _____, the need for medical advice, and the precautions necessary for the protection of others _____.

_____ Equipment and toys used by the child are washed with soap and hot water after the removal of the child.

Specific Observations or Other Comments

Evaluation

_____ How adequate are the isolation procedures?

<u>OTHER PREVENTIVE MEASURES</u>

Checklist

_____ In case of communicable disease in the child's family, the
school authorities are notified ____, and the child is kept
out of school during the period of incubation ____.

_____ Members of the staff with communicable diseases remain off
duty until danger of transmission is past ____ and abide by
the Sanitary Code in case of communicable disease in their
family ____.

_____ When children have been exposed to any communicable disease
from sources within the agency, only such new children as are
immune are accepted until the incubation period has elapsed ___.

_____ In case of epidemics the agency doctor or the Health Department
is consulted.

_____ All members of the staff are required to have a medical examination ____, including chest x-ray ____ and annual re-examina-
tions ____.

_____ The handling of food is satisfactory as shown by:
____ keeping of milk and other perishable foods under
refrigeration
____ sanitary dishwashing
____ exclusion of flies, roaches, rodents, etc.
____ sanitary disposal of garbage

_____ The housekeeping is satisfactory as indicated by:
____ clean walls, windows, floors, furniture and equipment
____ clean lavatories and toilets ____, ____ absence of odors
____ clean kitchen ____ dining facilities
____ clean sleeping facilities

Specific Observations or Other Comments

143

Evaluation

_____ How adequate are the miscellaneous measures for prevention of communicable disease?

_____ How satisfactory is the handling of food from the point of view of sanitation?

_____ How satisfactory is the housekeeping?

Promotion and Development of Healthful Living

The preschool child is in one of the most formative periods of life. Physical characteristics, attitudes and behaviours developed at this time may continue throughout life and affect his future growth and development. It is important, therefore, that experiences in which he is an active, or inactive participant, assist in the formation of a healthy behaviour pattern and the establishment of good physical health.

The promotion and development of healthful living is facilitated by good relationships and a wholesome atmosphere as well as by the specific health supervision of the child. Mutual understanding in health matters and cooperative planning between workers and parents lead to greater uniformity in their health teachings and practices as well as a better balanced daily program for the child. When adults adapt these activities and experiences to the child's interests and capacities, they not only become more meaningful to him, but provide him with greater security.

ADULT—CHILD RELATIONSHIP

Checklist

_____ The adult-child relationship is warm and friendly.

_____ Respect is shown for the child's personality.

_____ Control is maintained by other than autocratic procedure.

_____ Situations leading to emotional tensions are anticipated _____ and serious disturbances are avoided _____.

_____ Maladjustments are recognized _____, efforts are made to prevent them _____, and they are referred to experts when necessary _____.

_____ Instructions are given in terms easily understood by the child _____, and based on his level of growth and development _____.

_____ A sympathetic attitude is displayed toward injuries or other difficulties faced by the child.

_____ Care is exercised to avoid frightening the child or threatening his security either by procedure _____, or by remarks of workers or parents _____.

144

_____ Harmonious and cooperative relationships are maintained by
adults before the child?

Specific Observations or Other Comments

Evaluation

_____ How satisfactory are the adult-child relationships?

TEACHER—PARENT RELATIONSHIP

Checklist

_____ Parents and workers cooperate in coordinating the school and
home program for the child.

_____ Workers and parents confer both in the home _____ and in the
agency _____ about conditions affecting the welfare of the
child _____ .

_____ Group conferences are held for:
_____ parents
_____ parents and workers
_____ specialists to discuss special phases of the work

_____ Conferences with parents are conducted on their level of
understanding.

_____ Opportunities are provided for parent participation in the
school program _____ and to assist in planning it when
sufficiently prepared to do so _____ .

_____ Workers are familiar with community resources _____ , assist
parents in utilizing their services _____ and give proper
recognition to suggestions from parents.

Specific Observations or Other Comments

Evaluation

_____ How adequate are the teacher-parent relationships?

145

GENERAL HEALTH SUPERVISION OF THE CHILD

Checklist

_____ Admitting examination and report:-

_____ Written reports of medical examinations are on file for
each child including:
_____ a developmental and health history,
_____ clearly defined diagnosis, and
_____ recommendations

_____ When the medical examination takes place at the agency,
a responsible member of the family is present _____,
and consults with the doctor _____.

_____ When a responsible member of the family cannot be present,
a written report is sent to the parents _____, and a staff
member discusses the doctor's findings with the parent ___.

_____ The medical examination report is available to workers
_____, and is an integral part of the child's total
record _____.

_____ Workers confer with the doctor concerning his findings
and recommendations.

_____ The admitting examination is used to adapt the child's
experiences to his health needs and physical capacities
_____ and to institute remedial care _____.

_____ Medical follow-up services are provided for the child _____,
are continuous _____, and specialists are consulted when
necessary _____.

_____ Workers and parents assist in promoting the health of the
child by:
_____ Periodical measurements of weight _____ and height _____.

_____ Accurate observation _____ with recording by workers
_____ of any signs or symptoms of ill health _____
and changes in behaviour or growth _____.

_____ Use is made of information gained from any source
pertinent to child health _____ and their awareness
of the health aspects inherent in the various activities
of the program _____.

Specific Observation or Other Comments:

Evaluation

_____ How satisfactory is the health supervision of the child?

146

HEALTH VALUES IN DAILY ROUTINE

Checklist

_____ Toileting, washing and the drinking of water are carried out
so as to develop habits of good personal hygiene by encouraging:

_____ Elimination and voiding according to the child's rhythm

_____ Washing after toileting, before eating and as otherwise
needed

_____ Drinking water at regular intervals and in sufficient
amount

_____ The eating routine is utilized by the workers for development
of good eating habits and wholesome attitude towards foods by:

_____ Maintaining a calm and happy atmosphere

_____ Providing for child participation in preparing the
table and serving food when practicable

_____ Refraining from any form of coercion or reprimand

_____ Serving small portions _____, providing second helpings __

_____ Encouraging children to finish servings _____ making no
issue if they do not _____

_____ Introducing new foods singly _____, in a matter of fact
manner _____

_____ Table manners suited to the child's age taught _____,
accidents are not given undue attention _____

_____ Allowing sufficient time for eating (approx. 30 minutes)

_____ Play activities are designed to promote the physical, mental,
emotional, and social health of the child through:

_____ Adequate guidance and supervision

_____ A flexible program that can be adjusted to individual
interests and needs _____, and to the various age groups __

_____ Activities for:

_____ development of large and small musculature as
well as coordination

_____ development of motor skills such as swimming,
climbing, balancing, pushing and pulling

_____ creative and constructive experience such as draw-
ing, painting, modelling and building

_____ sensory experiences, manipulative, musical and
rhythmic

147

_____ dramatic and imaginative play

_____ Opportunities are provided for the child to:

    _____ learn to share and cooperate

    _____ develop initiative and self reliance

    _____ experience the satisfaction of successful achievement

    _____ develop a feeling of security in not being subjected
        to frustrating experiences

    _____ assume responsibility for his personal actions to the
        extent of his ability to do so

    _____ play outdoors under good hygienic conditions, including
        protection from dampness and cold_____ and accident _____

_____ Rest periods are suited to the child's needs.

_____ When naps are taken:

    _____ the length of the nap is adapted to the child's needs
    _____ the children are partially undressed
    _____ have individual bedding
    _____ the room is:
        _____ well ventilated
        _____ darkened
        _____ free from disturbing noises
        _____ not used as a thoroughfare during rest periods

    _____ short rest periods are provided:
        _____ after active or exciting play
        _____ before meals

_____ The workers endeavor to control the suitability of the child's
clothing to meet:

    _____ the requirements of the weather
    _____ free movement in normal activity
    _____ self help in dressing and undressing
    _____ changing after soiling

Specific Observations or Other Comments:

Evaluation

_____ How well is the daily routine utilized to promote the growth
and development of the child?

148

NUTRITION PROGRAM

Checklist

_____ A person with special training in nutrition plans the menus.

_____ The child's total diet is balanced by:

> _____ the inclusion of the dietary essentials necessary for the development of good nutrition of the child, i. e., proteins, carbohydrates, fats, minerals, vitamins, water

> _____ coordination of the agency's and the home diet by:

>> _____ conferring with mothers
>> _____ posting menus where mothers can consult them
>> _____ sending the menus home to the mothers
>> _____ regulating kinds and amounts of food on the basis of total intake of the child with due consideration to the amount of milk used in cooking

_____ All fresh milk is pasteurized or boiled _____ , and bottled or packaged milk is used for drinking purposes _____ .

_____ Other agencies are used when necessary in planning menus _____ , in securing adequate supply of milk and other foods _____ .

_____ Orange juice or a substitute is given daily.

_____ Cod liver oil or a substitute is given daily as prescribed by a doctor

_____ Food is prepared with consideration for preservation of nutritional qualities _____ , and digestibility _____ .

_____ Menus are varied.

Specific Observations or other Comments:

Evaluation

_____ How satisfactory is the diet?

149

Checklist

_____ First Aid for minor injuries is administered by a member of
the staff who has had First Aid Training.

_____ Standing medical orders covering any emergency are readily
available.

Specific Observations or Other Comments:

Evaluation

_____ How adequate are the provisions for first aid and emergencies?

150

CRITERIA FOR ESSENTIAL PHYSICAL FACILITIES AND ENVIRONMENT

Guiding Principles

Agencies giving day care to preschool children should be located in buildings and grounds which provide the physical facilities and environment conducive to healthful living and are easily accessible to patrons. They should be free from hazards or conditions detrimental to the health or safety of children, workers or parents.

The effectiveness and quality of the program are dependent to a large extent upon the physical facilities with which the staff must work. Ideally, buildings, playgrounds and equipment should be constructed to meet the specific purposes for which they are intended. If buildings or facilities originally devoted to other uses must be utilized, the structural changes and adjustments essential for carrying out the health program must be made.

Transportation of Children

GUIDING PRINCIPLES

In the transportation of children, provisions are made by the responsible carrier for optimum safety and comfort.

CONDITIONS AFFECTING SAFETY AND COMFORT

Checklist

_____ State or City laws are complied with.

_____ When children are transported by a school bus or private commercial carriers:

_____ the operator is properly licensed

_____ there is adequate insurance coverage

_____ the carrier is of standard construction

_____ the maximum number of children permitted by law is not exceeded

_____ an adult attendant, in addition to the driver, accompanies the children

Specific Observations or Other Comments:

Evaluation

_____ How well do transportation conditions provide for the comfort and safety of the child?

151

Site and Building

Checklist

_____ The building is within walking distance of patrons
_____ Transportation facilities are adequate
_____ Has a safe approach

_____ Quality of the environment:

_____ The immediate location is free from health hazards such as:
_____ inordinate noises
_____ excessive amounts of smoke
_____ excessive amounts of dust
_____ is not adjacent to warehouses, garages or factories
_____ light and air are not obstructed by nearby tall
buildings

_____ There is an enclosed playground
_____ with space of at least 75 square feet per child
_____ a safe and quick drying surface
_____ a balance of sunshine and shade

Specific Observations or other Comments

Evaluation

_____ How adequate are the conditions of safety and accessibility?

_____ How satisfactory are the playground facilities?

CONDITIONS AFFECTING SAFETY OF THE BUILDING

Checklist

_____ Local and State building codes and regulations are observed

_____ Traffic hazards about the building are controlled by established zones, police protection, etc.

_____ Appropriate safeguards are provided for:
_____ low windows
_____ open stairwells
_____ steam pipes
_____ radiators
_____ stairways

_____ There are no dead ends or pockets which could trap children in emergencies.

_____ Stairs and landings are safe in that they are:
  _____ in good repair
  _____ free from litter
  _____ well lighted

_____ Exits are ample in size _____, doors swing in direction of exit travel _____.

_____ Fire escapes _____, fire doors _____ are provided as needed

_____ Building is kept in good repair

Specific Observations or Other Comments:

Evaluation

_____ How adequate are the provisions for safety?

CONDITIONS AFFECTING HYGIENE AND CLEANLINESS OF THE BUILDING

Checklist

_____ No floor used by children is three feet below sidewalk level on all four sides.

_____ Floors are smooth _____, easily cleaned _____, and warm _____

_____ Walls and ceilings are light in color _____, free from glare _____, easily cleaned _____.

_____ Window shades are in good condition _____, are adjustable _____.

_____ One or more windows in the playroom and sleeping rooms open on a yard or court not less than 10 feet wide _____ and there are windows in all service rooms except storerooms _____.

_____ Tools and facilities for keeping the building clean and in good repair are provided.

Specific Observations and Other Comments:

Evaluation

_____ How adequate are its hygienic facilities?

153

Service Systems

Service systems have to be adjusted to meet the needs of a child-caring program in terms of size, sanitation and safety features. In buildings formerly used for other purposes, the equipment, fittings and furnishings should be rendered suitable for present use.

HEATING AND VENTILATION

Checklist

_____ There is an adequate heating system ____, the room temperature can be made uniform in winter ____, and maintained at approximately 68° to 70° ____.

_____ There is an accurate thermometer in each room, approximately three feet from the floor.

_____ There are at least 200 (preferably 300) cubic feet of air space per child in the playroom and sleeping room.

_____ Ventilation by window gravity includes:
____ deflectors
____ radiators under the windows

_____ The circulation of air is sufficient for comfort ____ and does not cause chilling drafts ____.

Specific Observations or Other Comments:

Evaluation

_____ How adequate are the heating and ventilating systems?

ARTIFICIAL AND NATURAL LIGHTING

Checklist

_____ The light is evenly distributed ____, is regulated according to needs ____.

_____ When artificial light is used, the source of light is:
____ enclosed in diffusing glassware
____ does not shine directly into the eyes of the children and workers
____ can be regulated

154

The intensity of light is measured _____ or estimated _____ and
is at least ten foot candles in the lightest part of the:
_____ playroom
_____ isolation room
_____ office
_____ examination room
_____ reception room
_____ kitchen

at least four foot candles (three feet from floor) in the:
_____ toilets
_____ stairways and landings
_____ corridors
_____ exits
_____ coat rooms

at least two foot candles in storeroom (on vertical plane
of the shelving) _____ .

Specific Observations or Other Comments

Evaluation

_____ How adequate is the lighting?

WATER SUPPLY

Checklist

_____ The source of water is satisfactory _____ and its temperature
can be controlled.

_____ Drinking facilities are accessible to
_____ playground
_____ playrooms

_____ and include either individual drinking cups, or
_____ a sanitary bubbler fountain 18 inches high
_____ one for every 30 children

Specific Observations or Other Comments:

Evaluation

_____ How adequate is the water supply?

155

Checklist

_____ Lavatory and toilet rooms are accessible to the:
_____ playrooms
_____ sleeping rooms
_____ playground
_____ with separate facilities for staff

_____ The rooms are large enough for four to six children to use at the same time under adult supervision.

_____ Floors and walls are of tile or non-absorbent material
_____ easily cleaned
_____ plumbing of an open sanitary type
_____ in good repair

_____ Supplies and equipment include:
_____ permanent toilet racks accessible to the child
_____ sanitary cabinet for paper towels, or _____ individual towels
_____ wash cloths
_____ combs
_____ provisions for keeping individual equipment separate
_____ at least one mirror

_____ Lavatory and toilet units are suitable in height to size of children _____, or platforms are provided _____.

_____ There is at least one toilet and lavatory unit for every 15 children.

_____ Toilets have hand operated flush valves _____, with non-breakable handles _____.

_____ Lavatories are:
_____ composed of durable material
_____ easily cleaned
_____ equipped with hot and cold water faucets
_____ valves which permit washing in running water
_____ with non-corrosive and non-breakable fittings

_____ Bathing facilities are provided for preschool children

_____ Hopper sinks are provided.

Specific Observations or Other Comments:

Evaluation

_____ How well do the lavatory and toilet facilities serve the purpose of hygiene?

156

LAUNDRY FACILITIES

Checklist

_____ Provision is made for care of soiled linen or clothing.

_____ There are facilities for washing and drying of linen and clothing.

Specific Observations or Other Comments:

Evaluation

_____ How satisfactory are the laundry facilities?

STORAGE FACILITIES

Checklist

_____ Storage facilities include:

_____ a storeroom adjoining the playroom or built-in cabinets in the playroom for orderly arrangement of equipment and supplies

_____ conveniently located space for storage of outdoor equipment

_____ conveniently located space for storage of cots, blankets, etc.

_____ storage space adjoining kitchen

_____ storage space for extra chairs needed for adult group meetings

Specific Observations or Other Comments:

Evaluation

_____ How adequate are the provisions for storage?

157

Room Facilities

While it is desirable to have separate rooms for the different kinds of activity, it is possible to use one room for more than one purpose without reducing the quality of the health program. For example, the same room may be used for playing, eating and sleeping. Space in the playroom or hallway may be equipped to care for children's wraps. The isolation room, when not in use for its major purpose, may be used for small activities or for quiet play for an over-excitable child.

It is good administration to make effective use of room facilities. However, considered judgment as well as ingenuity must be exercised in making multiple use of rooms if minimum interference with the effectiveness of the school program is to be achieved.

The furniture and equipment should be simple, sturdy and selected for the comfort of the child. Pleasant and harmonious colors make the room attractive and help to promote an atmosphere of well being.

Playroom

Checklist

_____ The playroom is separate from rooms used for other purposes.

_____ It is easily accessible to main corridors and grounds.

_____ It has exposure to sunlight from one _____, or more sides _____, and _____ the window area is at least 20 percent of the floor space.

_____ The floor area is at least 20 square feet per child.

_____ There are alcoves for quiet play _____, either built in _____, or by arrangment or placement of furniture.

_____ Shelves for toys and books are accessible to children

_____ Furniture and equipment are:
_____ easily cleaned
_____ suitable in size
_____ in good repair
_____ safe for children

_____ Play equipment is adequate for essential activities.

_____ Waste baskets are provided.

Specific Observations or Other Comments:

Evaluation

_____ How adequate is the playroom and its equipment for promotion of healthful living for the child?

158

SLEEPING ROOMS

Checklist

_____ Floor area in sleeping room is 30 square feet per child

_____ Furniture and equipment includes:
_____ cots
_____ washable pads when necessary
_____ sheets
_____ blankets

_____ Cots are placed at least two feet apart with two foot aisles.

Specific Observations or Other Comments:

Evaluation

_____ How satisfactory are the sleeping arrangements?

ISOLATION ROOM

Checklist

_____ There are provisions for simultaneous isolation of one child
out of each 25.

_____ The isolation room, or suitable room provided for this purpose,
is accessible to a toilet without coming in contact with other
children.

_____ It is located where the child can be easily supervised.

_____ The furniture and equipment include:
_____ a cot
_____ child's chair
_____ an adult chair
_____ sanitary waste can
_____ some easily sterilized toys

Specific Observations or Other Comments:

Evaluation

_____ How satisfactory are the isolation facilities?

159

EXAMINATION ROOM

Checklist

_____ The examination room, or suitable room provided for this purpose____, is accessible to office, reception room or corridor.

_____ It is free from disturbing noises

_____ The furniture and equipment include the following:
_____ examining table
_____ measuring apparatus
_____ scales
_____ eye chart (E)
_____ clinical thermometer
_____ first aid materials in a high locked cupboard
_____ desk chair
_____ two child's chairs
_____ child's table for psychological examination
_____ filing equipment
_____ sanitary waste can

Specific Observations or Other Comments:

Evaluation

_____ How adequate are the facilities for medical and psychological examinations?

OFFICE

CHECKLIST

_____ The office ____, and reception room _____ are accessible to main corridor.

_____ The furniture and equipment include:
_____ desk
_____ chair
_____ two adult chairs
_____ telephone
_____ filing equipment

SPECIFIC OBSERVATIONS OR OTHER COMMENTS:

Evaluation

_____ How satisfactory are the office facilities?

COAT ROOM

Checklist

_____ There are coat rooms _____, or built-in lockers _____ and
accessible to:
_____ main entrance
_____ playroom
_____ toilets
_____ playground

_____ Equipment includes:
_____ an open locker for each child
_____ a place for each child to sit
_____ a rack for drying wet outer clothing

_____ There are coat rooms for workers.

Specific Observations or Other Comments:

Evaluation

_____ How satisfactory are the coat room facilities?

KITCHEN

Checklist

_____ The kitchen is easily accessible to room where food is served
_____, near an outside entrance for delivery of supplies _____,
if adjacent to the playroom, it is guarded from it _____.

_____ The furniture and equipment include:
_____ stove
_____ refrigerator
_____ ventilating fan
_____ closed cabinet for dishes
_____ adequate working space
_____ utensils
_____ dishes necessary for preparing and serving food
_____ standard type sink facilities

Specific Observations or Other Comments:

Evaluation

_____ How adequate are the facilities for convenient and sanitary
preparation and serving of food?

161

SUPPLEMENT TO THE SURVEY GUIDE

FOR USE IN UNITS CARING FOR CHILDREN
UNDER EIGHTEEN MONTHS OF AGE

The supplement has been prepared for use in
day nurseries or other agencies caring for
infants and children under eighteen months
of age who are not ready for entrance in
the regular preschool program. Since the
basic health essentials are similar to
those for preschool children, the supplement is to be used in conjunction with the
general Survey Guide.

162

CRITERIA FOR ESSENTIAL ACTIVITIES

Guiding Principles

Infants and children under eighteen months of age have special
health requirements which are not entirely met by a health program
planned for preschool children. They have relatively less resistance
to disease; their digestive processes, muscles and bony structure are
less fully developed and their activities, as well as their habit
training, have been more limited. These differences are greater in
the case of young infants and become less marked as the age of
eighteen months is approached. However, agencies caring for infants
or any children under eighteen months should provide special facilities and activities designed to meet their peculiar needs.

Prevention and Control of Disease

IMMUNIZATION

Checklist

_____ Infants are vaccinated for smallpox at age three to six
             months

_____ Infants are immunized against diphtheria at age nine months

Specific Observations or Other Comments:

Evaluation

_____ How satisfactory is the immunization program?

SPECIAL PRECAUTIONS FOR INFANTS UNDER NINE MONTHS

Checklist

_____ Gowns are worn by:
             _____ doctors
             _____ nurses
             _____ attendants

_____ Masks are worn when handling the infant

_____ Visitors are not allowed in the nursery

163

_____ The formula is prepared and given according to approved
techniques, including the following:

_____boiling of bottles, nipples, caps and other equipment
used in preparing _____ and giving _____ the formula.

_____wearing of gown and cap while preparing the formula.

_____handling of individual bottles by filling_____,
capping_____, labeling_____, and keeping in refrigerator _____

_____keeping sterilized nipples in a sterile container
until used.

_____preparing formula in an unoccupied room_____with
sterile area for preparation of formula_____ by
person free from other duties _____.

Specific Observations or Other Comments:

Evaluation

_____ How adequately are these precautionary measures carried out?

Promotion of Wholesome Child Development

HEALTH SUPERVISION OF THE INFANT

Checklist

_____ The child is examined weekly by the doctor

_____ Any deviation from the normal, such as abnormal stools,
vomitting, refusal of formula, rash, or loss of weight is
reported to the doctor

_____ Doctor's orders are followed in relation to:
_____formula
_____orange juice
_____codliver oil
_____new foods (egg, cereal, vegetables, fruit juices, etc.)

Specific Observations or Other Comments:

Evaluation

_____ How satisfactory is the health supervision of the infant?

164

HEALTH VALUES IN THE DAILY ROUTINES

Checklist

_____ Social development of the infant is promoted by talking to him, encouraging him to talk, picking him up and holding him.

_____ Care is exercised not to frighten the infant by gentle handling, holding him firmly and avoiding sharp or sudden noises and abrupt movements.

_____ Care is exercised not to encourage the infant in activities beyond his muscular and structural development, such as sitting up, standing or walking.

_____ Attempts to hold cup or spoon, and other efforts at self-help are encouraged as the child shows readiness to perform these acts.

_____ Opportunity is provided for motor development and co-ordination by reaching, grasping, standing, crawling and walking.

_____ Security is developed by regular regime and by such devices as providing a toy from home.

_____ Bowel training is initiated when sufficiently mature (about 11 to 17 months)____, without coercion or compulsion ____.

_____ Voiding training is initiated after bowel training is established.

_____ The child's normal frequency is noted and regular bowel movements and voiding encouraged accordingly.

_____ Daily baths are given as necessary.

_____ Boiled water at room temperature is given between feedings.

_____ An approved method of feeding infant until doctor recommends regular preschool diet, i.e.
____warming the bottle to body temperature
____holding the infant in a comfortable position, well supported, (semi-sitting)
____feeding slowly (15 to 20 minutes)
____bubbling during and after feeding
____scraping or mincing meat
____straining or mashing vegetables and fruits
____gradual and natural weaning from bottle
____gradual introduction of coarse foods
____giving of zweibach, dry toast, etc.
____giving of codliver oil by dropper or spoon____, not mixed with other food____
____giving of orange juice by spoon, bottle or cup
____strained
____diluted with water

165

_____ Exercise is aided by:

     _____Coverings on cribs which permit freedom of movement

     _____Changing position of infant frequently

     _____Playing with infant and stimulating movement

_____ Fresh air and sunshine are provided by:

     _____Placing the crib outdoors for at least two hours a
day when the weather permits, with the child
adequately covered

     _____Sunbathing as prescribed by the doctor with eyes
protected from the sun

Specific Observations or Other Comments:

Evaluation

_____ How well are health values developed in the daily
routine?

166

CRITERIA FOR PHYSICAL FACILITIES

Guiding Principle

Since a special health program is required for the care of children under eighteen months of age, facilities designed especially for infants should be provided by agencies caring for children of this age.

Special Facilities

NURSERY

Checklist

_____ The nursery is separated from the room used by older children.

_____ It has two exits

_____ It is accessible to outdoor facilities

_____ There is an alcove (built-in or fenced off) for children learning to creep and walk.

_____ There are at least 30 square feet of floor area for each infant.

_____ There is a work table (5 x 3 feet) covered with washable material equipped with:
_____ a pad upon which to place the baby
_____ a thermometer tray with rectal thermometer
_____ a properly equipped bathing tray, including:
_____ olive oil
_____ safety pins
_____ boric acid solution
_____ talcum powder
_____ absorbent cotton _____ swabs
_____ soap
_____ individual towels _____ , wash cloths _____ , and combs _____

_____ There is an infant scale with pad.

_____ Miscellaneous equipment includes:
_____ tissues
_____ waste paper baskets
_____ covered laundry hamper
_____ high chairs
_____ chairs for attendants
_____ built-in cupboard or chests for storage of linen, diapers, clothing, etc.
_____ desk and file for infant charts

167

Specific Observations or Other Comments:

Evaluation

_____ How well is the nursery designed and equipped according to
these criteria?

OTHER FACILITIES

Checklist

_____ There is a diet kitchen or formula room with:

_____ work table

_____ equipment for sterilization of bottles, utensils, etc.

_____ bottle racks to hold formulae

_____ extra refrigeration for formulae

_____ cupboard for storage of formula material

_____ There are separate quarters for members of the staff living
on the premises.

Specific Observations or Other Comments:

Evaluation

_____ What is the quality of these facilities?

168

SPECIAL AND ADDITIONAL PERSONNEL

Guiding Principle

Because of the great importance of proper care of infants, no agency should assume the responsibility without an adequate staff of specially trained personnel.

Checklist

_____ There is a registered nurse _____, or a trained baby nurse _____.

_____ There is at least one trained nursery attendant for every eight babies, working under the supervision of the nurse.

_____ The domestic staff is adequate for the required cleaning, laundry, etc.

Specific Observations or Other Comments:

Evaluation

_____ How adequate is the personnel for the performance of the activities essential to the proper health care of infants?

169

BIBLIOGRAPHY

Nursery Schools

Alschuler, Rose H. - Edited by Children's Center. A handbook of practical
   information on the establishment of nursery schools in
   America, especially during wartime.   William Morrow & Co.,
   New York, 1942.

Andrus, Ruth, et al. Curriculum guides for teachers of children from two
   to six years of age. 293p N.Y. Day. c1936.

Baruch, Dorothy Walter, Parents and children go to school; adventuring in
   nursery schools and kindergarten. 504p. Chicago, Scott, c1939.

Blatz, William E., Millichamp, Dorothy, and Fletcher, Margaret. Nursery
   education, theory and practice. 365p. N.Y. Morrow 1935.

Bradbury, Dorothy E., and Skeels, Esther Leech. Bibliography of Nursery
   school education, 1935-1939. 64p. National Association for
   Nursery Education. 1939.

Foster, Josephine C., and Mattson, Marion L. Nursery-School Education.
   For teachers and parents on what we may expect in the well
   managed nursery school. 361p. N.Y. Appleton-Century. 1939.

Landreth, Catherine, Education of the Young Child; a nursery school manual.
   279p., John Wiley & Sons, Inc., N.Y. 1942.

Iowa, University of, Child Welfare pamphlets, Iowa City.
             No. 5. The young child and his education. Ruth Updegraff 1939
             No.10   How the child's mind grows. Beth L. Wellman, 1930
             No.17   What the kindergarten and nursery school have in
                     store for parent and child . George D. Stoddard
                     1933.
             No.46   A syllabus in nursery school education.
                     Ruth Epdegraff, 1935.
             No.57   The nursery school as a family aid. Grace Langdon
                     1936.

             The University of Iowa issues at irregular intervals,
             concise pamphlets of from eight to eighteen pages on
             various phases of child welfare. They are directed to
             parents and teachers. There are seventy-eight to date;
             some are particularly interesting to nursery school
             teachers and we have listed these.

National Association for Nursery Education. Essentials of nursery
   education, with special reference to nursery schools,
   prepared by Rose H. Alschuler, 32p. W514 East Hall,
   University of Iowa, Iowa City, 1941.

   Some ways of distinguishing a good nursery school. Folder.
   1938. Gives nineteen "pointers" for judging a nursery school.

Updegraff, Ruth, et al. Practice in preschool education. 408p. N.Y.
   McGraw-Hill, 1938.

Other Forms of Day Care

Kenny, Luna E., editor. A symposium: case work programs in day nurseries. 18p. N.Y. Child Welfare League of America and National Federation of Day Nurseries, 1937.

Health

Aldrich, C. A. and Mary M., Babies are Human Beings, N.Y. MacMillan 1938

Mohr, Edna, editor. Health program in the nursery school. Compiled and arranged by Jessie Craig, nutritionist, and Veronica Ryan, R.N., 16p. Chicago. Elizabeth McCormick Memorial Fund,1937.

Smith, Richard M., and Thom, Douglas A., Health; physical, mental and emotional. 286p. Boston. Houghton, 1936.

Stimson, Philip Moen. A manual of the common contagious diseases. A good text book for staff use. 3rd edition. 465p. Philadelphia. Lea and Febiger. c1940.

U.S. Children's Bureau. The healthy well-nourished child (1 to 6 years). Folder 17. Washington. Government. 1940. Your Young Child's Health (1 to 6 years). Folder 21. Washington. Government. 1940.

U.S. Public Health Service. Communicable diseases. A. M. Stimson. 111p. Washington. Government. 1939. (Miscellaneous publication 30).

Food and Eating Problems

Aldrich, Mary M., Feeding our old fashioned children. 112p. N.Y. MacMillan 1941.

American National Red Cross. Food and nutrition. 87p. Washington. American National Red Cross. 1942.

Borgeson, Gertrude M. Techniques used by the teacher during the nursery school luncheon period. 214p. N.Y. Teachers College, Columbia University. 1938. (Child-development monograph 24.)

Hann, Helen Nebeker, and Stiebeling, Hazel K. Food consumption of children at the National Child Research Center. 34p. Washington, Government. 1938. (U.S. Department of Agriculture Circular 481.)

Lowenberg, Miriam E., Your child's food. 299p. N.Y. McGraw-Hill. c1939. Menus which may be used by the entire family.

Lowenberg, Miriam E., Food for Children in Group Care, Children's Bureau Publication 285. Washington, D.C., 34p.

McCay, Jeanette B., Waring, Ethel B., and Kruse, Paul J., Learning by Children. At noon meal in a nursery school.

171

Sweeny, Mary E., and Buck, Dorothy Curts. How to feed children in
        nursery schools. 85p. Detroit. Merrill-Palmer School.
        1936. How to feed young children in the home. 68p.
        Detroit. Merrill-Palmer School. 1937.

Sweeny, Mary E., and Chatfield, Charlotte. Midday meals for preschool
        children in day nurseries and nursery schools. 47p.
        Washington. Government. 1932. (U.S. Department of
        Agriculture Circular 203.)

Educational Program

Alschuler, Rose H., and Heinig, Christine. Play; the Child's Response
        to Life. Advice on material for indoor and outdoor
        play. 256p. Boston. Houghton. 1936.

Biber, Barbara. Children's Drawings from Lines to Pictures. 43p., N.Y.
        Bureau of Educational Experiments. 1934.

Boettiger, Elizabeth, Children Play Indoors and Out, N.Y. E. P. Dutton
        c1938.

Johnson, Harriet M., The Art of Block Building. 48p. N.Y. Day. 1933.

Kawin, Ethel. The Wise Choice of Toys. Designed to teach parents what
        kinds of toys are most valuable for children of given
        interests, abilities and stages of development. Revised
        edition. 154p. Chicago. University of Chicago press. 1938.

Lambert, Clara. Play; a Yardstick of Growth. Covers the development of
        summer play schools and relation of play to environment.
        41p. N.Y. Child Study Association of America. 1938.

Shedlock, Marie L., The Art of the Storyteller. 287p. N.Y. Appleton-
        Century. 1936.

Thorn, Alice G. Music for young children. Describes is detail the four
        types of music participation of interest to children.
        158p. N.Y. Scribner. 1929.

Child Psychology and Development

Gesell, Arnold, et al. The first five years of life; a guide to the study
        of the preschool child. 393p. N.Y. Harper. c1940.

Isaacs, Susan, The Nursery Years. Describes typical situations between
        parents and children which appear as problems and prove
        to be indications of normal development. 138p. N.Y.
        Vanguard Press 1932.

Meek, Lois Hayden. Your Child's Development and Guidance - Told in
        Pictures. 166p. Philadelphia. Lippincott. 1940.

Jersild, Arthur, Child Psychology. Revised Ed. 591p. Prentice-Hall 1942.

Wolf, Anna W. M. Parents' Manual; a Guide to the Emotional Development
of Young Children. 331p. N.Y. Simon and Schuster. 1941.

War and the Young Child

Baruch, Dorothy, You, your Child and War. 234p. N.Y. D. A. Appleton-
Century. 1942.

Child Study Association of America. Children in Wartime; parents'
questions. 16p. N.Y. Association. 1942.

Dixon, Madeline, Keep them Human, 156p. N.Y. John Day. c1942.

Eliot, Martha M., Civil Defense Measures for the Protection of Children;
report of observations in Great Britain, February 1941. 186p.
Washington. Government. 1942. (Children's Bureau Publication
279.)

New York State Council of Defense and the State Departments of Education,
Health, Labor, Mental Hygiene, Social Welfare. Education
for Civilian Defense:
Bulletin No. 1 Community Programs of Child Care, Develop-
ment and Protection.
No. 2 Selection and Training of Volunteers as
Child Care Aids.
No. 3 Parents Prepare: Maintaining Family Morale
in Wartime.
Albany, State Council. 1942.

Proceedings of Conference on Day Care of Children of Working Mothers -
with special reference to defense areas. 84p. Washington
Government. 1942. (Bureau publication 281.)

Standards for Day Care of Children of Working Mothers. 20p. Washington.
Government. 1942. (Children in Wartime No. 3. Bureau
Publication 284.)

Wolf, H. W., Our Children Face War. Houghton Mifflin. Boston. 1942.

APPRAISAL OF THE TOTAL PROGRAM

Evaluations

_____ How well are the activities of the health program designed to prevent and control disease?

_____ How well are the activities of the health program designed to promote healthful living?

_____ How adequate are the physical facilities for supporting essential activities?

Points for Consideration:

_____ In what respects is the health program or use of facilities commendable?

_____ What situations or conditions hamper the effectiveness of the health program?

_____ In what ways does the agency feel it can use the services or help of the Department of Health or other agency?

_____ What recommendations and suggestions would be made for improvement of the health program?

174

CHILDREN IN WARTIME

OFFICIAL BULLETIN OF THE
COMMITTEE FOR THE CARE OF
YOUNG CHILDREN IN WARTIME

VOL. 1 - NO. 1   MARCH 5, 1942

INTRODUCING OURSELVES

This is the first bulletin of the COMMITTEE FOR THE CARE OF YOUNG CHILDREN IN WARTIME.

The Committee is made up of representatives of trade unions (AFL, CIO and independent), professional educational organizations, parents' groups, school faculties, and prominent individuals, all of whom believe:

1. That winning the war is all-important.
2. That the best and fastest way to win the war is to release the power of the American people for production, and
3. That the battle for production cannot be won with almost
   half of the nation's productive power--the women of
   America--unable to help.
4. That America's children must have the best care the
   nation can offer.

America will necessarily need more and more men to fight on her far-flung battle lines. Women must take their places on factory production lines, in offices, and in civilian defense. England found that to be so, Russia found it to be so.

This country has already started to absorb women into its industry in fast-increasing numbers. The COMMITTEE FOR THE CARE OF YOUNG CHILDREN IN WARTIME therefore proposes:

That the government (federal, state, city or any combination of the three) immediately establish CHILD CARE CENTERS where working mothers can leave their young children during the working day and feel assured that they will receive proper care and protection.

And further, that present facilities for children from six to fourteen be extended to all-day care.

CHILD CARE CENTERS WILL RELEASE THOUSANDS OF WOMEN FOR WORK.

CHILD CARE CENTERS WILL INSURE THE HEALTH, WELFARE AND EDU-
CATION OF OUR CHILDREN.

CHILD CARE CENTERS WILL BUILD AMERICA'S MORALE.

175

WHAT IS A GOOD NURSERY SCHOOL?

DO YOU KNOW THAT when four or more children between the ages of two and six play together regularly under supervision, they are considered a nursery school according to a law enacted in New York State in 1939? The law, which sounds stringent is actually a protection for preschool children. It aims to prevent untrained, poorly prepared people from setting up schools which do not meet minimum standards for the care of young children. All schools in New York City should be registered under regulations prescribed by the Board of Regents.

No school can be registered unless it meets with the standards of the Advisory Committee on Schools for Young Children which is cooperating with the New York State Department of Child Welfare and Parent Education.

A GOOD NURSERY SCHOOL SHOULD HAVE:

Permits from local Boards of Health and Building Departments to operate

Health supervision by a trained person; adequate provision for emergencies

Healthful and well planned arrangements for children to eat and rest

Adequate well-kept toilet facilities

Ample space indoors for the children to play freely, good light and ventilation, protection against safety hazards

Outdoor play space provided with equipment for active physical play; slides, sand box, climbing apparatus, boxes, boards, wheel toys, etc.

Teachers who like and understand young children; who can create a warm and happy atmosphere. This means teachers who have been trained according to the best modern practices for nursery age

Equipment suitable to young children's abilities and interests such as paints, clay, crayons, blocks, toys for playing house, dolls, hammers and nails, books, etc.

Teachers who can stimulate the children to genuinely creative play which yields them real pleasure and is also the most important means for their social and intellectual growth

A relaxed atmosphere where a child can grow at his own pace, find interesting things to do, grown-ups he can trust who will give him a good measure of freedom to follow his own impulses

Teachers who can control children without resorting to severe disciplinary threats or punishment

A program which provides opportunity for the children to learn a natural kind of give and take as they play freely together, enjoy common experiences and adjust to each other's personalities

Enough teachers to meet the needs of individual children and to provide interesting experience for the group as a whole

Grown-ups who know how to let children discover things for themselves and at the same time lead them to further discoveries; who can help the child fulfill his child-like curiosity about the world around him

Sufficient funds to insure fair salaries for teachers

Teachers who understand the importance of understanding and working with parents.

HOW TO GET A WPA NURSERY SCHOOL

If you provide part - quite a big part - the WPA, through the sponsorship of the Board of Education, will provide the rest of a WPA Nursery School. Here are the rules:

1. *General:* Find 25 children between the ages of two and five whose parents are in "relief status". Relief status is an elastic term. The Board of Education checks with local agencies to decide. There is no set income level. Income might be a bit higher than you suspect. *WPA provides some equipment.*

2. *Specifically:* You must provide space and equipment. Space must meet requirements of Health Department. You must have one toilet and wash basin to each 15 children. There must be one or two large rooms, cooking facilities and outdoor play space. Fire hazards must NOT exist - no wooden stairs, adequate fire-escapes, etc. Equipment must include small size cots, blankets, small tables and chairs, towels, bibs, washcloths, cooking utensils, tableware and play equipment such as slide, sandbox, blocks, paint, dolls, clay.

With equipment promised and the space and children lined up, write to Louis Herbert, Board of Education, 110 Livingston Street, Brooklyn. The Board of Education and the Department of Health will then check space, equipment and applicants.

If these are okay, the WPA through the Board of Education will supply: A head supervisor and about three teachers for 25 children; daily medical inspection; food for lunches.

Mr. Herbert is very sympathetic to all nursery school projects including WPA. He treats applications with interest and respect but he has an equal respect for standards so your space and equipment must be adequate. Firetraps won't do. Big cots sink in the middle.

Any group may set out to get one of these WPA Nursery Schools but it must be clearly understood that children cannot be limited to only one group. First come, first served. *Restrictions make these schools of little use to mothers in defense industries. Space being almost impossible to find gratis nothing happens -*

177

WHAT YOU CAN DO –

1. Support the Dorn-Johnson Bill

    Write to:

    > Honorable Irving M. Ives, Chairman of Assembly
    >   Committee on Defense, Albany, New York
    > Honorable Abbott Low Moffat, Chairman of Assembly
    >   Committee on Ways and Means, Albany, New York
    > Honorable Fred A. Young, Chairman, Senate Committee
    >   on Public Education, Albany, New York
    > Honorable Wheeler Milmoe, Chairman, Assembly Com-
    >   mittee on Public Education, Albany, New York
    > Honorable Francis A. Dorn, New York State Assembly,
    >   Albany, New York
    > Honorable Robert E. Johnson, New York State Assembly,
    >   Albany, New York

2. Get your organization to affiliate with the Committee and send
    delegates to our meetings

3. Organize a committee in your own neighborhood and send delegates
    to our meetings

4. Write letters telling of your interest in CHILD CARE CENTERS and
    what they would mean to you –

    To:

    > The Newspapers – The Governor – The Mayor –
    > James Marshall, President, New York Board of
    > Education, 110 Livingston Street, Brooklyn, N.Y.
    > John W. Studebaker, Office of Education in War-
    > time Commission, Washington, D.C.

Committee for the Care of Young Children in Wartime
535 Fifth Avenue, Room 1106, New York City

uopwa#16

Repealed and Reenacted Feb. 8, 1943
Amended Nov. 26, 1946

SECTION OF SANITARY CODE AND REGULATIONS
GOVERNING AGENCIES GIVING DAY CARE TO CHILDREN

Section 198. Agency giving day care to children defined; conduct thereof regulated; permit required.

1. It shall be unlawful to conduct an agency giving day care to children in the City of New York without a permit therefor issued by the Board of Health, or otherwise than in accordance with the terms of said permit and with the regulations of said board.

2. The term "Agency giving day care to children" shall mean and include any institution or place, whether known as a day nursery, nursery school, kindergarten, child play or progressive school or under any other name, which for compensation or otherwise, receives for temporary custody with or without stated educational purpose, during part or all of the day, apart from their parents, four (4) or more children under six (6) years of age and not of common parentage.

3. A permit under this section shall not be required for a nursery school or kindergarten attached to, and conducted by the public school authorities or an established religious group as a part of, an elementary school in accordance with Section 200 of the Sanitary Code, but such nursery school or kindergarten shall be maintained in conformity with the regulations hereunder relating to agencies giving day care to children.

(Repealed and reenacted February 9, 1943 and amended March 14, 1944)

Regulation 1. Application for Permit.

An organization, corporation, partnership, or individual proposing to operate a day care agency shall:

1. Make application in person to the Bureau of Child Hygiene of the Department of Health and fill out and submit on a form supplied by the Department information concerning the proposed agency. At the same time the owner or his agent shall submit:

(a) Floor plan showing all of the rooms, indicating uses for child caring purposes in said agency.

(b) A statement of the purpose of the agency and a description of the program and activities designed to carry out these purposes.

(c) A statement of the method to be used in admitting children for care.

(d) Evidence of a reasonably secure financial position to permit compliance with these regulations.

2. Before the permit is issued the Department of Housing and Buildings and the Fire Department shall approve the premises in question as to safety for the use intended.

179

3. No such agency shall be conducted in a factory, mercantile or business building, or be located above the third floor unless an elevator is provided.

Regulation 2. Permits, Posting Thereof.

The permit issued by the Board of Health shall be good for two (2) years unless sooner revoked and is not transferable. Such permit shall be posted in a conspicuous place in the entrance lobby or the reception room of the premises to which it applies.

PHYSICAL PLANT

Regulation 3. Rooms.

(a) Rooms used by children under two (2) years of age must be entirely apart from those used by other children. Rooms used by children over eight (8) years of age must be entirely set apart for their exclusive use while they are in the building.

(b) No room used for the care of children shall be so located that the floor on any of the four sides is more than three feet below the surface of the ground surrounding the building.

(c) The minimum allowance of space for each child in a play room shall be 20 square feet of floor space and 200 cubic feet of air space.

(d) Every room used for child-caring purposes shall have one or more windows opening upon a public thoroughfare, or a yard or court not less than 10 feet in depth and extending the length or width of the building.

(e) Adequate ventilation by natural or mechanical means shall be provided in each room.

(f) All parts of the building used by the children shall be adequately lighted and heated. The use of gas for lighting or heating in the children's quarters is prohibited.

(g) When the street temperature is less than fifty-five (55) degrees Fahrenheit, a temperature of between sixty-eight (68) and seventy-two (72) degrees Fahrenheit shall be maintained in all rooms used by the children except when sleeping. An accurate thermometer shall be hung in each room approximately three (3) feet from the floor.

(h) All walls, ceilings and floors shall be finished so as to be readily washable. Rooms shall not be swept or dusted while occupied by the children. Heavy draperies, upholstered furniture, carpets or other articles that hold the dust are prohibited in rooms used by children.

(i) All parts of the premises and all furnishings and equipment and materials used shall be kept at all times in a sanitary condition free from flies, rodents and other vermin.

(j) A lighted room or compartment shall be provided sufficiently large and so arranged that a child's outer garments may be hung separately.

(k) A properly ventilated space acceptable to the Department of Health shall be available for the temporary isolation of any child having symptoms of sickness, pending proper disposition of the case.

180

Regulation 4. Equipment and Furnishings.

(a) Educational and Recreational Equipment.-
Such material shall be clean, safe, and easily accessible to the children
at all times. Such equipment shall be free from sharp, loose or pointed
parts and all paints used thereon shall be lead free. It shall include play
materials appropriate to the stage of development of the children under care,
and designed to foster physical and motor development and creative play.

(b) Sleeping facilities.- A separate crib, canvas or metal cot or slat bed unit
shall be provided. Cots and slat beds must be so placed as to provide at
least 2 feet of space on all sides except that adjacent to a wall. If not
so placed each cot or slat bed shall be provided with a screen or partition
extending at least eight inches above the bottom and running the full length
of the cot or slat bed. Pillows and mattresses are prohibited for children
unless entirely covered by a moisture-proof material. Sheets on cribs shall
be provided for children two (2) years old and under. Sufficient blankets
shall be provided for all children to maintain adequate warmth during rest
and sleeping periods.

(c) Toilet facilities.- There shall be provided within the building convenient
to class or play room an adequate number of stationary washbasins with water
and waste connections and flush toilets, each of such height and size as to
be easily used by the children. If large equipment is installed, platforms
or steps shall be provided so that the children may use such equipment without assistance. Where new equipment is being installed or replacements made,
toilet seats with open fronts and of low height and small size so as to be
easily and safely used without necessitating steps or platforms should be
secured. The minimum allowance of toilet facilities shall be one flush

toilet and one stationary washbasin for every 15 children. An adequate supply of hot and cold running water shall be provided and the plumbing shall
be of the open sanitary type. If the agency is used by children of six (6)
years of age and over, toilets shall be separated by partitions at least
four feet high and shall not be used by boys and girls at the same time, and
a minimum of one toilet and one stationary washbasin for each 25 children
shall be provided.

(d) Washing facilities. - Soap and individual wash cloths and towels shall be
provided and arrangements made to keep all toilet articles separate. The
use of hair brushes is prohibited. If combs are used individual combs must
be provided.

(e) Drinking water.- Drinking water supplied by sanitary means shall be easily
accessible to class or play room, and individual drinking cups shall be provided. If bubble fountains are provided there shall be one for each thirty
(30) children. If water supply other than the public supply is used, it
shall be approved by the Department of Health.

(f) Care of diapers.- All soiled nursery linens, including diapers and articles
of infant clothing, shall be freed from fecal or other material and shall be
then immediately placed in a covered receptacle provided for this purpose.
Thereafter, they shall be thoroughly washed and sterilized by boiling in
water for 15 minutes or by any other approved method of sterilization, or if
removed from the premises before such sterilization, similar service shall
be provided by a laundry operating under a license issued by the Department
of Licenses of the City of New York. This procedure shall be so accomplished
that there shall be no opportunity for contaminating food or infecting
children.

181

(g) Eating. - Provision should be made for comfort during meals. Tables and chairs of proper height and size and adequate eating equipment that the child can handle easily shall be provided.

(h) Clothing.- Sufficient clothing for younger children shall be provided for wear in the agency to redress children in case of accident or if any should come in an uncleanly condition. All such clothing shall be thoroughly washed before being used for another child.

(i) First-aid.- An approved Red Cross first-aid kit shall be provided and kept completely stocked for emergency treatment, and readily available at all times and at least one staff member of those in charge of the children shall be qualified to administer first-aid.

Regulation 5. Care of Foodstuffs and Utensils.

(a) All foodstuffs shall be kept in clean covered receptacles.

(b) Milk shall be kept at a temperature below fifty (50) degrees Fahrenheit, and if purchased otherwise than in bottles, it must be transferred to sterile covered receptacles out of which it may be served without ladling.

(c) Milk bottles, nipples, and cooking utensils used in infant feeding shall be cleansed and sterilized in accordance with the physician's directions.

(d) Garbage receptacles, covered and of adequate size, shall be provided and the contents removed from the premises daily. The receptacles shall be cleaned (scalded) after emptying.

(e) Adequate refrigerators shall be supplied for food required to be kept at low temperatures.

Regulation 6. Admissions.

The number of children specified in the permit is the maximum number permitted in the agency at any one time.

The following children shall not be admitted:

(a) Children with frequent epileptic seizures or an objectionable physical or mental condition.

(b) Children with any communicable disease.

(c) Children between the ages of nine (9) months and ten (10) years of age who have not been given prophylaxis respectively against smallpox and diphtheria. Exception may be made provided parent or guardian gives written consent for such prophylaxis. In such case a child shall be given prophylaxis within a reasonable time after admission unless there are medical contra-indications, in which case a doctor's certificate stating such contra-indications shall be submitted when child is admitted.

(d) A nursing child shall not be admitted unless specific approval of the agency's physician has been secured.

Regulation 7. Health and Medical Care.

1. Examinations.- Each child shall be given a complete medical examination by a physician before admission to the agency. A written record of such examination shall

be filed with the agency, and shall include certification of freedom from communicable disease, measurement of weight and height, and recommendations for necessary medical treatment and special regimen as to diet, rest, etc. Each pre-school child shall be re-examined by a physician at least every six (6) months, and a record of such examination, including measurement of weight and height, shall be filed with the agency.

2. Morning inspection. - Such inspection shall be made by a person familiar with the child and competent to recognize, symptoms of communicable disease and ill health.

3. Communicable disease.

(a) If any child in the agency develops symptoms of illness, he shall be isolated from the other children until he can be seen by a physician or safely removed from the agency. If the symptoms point to a communicable disease enumerated in Section 86 of the Sanitary Code, notice shall be given to the Bureau of Preventable Diseases by telephone, and the parent or guardian notified.

(b) Children, directors, teachers or other agency personnel with a communicable disease, or who have recently recovered from a communicable disease, or in whose family there is a communicable disease, mentioned in Section 94 of the Sanitary Code, shall not be permitted to attend a day care agency unless evidence appropriate to the particular case as hereinafter specified is presented.

   (1) In the case of recovery from typhoid or paratyphoid fever, and in the case of recovery from or contact with diphtheria, or smallpox, either the Department of Health form 302-V, or the Department of Hospitals form SR-3063-A, issued by a duly authorized representative of the respective Department.

   (2) In the case of recovery from meningococcus meningitis, poliomyelitis or streptococcal sore throat, including scarlet fever, either the Department of Health form 302-V, or the Department of Hospitals form SR-3063-A, issued by a duly authorized representative of the respective Department, or a physician's written and signed statement certifying the individual's recovery and freedom from disease in communicable form. Contacts of cases of meningococcus meningitis, poliomyelitis and streptococcal sore throat, including scarlet fever, are not excluded from the agency.

   (3) In the case of recovery from measles, mumps, German measles, chicken pox, or whooping cough, either the Department of Health form 302-V, or the Department of Hospitals form SR-3063-A, issued by a duly authorized representative of the respective Department, or a physician's written and signed statement certifying recovery and freedom from disease in communicable form. If no such certificate is presented, the individual may be readmitted if the period of isolation as specified in the regulations under Section 89 of the Sanitary Code is completed. These periods are as follows:

      Measles - Five days after appearance of rash.
      Mumps - Until all swelling of the affected glands has disappeared.
      German measles - Five days after appearance of rash.
      Chicken pox - Seven days from onset (appearance of rash).
      Whooping cough - Twenty-one days after whoop appears.
      Contacts of cases of measles, mumps, German measles, chicken-pox, or whooping cough are not excluded from the agency.

4. Accidents and serious illness. - When cases of accident or serious illness

call for immediate medical care, the agency shall be responsible for securing that care, notifying parent or guardian of child.

5. Rest.-Quiet periods totalling at least one hour daily must be provided for each child, part or all of which should be taken lying on a cot adequately covered. The room should be well ventilated and an attendant on duty.

6. Outdoor play space.

(a) A safe and sanitary outdoor play space shall be available.

(b) Except in inclement weather and in the case of individual children where the physician advises otherwise, children under two (2) years of age shall be placed out of doors a part of each day at a time when the outdoor play space is not in use by older children.

(c) Outdoor play under supervision for at least two (2) hours daily shall be required for all children over two (2) years except during inclement weather or unless otherwise ordered by the agency physician.

7. Diet.- Nourishing food following a standard dietary acceptable to the Department of Health and adapted to the different age groups shall be provided at intervals not exceeding four hours. If an agency provides care for more than six (6) hours a hot meal served at noon and a daily allowance of at least a pint of milk a day are required.

Regulation 8. Staff.

(a) Constant and competent supervision must be provided for all children. The executive in charge should be a competent administrator with a knowledge of child development and behavior and shall have the capacity and responsibility for training other members of the staff. Training should include work with children under professional supervision, work with parents, a knowledge of community resources and how to use them. Such executive should also have demonstrated ability to make practical use of such training. All members of the staff should be friendly and emotionally stable, and have a sympathetic understanding of family and children's problems. The board, officers, or other persons having charge, management or control of an agency shall require of all executives and other employees who work in the agency and come in contact with the children, when appointed and annually thereafter, a certificate from a physician certifying such teacher or other employees to be free from disease in communicable form. Such certificate shall be based on a medical examination and chest x-ray, with such laboratory tests as may be indicated, and shall be kept on file.

(b) At least one (1) attendant shall be provided for each eight (8) children under two (2) years; one (1) for each fifteen (15) children from two (2) to four (4) years of age; one for each twenty-five (25) children from four (4) to six (6) years of age and one (1) for each thirty (30) school children over six (6).

Regulation 9. Records.

A permanent register shall be kept of the name, home address and birth date of each child admitted; the names and home address of the parents or guardian, the place at which said parent can be reached in case of an emergency, during the hours when the child is in care of the agency, the date of admission, date of discharge with reason therefor.

A daily record shall be kept of children admitted.

Regulation 10. Inspection.

An agency and its records shall be open at all times for inspection by a duly authorized agent of the Department of Health.

Regulation 11. Additional Special Provisions Affecting Children Under Eighteen (18) Months of Age.

1. Medical care.- Infants under one year shall be seen by the agency's physician at least once a week and weight records shall be made weekly for such a child.

2. Diet.- The diet of children under eighteen (18) months of age shall be regulated by the agency's physician, who shall prescribe a regimen including feeding formula and feeding intervals for each infant under one year. All formulae shall be prepared under sanitary conditions and no formula shall be changed without the approval of the physician. If a child is already under regular medical supervision, the agency's physician shall consult with the physician providing this supervision to reach agreement on feeding advice.

3. Staff.- Where children under eighteen (18) months of age are cared for, a trained babies' nurse immediately responsible for their care and a physician who can supervise in detail the diet and progress of each infant shall be provided.

Regulation 12. Discretion of the Board.

If there are practical difficulties or unnecessary hardships in carrying out the strict letter of these regulations in any day care agency existing at the time these regulations take effect, the Board of Health in its discretion and in a specific case may modify any provision in harmony with their general purpose and intent and upon such conditions as it may deem necessary for the children's welfare.

(Repealed and reenacted February 9 1943 and amended November 26, 1946).

LEGISLATIVE TRENDS IN NURSERY EDUCATION

Cornelia Goldsmith

1944

"The training and educational programs of the Army, the Navy and
civilian agencies during this war have broadened our conception of the role
that education should play in our national life. The records of selective service
reveal that we have fallen far short of a suitable standard of elementary and
secondary education. If a suitable standard is to be maintained in all parts of
the country, the Federal Government must render aid where it is needed. Such
financial aid should involve no interference with state and local control and
administration of educational programs. It should simply make good our obligation
to all our children" - from President Roosevelt's message to Congress.

New educational legislation on both the Federal and the State levels
is at present pending. Increased financial support to education, including
nursery schools and kindergartens, and reapportionment of school monies are vital
and necessary throughout the length and breadth of our land. Inequalities of
educational opportunities for our children are intolerable in a true democracy.
What is sound educational policy and procedure for children in any given area is
equally sound for children in another area, as well as for children of every race,
color or creed.

Our schools today are facing a critical situation. Increasing costs
of education have been rising steadily. Teachers' salaries have not kept up
with the increased living costs. Children have suffered also through the serious
dislocations of our population due to the war. It is urgently necessary that the
Federal Government give support to the states for the establishment and maintenance
of nursery schools and kindergartens, as well as elementary, secondary and adult
education schools throughout the country. It is high time that we comprehended
fully and put officially into effect our conviction that education begins with
the toddler and is a continuous, never-ending process through adulthood. To
develop the fullest potentialities of our citizenry and therefore of our nation,
education must be available without arbitrary age limitations or favoritism toward

186

special groups or those in more fortunate geographical areas. It is essential
that the Federal Government equalize opportunities for education throughout all
the states. Nursery schools should be included in any such Federal legislation.
Only thereby will education become a continuous process, as life is a continuous
process, and prevail as it should wherever life exists.

In New York State Governor Dewey has recommended a revision of the
outmoded Friedsam formula and has named a commission to recommend a new basis for
the apportionment of school funds. As Governor Dewey has stated "The future of
our State rests with the children. To the extent that adequate education is
supplied to those children they grow to full developed maturity and good citizenship. No one other thing in our State is as important. In the immediate present,
it is second to no objective except that of the war effort."

Full state aid for kindergartens is another matter that will come
before the New York State legislature and needs the fullest possible support.
State aid has been available for kindergartens only two years and has been
granted on half-day attendance - in other words, they have until now received
only half state aid.

The cost of good nursery schools is high - and undoubtedly requires
Federal and State aid to provide and equalize the establishment and maintenance
of Child Care Centers wherever they are needed throughout the country. The need
for nurseries will undoubtedly continue after the war. When the war ends they
will no longer be emergency centers set up primarily for the benefit of working
mothers. Instead, they will come into their own as educational institutions focusing
on the development of the pre-school child, whom we are at last recognizing as a
"school child" of significant and primary importance. Nursery schools are undoubtedly
an essential part of "our obligation to all our children", and are thus "the next
step in public education."

In New York City the establishment of the Day Care Unit in the Bureau
of Child Hygiene of the City Department of Health is making it possible to put

187

into effect a new city law requiring that every Child Care Center meet definite minimum standards in order to receive a permit to operate. With the help of this new law, and a special staff to put it into effect, support is given to all other standard-raising groups in the city. Thus a new leaven is at work in New York City to provide adequate conditions for the group care of all young children!

According to Katherine Lenroot, Chief of the U. S. Children's Bureau: "Evidence of the serious inadequacies in the health protection and medical care available to the children of this country is found in the rejection in a recent period of nearly 50 percent of the men examined for the armed forces. The ground-work for national health and physical fitness must be laid through a program that begins with prenatal care for the mother and extends through all the stages of infancy, childhood, and adolescence. Money invested in a comprehensive program that would assure access to health services and medical care for all, and in a nutritional program directed toward an adequate level of nutrition for all child-ren and youth, would contribute more to physical fitness and national preparedness than any other one measure."

To quote also from Grace Abbott's discussion of the administration of child-welfare services:

"The danger is always that the children's program, although of basic importance, may be overlooked or ignored as the pressure of numbers receiving general relief or old-age assistance and of the public interested in the aged and unemployed may absorb the attention of Federal, State, and county directors to the exclusion of other important and necessary programs.

"Except for the fact that the Social Security Act provided for the Federal grants-in-aid for child-welfare services and thus made possible increases in the professional staff of the child-welfare divisions or bureaus in the State departments as well as more assistance for county programs, the children's services, although better developed than the general public welfare services before the depression, might not have shared in the general advance of the last few years.

"Children, it should be repeated, are not pocket editions of adults. Because

188

childhood is a period of physical and mental growth and development, a period of preparation for adult responsibility in public and private life, a program for children cannot be merely an adaptation of the program for adults, nor should it be curtailed **during** the periods of depression or emergency expansion of other programs."

CITY OF NEW YORK - DEPARTMENT OF HEALTH
BUREAU OF CHILD HEALTH
DIVISION OF DAY CARE AND FOSTER HOMES

GUIDE REGARDING PERMIT PROCEDURE FOR DAY CARE AGENCIES
(Based on Section 198 of the Sanitary Code)

I. Applicant submit to the Division of Day Care and Foster Homes - Bureau of Child
    Health the following:
       (whether for first application or application for renewal of permit)

    1. Forms
          (a) Application (form #473K).....1 copy
          (b) Supplementary Information Record (form #460K).....1 copy
          (c) Day Care Agency Personnel Form (form #474K).......1 copy
    2. A complete floor plan indicating:
                   location of floors, dimensions (in feet) of indoor
                   space used, location of toilets and washbasins,
                   doors and windows, location and dimensions (in feet)
                   of outdoor space.
    3. Statement of financial position and anticipated annual budget.
    4. Typical three-week menus, including lunch, morning and afternoon snacks.
    5. Program of typical day's activities.
    6. Sample registration forms, agency brochure or catalogue.
       The above information should be submitted in person by new applicants.

II. Essentials of Section 198 of the Sanitary Code:
    1. The children should be under constant and competent (qualified) supervision.
    2. An accurate record of all children admitted should be kept.
    3. An accurate daily record of attendance for all children should be kept.
    4. A current, accurate and complete health record should be kept in the agency,
       for every child.
    5. The building and premises should be maintained in a safe and sanitary
       condition.
    6. Every child should have his own:
                          cot
                          locker
                          chair
                          blanket
                          sheet
    7. Temperature should be maintained between 68 degrees and 72 degrees F. in
       every room used by the children.
    8. There should be an accurate thermometer in every room and all the radiators
       should be covered.
    9. The stairwells and windows should be protected.
   10. Drinking, toilet and washbasin facilities should be readily available for the
       exclusive use of the children.
   11. There should be appropriate and sufficient indoor and outdoor equipment and
       play materials for each age group.
   12. The entire staff - all those who come in direct contact with the children -
       should have annual chest x-rays and annual physical examinations.

Permit is valid for 2 years only for premises and number of children specified
thereon. At no time shall there be in attendance more children than so specified
on the permit. Notify Division of Day Care and Foster Homes immediately of any
proposed change in ownership, location, in teaching personnel, and of contemplated
increase in registration of children or any structural changes.
Become thoroughly familiar with all regulations of Section 198 of the Sanitary
Code in order that the requirements will be met and sustained, at all times.
     JAN 15, 1952.
ChH 50

190

Mar. 23, 1959

~~Excerpts from~~

N E W   Y O R K   C I T Y

H E A L T H   C O D E

re Day Care Services

in THE CITY OF NEW YORK

ROBERT F. WAGNER
Mayor

GEORGE JAMES, M.D.
Commissioner of Health

Enacted by the Board of Health of
The City of New York on March 23, 1959

Available from
Bureau of Child Health
Division of Day Care, Day Camps
and Institutions
100 Centre Street, Room 1420A
New York 13, New York
Tel. WOrth 4-3800, Ext. 897

191

ARTICLE 45   GENERAL PROVISIONS GOVERNING DAY CARE SERVICES, SCHOOLS AND CHILDREN'S INSTITUTIONS

Section

Introductory Notes

Article 45 covers some of the subject matter presently contained in S.C. §§198, 200 and 203 and the Regulations thereunder. Numerous provisions of S.C. §§198, 200 and 203 and Regulations which imposed similar requirements for day care agencies, schools and shelters have been combined in this article to apply to all three types of institutions, thereby avoiding much duplication and needless inconsistencies contained in the prior code. With only a few relatively minor substantive changes, it was possible in many instances to arrive at a single standard for day care services, schools and children's institutions. In those instances where, by reason of differences among the kinds of establishments covered it was not feasible to arrive at a single standard, the provisions separately applicable to day care services, schools and children's institutions were placed in the respective articles (47, 49 and 51) dealing with the kind of establishment involved. Note, however, that Article 45 does not apply to family day care which is regulated by Article 53.

Some of the important changes are as follows. Day care service is defined so that a group does not become such a service until there are six or more, instead of four or more, children enrolled. The care of fewer than six unrelated children is governed by Article 53. A group which meets for less than five hours a week or which operates for less than one month a year is not, by definition, a day care service and is not regulated under this article. The term "children's institution" is used instead of "shelter" and the definition is expanded to include institutions giving care to children who are maintained on a permanent basis, rather than merely on a temporary basis as in the prior code. The provisions governing the use of rooms in cellars and basements are made uniform and are clarified. The lighting provisions are expanded by the adoption of higher lighting standards based upon a foot-candle requirement for various kinds of activities; the new standards are applicable only to new construction and, when possible, to renovated premises. A single heating standard is adopted as well as a common provision governing drinking water. Numerous differences in the prior requirements governing the use of lavatories by children of different sexes, and concerning the height of the partitions between toilets are eliminated; because the needs of day care services, schools and children's institutions in regard to the number of toilets required in each are necessarily different, however, the required numbers are specified in Articles 47, 49 and 51. All of the institutions regulated will have to comply, in serving or storing food, with the provisions of Articles 81, Food Handling and Food Establishments, and 87, Restaurants and Other Eating Places. Compliance with these articles will not impose any major obligations on such institutions which have not had to be met before.

§45.01 Definitions

When used in this article and in Articles 47, 49 and 51:

(a) Day care service means any service which during all or part of the day regularly gives care to six or more children, not of common parentage, who are under six years of age, whether or not the care is given for compensation, whether or not it has a stated educational purpose, and whether the service is known as a child care center, day nursery, day care agency, nursery school, kindergarten, play school, progressive school or by any other name. The total number of children receiving care shall be counted, including children or foster children of the owner or person in charge, in determining the applicability of this definition. The term day care service shall not, however, include a service which gives care to children for five hours a week or less or a service which operates for one month a year or less.

(b) School means a public or private elementary or junior high school where more than six children are received for instruction, but does not include a day care service attached to an elementary or junior high school.

(c) Children's institution means a place, other than a boarding home or children's hospital, where, for compensation or otherwise, six or more children, not of common parentage and under 16 years of age are received for day and night care apart from their parents or guardians.

NOTES: Subsection (a), day care service, is derived from S.C. §198(2).

The minimum number of children necessary to constitute a day care service is raised from four to six. The care of fewer than six children is regulated by Article 53, Family Day Care. Since recent studies have shown that family day care is preferable for children under two years of age, such children cannot be admitted to a day care service (see sections 47.07(a) and 53.03).

The term "day care service" replaces "day care agency" since the former is more accurately descriptive. The definition of "day care service" is broader than the definition of "day care agency" in S.C. §198(2)(b). The latter did not include the private person who cared for six or more children in his own home with his own child a member of the group, or the private person who ran a group without remuneration; both of these are included under the definition of "day care service" in this subsection.

The words "regularly gives care" and the last sentence are added so as to exclude from coverage Sunday schools, groups meeting for occasional outings, dance or music classes meeting for short periods of time, summer groups operating for less than one month, and persons who may occasionally care for a neighbor's children.

Subsection (b), school, is new and replaces the definition found in S.C. §200(3). The definition reflects the long established administrative interpretation of S.C. §200(3) which included junior high schools.

Subsection (c), children's institution, is in part derived from S.C. §203(2) where "shelter" was defined. The difference between a shelter as defined in S.C. §203(2) and a children's institution as here defined is that in the former children were received for care for a period not exceeding three months, while the new definition includes institutions providing long term as well as short term care. Boarding homes and children's hospitals are excluded from coverage.

§45.03 Statement of policy; scope of Article 45

(a) It is hereby recognized that other State and City agencies, including among others, the Board of Education, the State Department of Social Welfare, and the State Department of Health, have important functions in areas relating to the health and welfare of children. The Department shall, therefore, as far as possible, administer the provisions of Articles 45 through 51 of this Code with due regard to the duties and responsibilities of such other agencies, and shall, as far as possible, coordinate its activities with theirs. The provisions of these articles are not intended and shall not be construed to interfere with the teaching of religion. It is further recognized that experimentation and the testing of new ideas are of great importance in raising standards relating to day care services, schools and children's institutions. The provisions of Articles 45 through 51 of this Code shall not be interpreted to favor any specific doctrine of child care or early childhood education, but shall be applied so as to permit experimental programs of all kinds consistent with the health, safety and welfare of children.

(b) The provisions of Article 45 of this Code shall apply to day care services, schools and children's institutions and the provisions of section 45.09(b), (c) and (d) shall also apply to public and private high schools.

NOTES: This section is new.

§45.05 Copy of Code to be kept and made available

The person in charge of a day care service, school or children's institution shall keep a copy of this Code and shall make it available to all personnel.

NOTES: This section is derived from S.C. §200 Reg.4(part) and §203 Reg. 2(f) but is expanded to require a copy of the full Code to be kept.

§45.07 Admissions

A child who has not been successfully vaccinated against smallpox when there are no medical contraindications shall not be admitted to a day care service, school or children's institution, except that if his parents or guardians consent in writing to a vaccination to be given upon admission, such child may be admitted and vaccinated without undue delay.

NOTES: This section is derived from S.C. §198 Reg. 6(c)(part), §200 Reg. 20(a) and §203 Reg. 20(c)(part). The reference to medical contraindications is derived from S.C. §198 Reg. 6(c). The reference to admission upon parental consent to vaccination is derived from S.C. §203 Reg. 20(c) and §198 Reg. 6(c). The inclusion of the clause on medical contraindications and parental consent is not inconsistent with Public Health Law §2130(1) which has no similar exceptions; all children who do not present medical contraindications will be vaccinated either before or upon admission.

The requirement for vaccination imposed by the State Public Health Law has been held constitutional and the parents of unvaccinated children who were excluded from school have been convicted of failing to send their children to school as required by the Education Law, *Viemeister v. State,* 179 N.Y. 235, 72 N.E. 97 (1904) ; *People v. Ekerold,* 211 N.Y. 386, 105 N.E. 670 (1914) ; *Shappee v. Curtis,* 142 App. Div. 155, 127 N.Y.S. 33 (3rd Dept. 1911) ; *People v. McIlwain,* 151 N.Y.S. 366 (Delaware County Court 1915) ; *In re Whitmore,* 47 N.Y.S. 2d 143 (Dom. Rel. Ct. 1944). See also: *Jacobson v. Massachusetts,* 197 U.S. 11 (1905) and *Zucht v. King,* 260 U.S. 174 (1922).

The provisions of S.C. §198 Reg. 6(a) and §200 Reg. 20(b) pertaining to the exclusion of children who have frequent epileptic seizures or who are mental defectives or deficients have been omitted as undesirable.

§45.09 Staff

(a) Constant and competent supervision by an adequate staff shall be maintained for all children in a day care service, school or children's institution. No child or group of children shall be unsupervised at any time.

(b) The owner or person in charge of a day care service, school or children's institution or public or private high school shall not permit an employee to work when he is required to be excluded pursuant to section 11.63. After having a communicable disease, a person in charge, teacher or any other person who associates with children shall not return to work until:

(1) He presents a certificate of recovery issued by the Department, if he was a case of tuberculosis, a case or carrier of typhoid or paratyphoid A or B fever, or a case, carrier or household contact of diphtheria or smallpox; or,

(2) After the period of isolation, if he was a case of measles, mumps, German measles, chicken pox, whooping cough, streptococcal sore throat including scarlet fever, meningitis or poliomyelitis; or,

(3) He presents a certificate of recovery issued by the Department or a physician's written statement, if he was a case or carrier of any other disease reportable pursuant to section 11.03. The statement shall indicate that he is free from disease in communicable form and that the period of isolation or exclusion required by Article 11 has ended.

(c) A person in charge, teacher, volunteer worker or any other person who regularly associates with children shall not be permitted to work in a day care service, school, children's institution, or public or private high school, unless an X-ray examination is made of his chest before he begins employment and thereafter at such intervals as may be prescribed by the Department as necessary for the protection of children. The X-ray film shall either be taken by the Department or by a private physician. Within 30 days after an X-ray film is taken by a private physician, it shall be properly identified and submitted to the Department together with certificates on forms furnished by the Department. After a satisfactory X-ray film has been taken or received by the Department, a certificate of compliance shall be issued and kept on file by the day care service, school, children's institution, or public or private high school so long as the person is employed and two years thereafter. When, in the opinion of the Department, an X-ray film is unsatisfactory or discloses a condition which cannot properly be evaluated on a single X-ray, the person to whom the X-ray film relates shall be further X-rayed and, if the Department requires, shall be given further periodic medical and laboratory examinations.

195

(d) No person in charge, teacher or other person who regularly associates with children shall be permitted to work in a day care service, school, children's institution, or public or private high school unless he is healthy and capable of carrying out the responsibilities of his job.

(e) All employees, whether or not they are directly concerned with the care of children, shall be regularly instructed in the protection of children during emergencies such as accidents, fires or air raids.

NOTES: Subsection (a) is derived without substantive change from S.C. §§198 Reg. 8(a) (part), 200 Reg. 19(e)(part) and 203 Reg. 19(f). The requirement of having an attendant on duty while the children are resting or sleeping in S.C. §198 Reg. 7(5) is merged in the broad requirement of this subsection.

Subsection (b) is derived from S.C. §198 Reg. 7(3)(b), §200 Regs. 19(b) and (c) and 22(f) and §203 Reg. 19(c). The subsection now permits the return of cases of streptococcal sore throat, meningitis and poliomyelitis at the end of the period of isolation without a certificate or physician's statement. Isolation for these diseases ends at the termination of the febrile period. The requirement in subdivision (3) that the physician's statement indicate that the period of isolation or exclusion is ended, is new.

Subsection (c) is derived from S.C. §198 Reg. 8(a)(part), §200 Reg. 19(a), §203 Reg. 19(a) and §87 Reg. 10(a)-(d). S.C. §87 Reg. 10(f) is the basis for section 11.47 (d). Persons in charge, volunteers and other persons (such as bus drivers who may be employed by a contract carrier) are now required to be X-rayed as well as employees. S.C. §87 Reg. 10(e), which required the Department to notify the employer, is deleted because the Department may take such action without specific direction. The provision on the length of time the records are to be kept is new.

The requirement for X-ray examinations has been held constitutional. *Conlon v. Marshall*, 185 Misc. 638, 59 N.Y.S. 2d 52; *aff'd without opinion* 271 App. Div. 972, 68 N.Y.S. 2d 438 (2d Dept. 1945).

Subsection (d) is new.

Subsection (e) is derived without substantive change from S.C. §198 Reg. 4(i) (part), §200 Reg. 19(d) and §203 Reg. 19(d).

§45.11 Physical facilities

(a) A day care service, school or children's institution shall not be conducted in a factory, mercantile or business building, unless the premises are approved by the Department. Such approval shall not be granted unless the premises and the area surrounding the premises are free from fire, traffic or other safety hazards.

(b) A child shall not be kept for any period of time in a cellar as defined in §C26-30.0 of the Administrative Code. A child shall not be permitted to remain for any period of time in a basement as defined in §C26-22.0 of the Administrative Code when one side of the basement is more than three feet below the surface of the ground surrounding the building, without the prior approval of the Department. Such approval shall not be granted to a day care service, school or children's institution which receives a permit for the first time after the effective date of this Code, or which is in a building erected or renovated after the effective date of this Code.

(c) All parts of a building used for the care of children shall be adequately lighted by natural or artificial means. All lighting shall be evenly distributed and diffused, free from glare, flickering or shadows. Background surfaces shall be of a dull finish in colors providing low brightness differences and low contrasts. In a day care service, school

196

or children's institution located in premises constructed after the effective date of this Code, the amounts of light required by subdivisions (1) through (5) of this subsection shall be provided and maintained at the children's activity level. In a day care service, school or children's institution located in premises constructed on or prior to the effective date of this Code, the requirements of subdivisions (1) through (5) of this subsection shall be complied with as far as practicable when the premises are renovated or altered. The lighting standard is as follows:

(1) Fifty footcandles of light in drafting, typing or sewing rooms and in all classrooms used for partially sighted children;

(2) Thirty footcandles of light in all other classrooms, study halls or libraries;

(3) Twenty footcandles of light in recreation rooms;

(4) Ten footcandles of light in auditoriums, cafeterias, locker rooms, washrooms, corridors containing lockers; and,

(5) Five footcandles of light in open corridors and store rooms.

(d) When the outside temperature is less than 55 degrees Fahrenheit, and the children are on the premises, a temperature of between 68 degrees and 72 degrees Fahrenheit shall be maintained in all parts of the building used by the children, except when the children are sleeping. Heating apparatus shall be equipped with adequate protective guards. Gas space heaters shall not be installed or used without the approval of the Department. Kerosene heaters are prohibited.

(e) A lighted and ventilated room or compartment shall be provided, sufficient in size and arranged so that each child's garments may be hung separately and within his reach.

(f) Drinking water shall be available near classrooms and play-rooms and easily accessible to the children. Except when bubbler fountains are used, individual drinking cups shall be provided within reach of the children. If bubbler fountains are used, they shall be of the angle jet type with suitable guards and shall have water pressure which is sufficient to raise the water high enough above the spout to avoid contamination.

(g) Walls, ceilings and floors shall be finished so that they may be cleaned readily. The premises, furnishings and equipment shall be kept clean. While occupied by children, rooms other than workshops shall not be swept or dusted. No room used for children shall be cleaned by dry sweeping. When quarters are provided for the staff or attendants, they shall be kept clean at all times.

(h) Indoor and outdoor play areas shall be available for the use of the children. Such play areas shall be safe, clean, easily accessible, adequate in size and suitable for the needs of the children. A shady area shall be available in outdoor play areas used during the summer months.

(i) Toilets shall be provided convenient to playrooms, class rooms and dormitories and the number of such toilets shall be as prescribed by sections 47.13 for a day care service, 49.07 for a school or 51.09 for a children's institution. In a lavatory for boys six years of age and over, urinals may be substituted for not more than one-third of the number of toilets required. When such substitution is made, one urinal shall replace one toilet so that the total number of toilets and urinals shall in no case be less than the number of required toilets. Toilets and urinals shall be of such height and size as to be usable by the children without assistance.

(j) Separate lavatories shall be provided for boys and girls six years of age and over, and a partition no less than five feet six inches high shall separate the toilets in such lavatories. In a day care service, school or children's institution located in premises constructed after the effective date of this Code, separate lavatories shall be provided for the persons in charge, staff and other employees.

(k) Wash basins with an adequate supply of hot and cold running water shall be provided in or adjacent to lavatories, and the number of such wash basins shall be as prescribed by sections 47.13 for a day care service, 49.07 for a school and 51.09 for a children's institution. When an extended wash basin with several faucets supplying tempered water is used, each faucet shall be considered as meeting the requirement for one wash basin.

(l) Plumbing shall be installed only by a licensed master plumber and shall be free of cross-connections and other hazards to health.

(m) Proper and sufficient ventilation, by natural or artificial means, shall be provided in each room used by the children pursuant to section C26-266.0 of the Administrative Code. The windows, inlets and outlets shall be located and the rate of air flow shall be controlled so as not to subject the children to drafts.

(n) Windows in rooms above the ground floor shall be safely guarded when the window sills are so low as to present a safety hazard to the children.

NOTES: Subsection (a) is derived from S.C. §198 Reg. 1(2)(part) as amended on April 21, 1958, §200 Reg. 2 and §203 Reg. 1(c). The use of factory, mercantile or business buildings which was previously completely prohibited is now permitted under certain circumstances.

Subsection (b) is derived from S.C. §198 Reg. 3(b), §200 Reg. 5 and §203 Reg. 4, with several changes resulting in the consolidation. Cellar rooms (*i.e.*, rooms with more than one-half of their height underground) cannot be used for any purpose, even in schools. A basement (*i.e.*, a story partly underground but having at least one-half of its height above ground) may be used only with the approval of the Department if one of its sides is more than three feet below the ground. After the effective date of this Code, a new day care service, school or children's institution or one in new or renovated premises cannot use such a basement for any purpose.

Subsection (c) is derived from S.C. §198 Reg. 3(f)(part), §200 Reg. 8 and §203 Reg. 6(part), but is considerably expanded by the establishment of new lighting standards. The standards in the subdivisions are based upon the recommendations of the Illuminating Engineering Society and American Institute of Architects, and the National Society for the Prevention of Blindness, approved by the American Standards Association. The standard is to apply to new construction and as far as practicable in buildings renovated after the effective date of this Code. All lighting is required to be free from flickering, glare or uneven diffusion, and background surfaces are to have a suitable finish.

Subsection (d) is derived from S.C. §198 Reg. 3(f) and (g), §200 Regs. 8(part) and 9 and §203 Regs. 6(part) and 7. Although each of these regulations differed in regard to the temperature to be maintained, they have been combined so as to provide a single standard, in keeping with the November 30, 1956 amendment to S.C. §225. The standard of 68°—72° F. is to be maintained only when the outside temperature drops below 55 degrees; without the latter provision this subsection might be construed as requiring air conditioning in the summer months. The provision requiring protective guards for heating apparatus is new. The provision prohibiting the use of gas for heating without permission of the Department has been changed so as to relate only to gas space heaters. Central gas heaters may be used. The provisions prohibiting the use of gas for lighting and cooking have been eliminated. The requirement for hanging a thermometer at a certain level above the floor is omitted.

Subsection (e) is derived from S.C. §198 Reg. 3(j), §200 Reg. 11 and §203 Reg. 9. The only change is to add the requirement that the clothes be hung within reach of the children.

Subsection (f) is derived from S.C. §198 Reg. 4(e), §200 Reg. 13 and §203 Reg. 10. Water is not only required to be near classrooms and playrooms but also easily accessible to the children. Cups must also be within their reach. The requirement of S.C. §198 Reg. 4 that the water be from a public supply is omitted as unnecessary. See Article 141, Drinking Water. The ratio of one bubbler fountain per 100 children has been omitted as unrealistic, since there never was a requirement that bubbler fountains be used. The last sentence is new.

Subsection (g) is derived from S.C. §198 Reg. 3(i) and (h)(part), §200 Regs. 16(a)(part), 17 and 19(f), and §203 Regs. 13(a)(part), 17 and 19(g) without substantive change. The words "other than workshops" were added because it may be desirable to have the pupils sweep workshops after completion of their work. See Article 151, Rodents, Insects and Other Pests; section 151.03 requires premises to be free of rodents and insects and free of harborages for such pests.

Subsection (h) is derived from S.C. §198 Reg. 7(6)(a), §200 Reg. 15(a)(part) and §203 Reg. 12(part). The changes require the play areas, both indoor and outdoor, to be adequate and accessible. Shade is required in outdoor areas used in the summer. The requirement in S.C. §203 Reg. 12 for a playroom separate from a nursery or dormitory is eliminated.

Subsection (i) is derived from parts of S.C. §198 Reg. 4(c), §200 Reg. 14 and §203 Reg. 11. Since the needs of day care services, schools and children's institutions differ in regard to the ratio of the number of toilets to the number of children, the ratios are left to the separate articles and an appropriate cross-reference is made here. In regard to urinals in lavatories for boys, the provisions of the Code were quite inconsistent: S.C. §198 did not mention them; S.C. §200 Reg. 14(b) required at least one-fourth of the required number of fixtures to be water closets [sic]; S.C. §203 Reg. 11 provided that urinals could be substituted for toilets, but required that the number of water closets could not be reduced below two-thirds the required number; §C26-1279.0 of the Administrative Code requires schools to provide water closets [sic] for at least one-fourth of the required number of fixtures, while at the same time providing that when urinals are substituted for toilets the number of toilets shall not be reduced below two-thirds the required number. There appears to be an error in S.C. §200 Reg. 14(b) and §C26-1279.0 of the Administrative Code in that the words "water closet" appear where the word "urinal" should have been used. The provisions of this subsection represent the true intention of the law. Urinals are not required. For definitions of toilet and urinal see section 1.03; they must be water-flushed and connected to a private or municipal sewage disposal system.

Subsection (j) is derived from parts of S.C. §198 Reg. 4(c), §200 Reg. 14 and §203 Reg. 11. The provisions of the prior regulations concerning the use of lavatories in day care services, schools and children's institutions differed considerably and were largely inconsistent. In arriving at the single standard set forth in this subsection, several changes were made which better reflect present-day attitudes. Separate lavatories are now required for boys and girls over six years of age and all provisions on contemporaneous use by younger boys and girls are omitted. The Sanitary Code contained several different standards. S.C. §198 Reg. 4(c) did not require separate lavatories but prohibited contemporaneous use by both sexes over age six. S.C. §200 Reg. 14, provided for separate lavatories for children over age six, and allowed children between four and six to use the same lavatory if boys and girls did not use it at the same time; but if used at the same time (in violation of the preceding sentence) partitions were required. S.C. §203 Reg. 11 required separate lavatories only for children over eight years and boys and girls from four to eight could not use the lavatory at the same time. This subsection also contains a single standard for partitions instead of the variety of requirements in the former code: S.C. §198 Reg. 4(c) required a partition four feet high in a lavatory used by children over six years of age; S.C. §200 Reg. 14(c) required a partition four feet high in lavatories used by both sexes at the same time and a partition five feet six inches high in lavatories used by children over six years of age; and S.C. §203 Reg. 11 required a partition four feet high in a lavatory for children between four and eight years of age and a partition five feet high in lavatories used by children over eight years of age. The last sentence is new. For a definition of lavatory see section 1.03(n).

Subsection (k) is derived from parts of S.C. §198 Reg. 4(c), §200 Reg. 14(d) and §203 Reg. 11. The requirements for wash basins in day care services, schools and children's institutions are so different that the number of fixtures required is left to the articles specified. The last sentence is new. Wash basin is defined in section 1.03(o) ; it must be connected to a private or municipal sewage disposal system.

Subsection (1) is new.

Subsection (m) is derived from S.C. §200 Reg. 7(a), §198 Reg. 3(e) and §203 Reg. 5(b). The detail of §203 Reg. 5(b) in regard to cubic feet of air per hour is deleted. S.C. §200 Reg. 7(a) referred for its ventilation standard to the Administrative Code. The index for ventilation contained in §C26-266.0(4) of the Administrative Code pertains specifically to schools. Day care services and children's institutions are now required to meet the same standards as schools. The subsection also results in the deletion of cubic foot requirements in S.C. §198 Reg. 3(c) and §200 Reg. 7(b).

Subsection (n) is new. The provisions of S.C. §§198 Reg. 3(d), 200 Reg. 7(a) and 203 Reg. 5(a) relating to windows opening on a yard or court are omitted. See Administrative Code §§C26-261.0 and C26-269.0.

§45.13 Equipment and furnishings

(a) All equipment and furnishings used shall be readily washable or otherwise easily cleaned. Furnishings which are likely to collect excessive amounts of dust, such as heavy draperies, upholstery or carpets, shall not be used in rooms occupied by children, but such furnishings may be used for educational purposes if they are kept clean.

(b) Tables and chairs and other equipment shall be appropriate for the size and needs of the children who use them and shall be readily washable.

(c) In the indoor and outdoor play areas, sufficient play equipment shall be provided which is appropriate to the stage of development of the children and which is designed to foster physical and motor development. The equipment shall be easily accessible to the children, readily washable, clean, in good repair and free from hazards such as sharp or pointed parts, or toxic or poisonous finishes or materials.

(d) A first aid kit, completely stocked for emergency treatment of cuts and burns, shall be provided and shall be easily accessible for use. The first aid kit shall be kept out of the reach of young children.

(e) Soap and individual paper or cloth towels or sanitary driers shall be provided adjacent to wash basins and within easy reach of the children. If combs or washcloths are provided, each child shall have such articles for his exclusive use.

NOTES: Subsection (a) is derived without substantive change from S.C. §198 Reg. 3(h) (part), §200 Reg. 16(a) (part) and §203 Reg. 13(a) (part). The exception for educational purposes was added so as to exempt a classroom in which home economics is taught.

Subsection (b) is derived without substantive change from S.C. §§198 Reg. 4(g), 200 Reg. 16(b) (part) and 203 Reg. 13(b) (part).

Subsection (c) is derived without substantive change from S.C. §198 Reg. 4(a),

§200 Reg. 16(b)(part), §203 Reg. 13(b)(part) and §203 Reg. 12(part). The changes are as follows: Specific mention is made of "indoor and outdoor areas" to assure that materials will be available in every play area; the language relating to sufficiency and appropriateness for development is new; the requirement that equipment be "free from hazards" is expressly stated and the requirement that the equipment be "in good repair" replaces the prohibitions on "loose" parts; the requirement of lead-free paint is changed to a prohibition of poisonous finishes or materials. See in this connection Article 173, Hazardous Substances, section 173.13.

Subsection (d) is derived from S.C. §198 Reg. 4(i)(part), §200 Reg. 16(c) and §203 Reg. 13(e).

Subsection (e) is derived from S.C. §198 Reg. 4(d)(part), §200 Reg. 14(d) (part) and §203 Regs. 11(part) and 13(d)(part). The words "adjacent to wash basins and within easy reach of the children" are new. Common towels cannot be used under section 181.05.

§45.15 Care and preparation of food

(a) When food is stored or served to children in a day care service, school or children's institution, the provisions of Articles 81 and 87 of this Code shall be complied with.

(b) The food supplied to children shall be wholesome, of good quality, properly prepared, sufficient in amount, varied according to a diet approved by the Department of Health or the State Department of Social Welfare and served at regular hours.

(c) Milk shall be kept at a temperature below 50 degrees Fahrenheit.

(d) A child under 12 years of age shall not be permitted to remove the caps from bottles or containers of milk intended for other persons or permitted to assist in the dispensing of milk except under adequate supervision.

NOTES: Subsection (a) is in part derived from S.C. §198 Reg. 5(a), (d) and (e), §200 Reg. 18(a), (b), (e) and (f) and §203 Reg. 18(a), (d) and (e), but is much broader in scope in requiring food in day care services, schools and children's institutions to be stored and handled pursuant to Article 81, Food Handling and Food Establishments, and Article 87, Restaurants and Other Eating Places. A lunchroom in a day care service, school or children's institution is a "food establishment" under section 81.03(a) and an "eating place" (not a restaurant) under section 87.01(b).

Subsection (b) is derived without substantive change from S.C. §200 Reg. 18(d) and §203 Reg. 18(c) and from S.C. §198 Reg. 7(7)(part). The reference to the State Department of Social Welfare is new.

Subsection (c) is derived from S.C. §198 Reg. 5(b) and S.C. §203 Reg. 18(b) (part). The reference to milk "purchased otherwise than in bottles" is deleted because ladling from large milk cans is no longer practiced.

The last sentence of S.C. §203 Reg. 18(b) dealing with infants' bottles and nipples has been incorporated into section 51.15(b). A similar provision in S.C. §198 Reg. 5(c) has been deleted.

Subsection (d) is derived without substantive change from S.C. §200 Reg. 18(c) and §203 Reg. 18(b)(part).

The portion of S.C. §200 Reg. 18(c) calling for the sanitary use of drinking straws, is here omitted; it is covered by section 87.11 which was derived from S.C. §144a. Also see section 181.07 on common eating and drinking utensils.

§45.17 Health and medical care

(a) A health inspection of all children shall be made daily by a responsible person who is familiar with the children and who is able to recognize signs of ill health.

(b) The person in charge of a day care service, school or children's institution shall isolate cases and carriers of communicable disease and provide facilities for their isolation pursuant to section 11.57.

NOTES: Subsection (a) is derived without substantive change from S.C. §198 Reg. 7(2) and §200 Reg. 22(c).

Subsection (b) is derived in part from S.C. §198 Reg. 7(3)(a)(part), S.C. §200 Regs. 10 and 22(c)(part) and (d), and S.C. §203 Reg. 21(d)(part). The provisions of S.C. §203 Reg. 8 are omitted because the subject is covered in section 11.57(d) and (f). A day care service or school must provide rooms for temporary isolation pursuant to section 11.57(i) and a children's institution must provide room for isolation pursuant to section 11.57(f). Children must be isolated in accordance with section 11.57. Reports of communicable diseases or conditions must be made pursuant to sections 11.03 and 11.05.

§45.19 Records

Day care services, schools and children's institutions shall keep a current record containing the name, home address, date and place of birth, the date of admission and the date of and reason for the discharge of each child, and the names and home and emergency addresses of parents, guardians, or agency which placed the child.

NOTES: This section is derived from S.C. §198 Reg. 9, §200 Reg. 23(part) and §203 Reg. 23(part) with the addition of the word "current". The portions of S.C. §§200 Reg. 23 and 203 Reg. 23 and S.C. §§198 Reg. 10, 200 Reg. 24 and 203 Reg. 24 relating to the power of the Department to inspect the premises and records of day care services, schools and children's institutions are here omitted; the power is contained in Article 3 of this Code.

§45.21 Modification of provisions

When the strict application of any provision of this article or Articles 47, 49 or 51 presents practical difficulties, or unusual or unreasonable hardships, the Commissioner in a specific instance may modify the application of such provision consistent with the general purpose and intent of these articles and upon such conditions as in his opinion are necessary to protect the health of the children. The denial by the Commissioner of a request for modification may be appealed to the Board in the manner provided by section 5.21.

NOTES: This section is derived from S.C. §198 Reg. 12, §200 Reg. 25 and §203 Reg. 25. It is changed so as to empower the Commissioner to authorize modification.

ARTICLE 47   DAY CARE SERVICES

Introductory Notes

Article 47 covers some of the subject matter contained in S.C. §198 and Regulations thereunder. Many provisions of S.C. §198 and Regulations are integrated in Article 45, since they are applicable to schools and children's institutions as well as to day care services.

Nursery schools or kindergartens attached to public elementary schools or established religious organizations are required to comply with the provisions of this article even though they do not need permits (section 47.03). A new system of issuing permits to day care services is adopted: Upon application for a permit, the Department may issue a temporary permit which will allow the service to operate lawfully for a period of time prior to the issuance of a final permit so that the Department can observe the service in actual operation (section 47.05). Staffing requirements with standards based upon existing administrative agreements btween the City and State are added (sections 47.09 and 47.11). Prophylaxis against tetanus, pertussis and poliomyelitis is now required in addition to diphtheria (section 47.07). The provisions governing the use of cots have been modified but are similar to the provisions concerning cots in Article 49 (section 47.15). There is a new section dealing with the transportation of children between their homes and the day care service (section 47.23).

All regulations pertaining to children under two years of age are omitted (S.C. §198 Regs. 3(a)(part), 4(b)(part), 4(f), 5(c), 7(6)(b) and 11), because such children are not permitted in day care services (section 47.07).

The Rules of the State Board of Social Welfare on the Day Care of Children adopted on February 15, 1955, pursuant to Social Welfare Law §390 do not apply in the city of New York. They have, however, been considered in the preparation of this article as have the requirements of the State Education Department for voluntary registration of non-public nursery schools and kindergartens.

§47.01   Scope

The provisions of this article apply to all day care services, and the requirements of this article shall be in addition to the requirements to be met by day care services pursuant to Article 45.

NOTES: This section is new.

§47.03   Permit required; exception

No person shall conduct a day care service without a permit or temporary permit issued by the Commissioner, but a permit shall not be required for a nursery school or kindergarten conducted by the Board of Education or by an established religious organization as part of an elementary school; such a nursery school or kindergarten shall, however, comply with the other provisions of this article and Article 45.

NOTES: This section is derived from S.C. §198(1) and (3). A reference to temporary permits has been added so as to allow a day care service to operate with such a temporary permit which may be issued upon submission of an application for a permit pursuant to section 47.05(b). The Department may observe the operation of the day care service pursuant to section 47.05(c) prior to issuing a regular permit.

§47.05 Permit; application, issuance and renewal

(a) An application for a permit to conduct a day care service shall be submitted by the person or persons who propose to operate the service. The application shall include:

(1) A sketch of the premises, with measurements, showing all of the rooms, their dimensions and the uses for which they are intended;

(2) A sketch, with measurements, of the outdoor play space indicating its location in relation to the indoor premises, and a plan for the use of such space;

(3) A statement of the purposes for which the service is conducted;

(4) A description of the program of indoor and outdoor activities;

(5) Evidence of a reasonably secure financial position to permit compliance with the provisions of this Code; and,

(6) A statement of the method to be used in admitting the children.

(b) Upon submission of an application for a permit for a new day care service, the Department may in its discretion issue a temporary permit, which, unless renewed, shall be valid for six months or until the Department rejects the permit application, whichever period is the shorter.

(c) A permit shall not be issued or renewed unless the Department has observed a program in operation under a temporary permit or permit and, upon inspection, is satisfied that all the requirements of the Code have been met.

(d) An application for renewal of a permit shall include notice of any change which occurred since the submission of the previous application for a permit as to any information required by subsection (a) of this section.

(e) A permit or temporary permit shall specify the maximum number of children that may attend the service at any one time. The maximum number shall not exceed the number of children for which the indoor space and facilities are adequate under the provisions of this Code; the Department may, however, in its discretion specify on the permit a higher maximum number for attendance during the summer months upon consideration of the availability of additional outdoor space.

NOTES: Subsection (a) is derived from S.C. §198 Reg. 1(1) and (2). The phrase "person or persons who propose to operate the service" is used instead of "an organization, corporation, partnership, or individual proposing to operate". The requirement that dimensions be shown on the sketch is new, as is the requirement that the sketch specify the use of each room, whether or not intended "for child caring purposes", as heretofore. Subdivision (2) is new. The words "description of the program and activities to carry out these purposes" have been changed to "description of the program of indoor and outdoor activities." See Article 5, General Permit Provisions, for regulations concerning application, expiration, fees, revocation, transfer and renewal of the permit.

Subsection (b) is new. It permits a day care service to operate between the time of submission of an application for a permit and the time when action thereon is taken, so that the Department may observe the service in operation before a regular permit is granted. The issuance of a temporary permit is purely discretionary, and the Department may, for instance, refuse to issue a temporary permit if it has previously denied an application for a permit, or if it finds upon the face of the application that the applicant does not or cannot meet the requirements of the Code. The time limit of six months will encourage the applicant to comply promptly with all requirements blocking final approval of his permit, because renewal of the temporary permit may be refused.

Subsections (c), (d) and (e) are new.

The State Education Department has a program for the voluntary registration of non-public nursery schools or kindergartens which comply with the standards established by that Department. Information about the standards and application blanks can be obtained from the Division of Elementary Education, State Education Department, Albany, New York. Since the requirements of this article are in many respects similar to the standards of the State Education Department, day care services under permit and day care services operated by religious organizations as part of elementary schools may be eligible for voluntary registration by the State. It should be noted, however, that a few of the standards recommended by the State Education Department are more stringent than those required by the Code, *e.g.:* size of groups of children, indoor floor space, outdoor play space and minimum age of admission.

§47.07 Admissions

(a) No child shall be admitted to a day care service unless:

(1) He is two years of age or over;

(2) He has received a thorough medical examination within 30 days prior to admission, and a statement by the examining physician has been furnished to the day care service pursuant to subsection (b) of this section; and,

(3) He has received prophylaxis against diphtheria, tetanus, pertussis and poliomyelitis, when there are no medical contraindications, except that if his parents or guardians consent in writing to immunization, the child may be admitted and immunized without undue delay.

(b) The physician examining a child pursuant to subsection (a)(2) of this section shall furnish to the day care service a signed statement containing a summary of the results of the examination, the past medical history and, if a disease or abnormal condition is found, recommendations for exclusion or treatment of the child, or modification of his activities, or plans for the health supervision of a handicapped child.

(c) A day care service shall not have children in attendance in excess of the number prescribed in its permit.

NOTES: Subsection (a)(1) is new. Children under two years of age may not be cared for in a day care service. The care of such children in a home is regulated by Article 53, Family Day Care. In accordance with this policy, all references to children under age two and requirements for their care, previously found in S.C. §198, are omitted from this article. See *e.g.:* S.C. §198 Regs. 3(a)(part), 4(b)(part), 4(f), 5(c), 6(d), 7(6)(b) and 11. Although it is recognized that as an ultimate goal it is not desirable to permit children under three years of age in a day care service, and many services now have a policy of not admitting such children, the presently practicable limitation of prohibiting only the care of children under two has been adopted.

Subsection (a)(2) is derived from S.C. §198 Reg. 7(1)(part). The time in which the examination is to be made is new.

Subsection (a)(3) is derived in part from S.C. §198 Reg. 6(c)(part) which related to prophylaxis against diphtheria. The requirement for prophylaxis against tetanus, pertussis and poliomyelitis is new. Vaccination against smallpox is covered by section 45.07.

Subsection (b) is derived from S.C. §198 Reg. 7(1)(part) but is broader. S.C. §198 Reg. 6(a) is omitted.

Subsection (c) is derived without substantive change from S.C. §198 Reg. 6 (para. 1).

§47.09   Staff

(a) An educational director shall be in charge of the program of a day care service. In addition to being a qualified teacher in early childhood education pursuant to subsection (b) of this section, an educational director shall have a minimum of two years experience as a group teacher in a program for children under six years of age. The educational director shall not have any teaching duties when there are more than 40 children enrolled in the service, or in the case of a day care service which is an integral part of a school with grades one to six or more, having a principal with no teaching duties, when there are more than 60 children enrolled in the service.

(b) No person shall be placed in charge of a group of children unless he is licensed by the City Board of Education as a teacher in early childhood education or is certified by the State Education Department as a teacher in the field of early childhood education, or unless he meets any of the following requirements:

(1) He is eligible for certification by the State Education Department as a teacher in the field of early childhood education, except for the citizenship requirement; or,

(2) He has been certified by another public or private certifying agency whose standards are equivalent to the standards of the State Education Department; or,

(3) He has a plan for obtaining, within a reasonable time, certification by the State Education Department as a teacher in the field of early childhood education, and his plan has been approved either by the State Education Department or by a college accredited by the University of the State of New York. In such case he shall submit to the Department a letter indicating the time necessary for completion of the training.

(c) A person in charge of a group of handicapped children shall be a qualified teacher in early childhood education pursuant to subsection (b) of this section and shall have additional, appropriate training for work with handicapped children.

(d) A person may be employed temporarily as an educational director or teacher while his certification approval by the State Education Department or other certifying agency is pending or while his plan for obtaining certification is pending approval.

(e) An assistant teacher shall be a mature person who has at least two years of college education or who is a high school graduate at least 19 years of age.

NOTES: The subject matter covered by this section was formerly in S.C. §198 Reg. 8. It has been substantially revised. Subsection (a) is derived in part from S.C. §198 Reg. 8. Subsections (b), (c), (d) and (e) are new. The standards are based upon existing administrative agreements between the City and State.

The requirements for a certificate as a teacher in early childhood education have been established in §131 of the Rules promulgated by the Commissioner of the State Education Department of the University of the State of New York. The candidate is required to have completed a four year curriculum approved for the preparation of teachers of early childhood education leading to a baccalaureate degree. The required curriculum must be of a college grade with approximately two years of liberal arts study and a specialization in early childhood education of not less than 36 semester hours in appropriate professional courses, 12 of which have been in supervised student practice teaching in the primary grades, the kindergarten and nursery school. The other 24 required semester hours are to give appropriate emphasis to the learning problems, behavior problems and instructional needs of young children. The courses include: history, principles, philosophy or problems of education (2 semester hours); child development (6 semester hours); methods and materials (6 semester hours); language arts or story telling (2 semester hours); creative arts (2 semester hours) and electives in early childhood education (6 semester hours).

The Board of Education of the City of New York has similar requirements for preparation for the license to teach early childhood classes. In addition, the Board of Education requires evaluation to be made by examinations conducted by the Board of Examiners including, but not limited to, a written test, an interview test and a teaching test.

This section requires the educational director and all teachers in charge of groups of children in day care services to be certified by the State Education Department or licensed by the Board of Education of the City of New York in the field of early childhood education, but permits several alternatives to certification, including acceptance of a person working toward State certification. Subsection (b)(3) allows a person who has an approved plan for obtaining certification to be employed as a teacher. Under this subsection, a person who lacks the required 12 hours of supervised practice teaching may also be employed. In this connection it should be noted that under the rules of the State Department of Education two full years of satisfactory teaching experience in an approved day care service may be substituted for all of the required 12 semester hours of supervised practice teaching, if one full term is devoted to teaching on each of the three levels; less teaching experience may be required for certification if the candidate also has some semester hours of practice teaching with which he can be credited. Furthermore, if a candidate meets all of the requirements except practice teaching on the primary level, a certificate restricted to nursery and kindergarten can be issued. Thus appropriate credit is given for on-the-job training.

Under a 1949 compact with the New England states, New Jersey, and a later compact with Pennsylvania, Delaware and Maryland, the State Education Department will certify teachers who are certified by those states or who are graduates of certain approved institutions in those states. Regulation 117(8) of the Regulations of the Commissioner of Education of New York State entitled "certification reciprocity" as amended on November 22, 1957, by the addition of subsection (b), provides:

"a. A teaching, supervisory or administrative certificate duly issued by the appropriate State authority in one of the New England States and New Jersey and currently in full force and effect shall be honored by the Commissioner of Education of the State of New York provided that the holder of such certificate shall have had

(1) Not less than three years of successful experience at the teaching, supervisory or administrative level for which transfer of certificate privilege is sought

(2) Basic preparation equivalent in length (though not necessarily in specific content) to the minimum preparation required in these regulations for the teaching, supervisory or administrative level in question

(3) In the case of supervisors and administrators, a program of study directed toward preparation for supervision and for administration equivalent

207

assistants to be provided for groups of children which were previously governed by S.C. §198 Reg. 8(b).

Subsection (c) is new. The subsection does not require the segregation of handicapped children when admitted to a service attended predominantly by normal children. It is intended to apply to a service that admits primarily handicapped children or to a service that has a special group for severely handicapped children when inadvisable to integrate them in a group for other children.

Subsection (d) is new. It permits the intermingling in a single group of children over two and under four years of age, or over three and under five years of age, or over four and under six years of age.

§47.13 Physical facilities

(a) The minimum allowance of space for each child in a playroom in a day care service shall be 30 square feet of wall to wall space.

(b) Rooms and facilities for children in a day care service shall be reserved for their exclusive use and shall not be shared with other children while the service is in operation.

(c) One toilet and one wash basin shall be provided for every fifteen children or fraction thereof admitted to the day care service.

(d) A day care service shall not be operated above the third floor of a building unless an elevator is provided.

NOTES: Subsection (a) is derived from S.C. §198 Reg. 3(c). The requirement has been changed to 30 square feet of wall to wall space instead of 20 square feet of floor space. Since "floor space" was interpreted by the Department to exclude space occupied by furniture, the new standard is not intended as a substantive change in space requirement, but solely as a more convenient method of measurement. The "wall to wall" method is used by other City and State agencies. See: Rules of the State Board of Social Welfare on Day Care of Children, 1955, §19.4(c)(1); Multiple Dwelling Code, Administrative Code §D26-2.2(10). The State Education Department recommends a higher standard (35 square feet of floor space per child exclusive of cloakrooms, isolation rooms, toilets and storage space) for voluntary registration. The cubic foot requirement is deleted since the ventilation requirement is adequately covered by section 45.11(m). Ninety-six percent of the licensed day care services now have from 30 to 89 square feet of wall to wall space for each child and only four percent of the services do not comply.

Subsection (b) is derived from S.C. §198 Reg. 3(a) which required separate rooms for children under two years of age and for children over eight years of age.

Subsection (c) is derived without substantive change from S.C. §198 Reg. 4(c) (part). Other provisions applicable to lavatories are contained in section 45.11(i), (j) and (k).

Subsection (d) is derived without substantive change from S.C. §198 Reg. 1(2) (part) as amended April 23, 1958.

§47.15 Clothing and equipment

(a) Sufficient and suitable clothing shall be available in a day care service so that children who soil their clothing may receive a change. All such clothing shall be thoroughly washed after each use.

(b) A separate, firm, sanitary cot shall be provided for each child who spends more than four hours a day in the service. Cots shall be placed at least two feet apart unless separated by a screen or partition. Pillows and mattresses shall not be used. A clean sheet shall be provided for the exclusive use of each such child. Blankets which are sufficient to maintain adequate warmth shall be available for use by each such child and shall be used when necessary.

in semester hours (though not necessarily in specific content) to the minimum program prescribed in these regulations for certification

(4) Assurance of employment in the kind and grade of professional position in the public schools of the State of New York for which certification is sought.

"b. Graduates of baccalaureate programs in elementary education in institutions in the New England States and New Jersey, Pennsylvania, Delaware and Maryland shall be eligible for permanent certification in New York State provided that the program is approved by the State Department of Education in the State in which the institution is located and the institution is accredited by a regional or national accrediting agency."

Further information about certification under this Compact and a list of approved institutions can be obtained from the Bureau of Teacher Education and Certification, State Education Department, Albany 1, New York.

The object of this section—professionally trained staff—has been substantially achieved in the more than 500 licensed day care services under S.C. §198. As of January, 1959, 1,160 teachers and directors in the licensed day care services (78.6%) were fully qualified (certified by the State Education Department), 20.2% were working towards certification under approved plans and 1.2% were not qualified under these provisions.

§47.11 Groups

(a) A teacher qualified pursuant to section 47.09(b) shall be in charge of each group of no more than:

(1) Ten children, if the children are two and over and under three years of age; or,

(2) Fifteen children, if the children are three years and over and under four years of age; or,

(3) Twenty children, if the children are four years and over and under five years of age; or,

(4) Twenty five children, if the children are five years and over and under six years of age.

(b) In addition to a teacher qualified pursuant to section 47.09(b), an assistant teacher shall be provided for each group of children when:

(1) The group has more than five children two years and over and under three years of age; or,

(2) The group has more than 10 children three years and over and under four years of age; or,

(3) The group has more than 12 children four years and over and under five years of age; or,

(4) The group has more than 15 children five years and over and under six years of age.

(c) The ratios of teachers and assistant teachers to the number of children in a group of handicapped children shall be determined by the type and severity of the handicaps and shall be subject to the approval of the Department, but the number of teachers and assistants shall not be fewer than the number required by subsections (a) and (b) of this section.

(d) Children in two contiguous age categories specified in subsection (a) of this section may be placed in one group. When children in different age categories are so intermingled, the requirements for supervision applicable to the age of the majority of the children in the group shall apply.

NOTES: Subsections (a) and (b) contain new standards for the teachers and

(c) Hair brushes shall not be provided or used.

NOTES: Subsection (a) is derived without substantive change from S.C. §198 Reg. 4(h).

Subsection (b) is derived from S.C. §198 Reg. 4(b) and S.C. §200 Reg. 15(c) with some changes. Cots, sheets and blankets are not required for all children, but only for children who spend more than four hours a day in the service. The use of pillows and mattresses is absolutely prohibited. The reference to cribs and slat beds is deleted. Individual sheets are required for every child. The provision on blankets is changed so as to require availability and use only when necessary.

Subsection (c) is derived from S.C. §198 Reg. 4(d)(part), the remainder of which is found in section 45.13(e).

S.C. §198 Regs. 4(f) and 5(c) on diapers and milk bottles are deleted because children under age two may no longer be admitted to a day care service.

§47.17 Food; rest periods; outdoor play

(a) Sufficient, nourishing food following a diet acceptable to the Department shall be provided for the children.

(b) Each child in full time day care shall have a quiet, relaxed period of approximately one hour a day. Shorter, comparable periods of quiet and relaxation shall be provided for each child who spends less time in the service.

(c) Adequate periods of outdoor play shall be provided daily for all children, except during inclement weather.

NOTES: Subsection (a) is derived from S.C. §198 Reg. 7(7)(part). The provisions of S.C. §198 Reg. 11(2) have been omitted because they pertained to infants. The requirement for a hot meal, milk and food every four hours is deleted. The subsection supplements section 45.15(b) which requires food, when served to be wholesome, of good quality, properly prepared, and varied.

Subsection (b) is derived from S.C. §198 Reg. 7(5) with some changes. The regulation requiring the children to spend "part of" the one hour rest period lying on the cots is deleted.

Subsection (c) is derived from S.C. §198 Reg. 7(6)(c). A part of the day must be used for outdoor play; the rigid requirement for two hours a day of outdoor play is deleted. S.C. §198 Reg. 7(6)(b) is omitted since it dealt with children under two years of age.

§47.19 Health and medical care

(a) Each child shall be given a complete medical examination by a physician every six months after admission if he is under five years of age, or once a year if he is five years and over and under six years of age.

(b) When a child is injured or becomes ill under such circumstances that immediate medical care is needed, the person in charge shall obtain necessary emergency medical care and shall notify the parents or guardian of the child. The name, address and telephone number of the physician or hospital to be called in an emergency shall be conspicuously posted.

(c) The person in charge of a day care service shall not permit a child who is a case, contact or carrier of communicable disease to attend when required to be isolated or excluded by Article 11 of this Code. A child who has been a case, contact or carrier shall not be permitted to return to a day care service until:

(1) He presents a certificate of recovery issued by the Department, if he was a case of tuberculosis, a case or carrier of typhoid or

paratyphoid A or B fever, or a case, carrier or household contact of diphtheria or smallpox; or,

(2) After the period of isolation, if he was a case of measles, mumps, German measles, chicken pox, whooping cough, streptococcal sore throat including scarlet fever, meningitis or poliomyelitis; or,

(3) He presents a certificate of recovery issued by the Department or a physician's written statement, if he was a case or carrier of any other disease reportable pursuant to section 11.03. The statement shall indicate that he is free from disease in communicable form and that the period of isolation or exclusion required by Article 11 of this Code has ended.

NOTES: Subsection (a) is derived from S.C. §198 Reg. 7(1)(part) which required all children in day care services to have a medical examination every six months. The provision of S.C. §198 Reg. 11(1) concerning medical examination of infants is omitted since it dealt with children under two years of age.

Subsection (b) is derived from S.C. §198 Reg. 7(4). The last sentence is new.

The first sentence of subsection (c) is derived from S.C. §198 Reg. 6(b). It is comparable to section 11.63 which requires exclusion of staff members and employees who are cases, contacts or carriers of a communicable disease. The second sentence is derived from S.C. §198 Reg. 7(3)(b)(part). The provisions are the same as for the return of staff in section 45.09(b). (See notes to that section.)

§47.21 Attendance and medical reports

(a) A daily attendance record shall be kept.

(b) A current cumulative medical record shall be kept for each child. The record shall contain all defects and data disclosed by the medical examination given pursuant to sections 47.07 and 47.19, and a history of all illnesses, accidents, and other health data. The record shall be kept for at least two years after the child has left the service.

NOTES: Subsection (a) is derived without substantive change from S.C. §198 Reg. 9(part).

Subsection (b) is derived in part from S.C. §198 Reg. 7(1). The reference to records of accidents or illnesses is new.

This subsection is identical with section 51.21 governing medical records in children's institutions.

§47.23 Transportation

A day care service shall not use or contract for the use of a motor vehicle or omnibus for the purpose of transporting children to or from the service unless the motor vehicle or omnibus prominently displays an unexpired certificate of inspection issued by the Public Service Commission. A day care service which provides transportation facilities shall supervise the transportation so as to preserve the health, safety and comfort of the children. A transportation schedule shall be arranged so that no child will regularly travel more than one hour between his home and the place where the service is operated.

NOTES: This section is new. Pursuant to the authority of Public Service Law §61(14) the Public Service Commission in Case 11346, December 28, 1950, issued an order adopting rules and regulations governing omnibuses having a seating capacity of more than 11 adult passengers which are (1) used in the business of transporting

ARTICLE 49   SCHOOLS

Introductory Notes

Article 49 covers the subject matter contained in S.C. §200 and Regulations thereunder, except for those portions which are integrated into Article 45.

A nursery school or kindergarten, although attached to a school, will be maintained in compliance with the provisions applicable to day care services. This resolves the dilemma created by S.C. §200(3) which required such a nursery school or kindergarten to comply with both S.C. §198 and §200, although several of their provisions were conflicting. The cross-reference in S.C. §200 Reg. 3(b) requiring boarding schools to comply with S.C. §197 Regs. 5, 6, 7 and 9(a)—(f), which were applicable to boarding homes, has been changed to require compliance with the provisions of section 51.11, which pertains to children's institutions; the revised Code no longer contains regulations governing boarding homes; moreover, sleeping arrangements in boarding schools are more closely analogous to those in children's institutions than in boarding homes. See Introductory Notes to this title.

§49.01   Scope

The provisions of this article apply to all schools, and the requirements of this article shall be in addition to the requirements to be met by schools pursuant to Article 45. A nursery school or kindergarten attached to a school shall be maintained pursuant to Article 47. The provisions of section 49.15(d) shall also apply to public and private high schools.

NOTES: This section serves as a general cross-reference to Article 45; it is derived from S.C. §200(1) with some changes. S.C. §200(3) defined a school and included within the definition nursery schools or kindergartens attached to an elementary school, and provided that such nursery schools and kindergartens had to comply with the provisions of the Code applicable to both schools (S.C. §200) and day care services (S.C. §198). If read literally, it required these institutions to comply with numerous conflicting regulations, e.g. heating requirements, S.C. §198 Reg. 3(g) and S.C. §200 Reg. 9; use of basements, S.C. §198 Reg. 3(b) and S.C. §200 Reg. 5; floor space, S.C. §198 Reg. 3(c) and S.C. §200 Reg. 7(b); toilet facilities, S.C. §198 Reg. 4(c) and S.C. §200 Reg. 14; medical examinations, S.C. §198 Reg. 7(1) and S.C. §200 Regs. 20 and 21; drinking facilities, S.C. §198 Reg. 4(c) and S.C. §200 Reg. 13. Nursery schools and kindergartens will be required to comply only with Article 45 and Article 47, since they provide care for children under six years of age and fall within the definition of day care services. This permits the omission of certain provisions of S.C. §200 applying only to children under six years of age from Article 49; the omitted portions are transferred to Article 47, e.g. S.C. §200 Regs. 15(c), 19(e) (part) and 6(part). The fact that nursery schools and kindergartens will have to look to Article 47 for their regulation has no effect on the administrative functions of the appropriate bureaus of the Department.

The provisions of section 49.15(d), governing return to school after isolation or children for hire, (2) owned or operated by a private or public school, or a school district when used to transport school pupils, and (3) operated pursuant to a certificate of convenience and necessity issued by the Commission. By order of December 28, 1955, it was extended to such vehicles which are operated pursuant to a permit for contract carriage of passengers by motor vehicle issued by the Commission. In Case 9136, December 28, 1955, the Commission issued an order adopting rules and regulations governing motor vehicles having a seating capacity of not more than eleven adult passengers which fall into any of the four categories listed above. The rules contain detailed standards for the construction, maintenance and operation of the vehicles regulated, and include a requirement for an inspection and certificate of inspection. The first sentence of this section prohibits a day care service from using uninspected vehicles. The last two sentences are designed to encourage day care services to plan their routes and pick-ups so as to prevent accidents, provide staff and parents with adequate knowledge of the children's whereabouts at all times, and to prevent exposure of the children to motion sickness, fatigue, over-stimulation, restlessness and disturbing behavior resulting from unnecessarily long trips.

§51.21 Medical records

(a) A current cumulative medical record shall be kept for each child. The record shall contain all defects and data disclosed by the medical examinations given pursuant to sections 51.07(a) and 51.19(b), and a history of all illnesses, accidents and other health data. The record shall be kept for at least four years after the child leaves the institution.

(b) When a child is transferred to another children's institution, a copy of his medical record shall be forwarded together with a current medical summary by the institution's physician, including a report of any treatment in progress or recommended treatment.

NOTES: Subsection (a) is derived without substantive change from S.C. §203 Regs. 20(a)(part) and 23 (part).
  Subsection (b) is new. A report of the child's past and present health condition will accompany him when he leaves the institution.

§51.23 Visitors

Visiting of children in children's institutions shall be encouraged by scheduling as many visiting hours during each week as possible without undue interference with the institution's program. When possible, a member of the professional staff shall be available to speak to parents and guardians during visiting hours. Visitors with evidence of communicable disease shall be excluded.

NOTES: The subject matter of this section is derived from S.C. §203 Reg. 22 but reflects a change of policy in regard to visiting in institutions. Under this section visiting is to be encouraged and the prohibition of visits by others than parents is deleted. The requirements for glass doors, close supervision during visiting hours, and the use of protective gowns are deleted.

ARTICLE 53 FAMILY DAY CARE

Introductory Notes

Article 53 is new. It provides a program for the day care of children in small groups of not more than five in a home environment. The article establishes a procedure whereby persons who provide such family day care may voluntarily apply for a certificate of approval and a listing in the Department's registry of approved homes. The program is voluntary, except that only persons who hold a certificate of approval may give family day care to children under two years of age (sections 53.03 and 53.05). A person who holds a certificate of approval must maintain the standards required by this article (section 53.07(e)).

The new article reflects the policy that children under two years of age should be cared for in a home setting, rather than in a regular day care service. In addition, a certificate of approval cannot be issued to permit the care of more than two children under two years of age (section 53.07(c)).

Article 45 which contains general provisions applicable to day care services, schools and children's institutions does not apply to family day care. Therefore, the provisions for physical facilities, equipment and admissions applicable to family day care are found only in Article 53.

§53.01 Definition

When used in this article, family day care means the regular day time care of not more than five children apart from their parents or guardians, in the home of an unrelated family.

NOTES: This section is new. Aside from other differences, family day care is distinguished from a day care service regulated by Articles 45 and 47 in that the former means the care of fewer than six children while the latter covers six or more children. The article is intended to cover only "regular" day time care, that is, care on a continuing basis and not occasional baby sitting for a neighbor's children or other temporary arrangements.

§53.03 Certificate of approval; when required

No person other than a child's parent, stepparent, grandparent, brother, sister, uncle, aunt, first cousin, stepbrother, stepsister, niece, nephew, guardian appointed by a court, or an authorized public officer shall provide family day care, with or without compensation, for a child or children under two years of age without a certificate of approval issued by the Commissioner pursuant to section 53.07.

NOTES: This section is new. A person who is not within the degree of relationship here specified may not care for a child under two years of age without a certificate of

215

approval. Note that a certificate of approval cannot be granted for the care of more than two such children under two years of age (section 53.07(c)).

§53.05 Certificate of approval; voluntary application

A person who provides or intends to provide family day care to not more than five children, two years and over and under 16 years of age, and who intends to comply with the provisions of this article, may voluntarily apply to the Department for a certificate of approval pursuant to section 53.07.

NOTES: This section is new. It provides for a voluntary program of application for certificates of approval.

§53.07 Certificate of approval; application, issuance and conditions

(a) An application for a certificate of approval shall include:

(1) The name and address of the applicant;

(2) The number and age range of the children for whom care is or will be provided; and,

(3) The names and addresses of three persons, not related to the applicant by blood or marriage, who know the applicant's character and reputation.

(b) A certificate of approval shall not be issued unless:

(1) The applicant and all members of the household are persons of good character, habits and reputation and the home conditions present a satisfactory family environment;

(2) The applicant and all members of the household are in good health and have no disqualifying physical, mental or emotional conditions. These facts shall be evidenced on the original application and, if required by the Department, on renewal applications by written statements signed by a physician and based upon complete medical examinations made within 90 days prior to the date of application. The examinations shall include laboratory tests when indicated and a chest x-ray of each person over 15 years of age taken by the Department or by a private physician. When X-ray films are taken by a private physician, they shall be properly identified and submitted to the Department together with certificates on forms furnished by the Department. When, in the opinion of the Department, an X-ray film is unsatisfactory or discloses a condition which cannot properly be evaluated on a single X-ray, the person to whom the X-ray film relates shall be further X-rayed and, if the Department requires, shall be given further periodic medical and laboratory examinations. After a certificate of approval has been issued, chest X-rays of the holder of the certificate and of all members of the household over 15 years of age shall be taken whenever the Department requires for the protection of public health. The provisions of this subsection relating to chest X-rays taken in connection with an original application shall apply to such further chest X-rays;

(3) The applicant is under 60 years of age at the time of application. An applicant for renewal may be 60 years of age or over if she has held a certificate of approval prior to and continuously since her sixtieth birthday, but she shall submit biennially a written statement signed by a physician that she is in good health and has no disqualifying physical, mental or emotional condition; and,

(4) The applicant is in a reasonably secure financial position, does not work outside the home without the consent of the Department and does not conduct any business in the home or any homework which, in the opinion of the Department, may adversely affect the health of the children.

(c) A certificate of approval shall not be issued so as to allow more than two children under two years of age or more than five children under 16 years of age in the applicant's household, including the applicant's own children, children who are boarded out or placed out, and children receiving family day care.

(d) A certificate of approval shall be issued only to a woman. It shall be issued on a Department form and shall state the name and address of the person to whom it is issued, the number and ages of children for whom care is to be provided, and a statement to the effect that the person to whom the certificate is issued maintains an approved home suitable for the care of children.

(e) Sections 53.11 through 53.19 shall apply only to a person to whom a certificate of approval has been issued on a voluntary application and to a person required by section 53.03 to obtain a certificate of approval.

NOTES: Subsection (a) is new but is similar to S.C. §197 Reg. 1(b) which pertained to applications for boarding children. See Article 5, General Permit Provisions, for provisions on applications, expiration and revocation of certificates of approval.

Subsection (b) is new. Subdivision (1) is similar to S.C. §197 Reg. 3(a)(1), (2) and (3). Subdivision (2) is similar to S..C. §197 Reg. 3(a)(4). Subdivision (3) is similar to S.C. §197 Reg. 3(a)(5). Subdivision (4) is similar to S.C.. §197 Reg. 3(b) (1). Note that unlike S.C. §197 Reg. 3(b)(1), subdivision (b) (4) of this section does not prohibit a woman from obtaining a certificate of approval solely on the ground that she receives public assistance.

Subsection (c) is new.

Subsection (d) is new and is similar to S.C. §197 Reg. 2(a)(part).

Subsection (e) is new. All holders of certificates of approval, on voluntary application, are required by this subsection to meet the standards imposed by this article. Also, a person required to obtain a certificate of approval by section 53.03 must meet the standards of this article even if such person does not obtain the certificate in violation of section 53.03. See Article 5. General Permit Provisions, for regulations governing applications, expirations, revocations and renewals of certificates of approval.

§53.09   Registry of approved homes

The Department shall maintain and may publish a current registry listing the approved homes of all holders of certificates of approval issued by the Commissioner.

NOTES: This section is new. It requires the Department to establish a registry of persons who have certificates of approval issued by the Commissioner. The registry will be open to inspection by the public, which will in fact be encouraged to ascertain the qualifications of persons who operate family day care homes. The Department is given specific authority to publish the list of approved homes.

§53.11 Admissions

(a) The Department shall be notified on a form which it shall provide whenever a child is admitted to or discharged from a family day care home and whenever there are significant changes in the membership of the household.

(b) The total number of children admitted and the number of children admitted in each age group shall not exceed the applicable number prescribed in the certificate of approval.

(c) A child shall be given a complete medical examination by a physician at the time of admission to a family day care home or within 30 days thereafter. A child shall be given such immunization and such further, periodic medical examinations as the Department may require.

NOTES: This section is new.

§53.13 Physical facilities and equipment

(a) Premises shall be kept clean, sanitary, safe, comfortable, in good repair and free of fire hazards. The premises shall be heated by adequate and safe apparatus and the minimum temperature required pursuant to section 131.03 shall be maintained.

(b) Rooms used by children shall be well lighted and ventilated and shall have at least 30 square feet of wall to wall space for each child. A child shall not be permitted to remain for any period of time in a cellar as defined in §C26-30.0 of the Administrative Code. A child shall not be permitted to remain for any period of time in a basement as defined in §C26-22.0 of the Administrative Code, except that basement play rooms which are dry and well lighted and ventilated may be used with the approval of the Department.

(c) A separate, firm, sanitary cot shall be provided for each child two years and over and under six years of age who spends more than four hours a day in the home. A separate, sanitary crib or bassinet shall be provided for each child under two years of age. Cots, cribs and bassinets shall be placed at least two feet apart unless separated by a screen or partition. Pillows and mattresses shall not be used on cots. A clean sheet shall be provided for the exclusive use of each child and a cot, crib or bassinet used by a child under three years of age or by an enuretic child shall be covered by a moisture-proof material. Blankets which are sufficient to maintain adequate warmth shall be available for use by each child and shall be used when necessary.

(d) Sufficient, safe play materials and equipment appropriate to the age of the children cared for shall be available for their use.

NOTES: Subsection (a) is new. It is similar to S.C. §197 Reg. 5(a), (b) and (c). See Article 131, Buildings Generally, for provisions applicable to heating, gas appliances and basement and cellar occupancy.

Subsection (b) is new and is similar to S.C. §197 Reg. 9(a) and (c).

Subsection (c) is new and is similar to S.C. §198 Reg. 4(b).

Subsection (d) is new.

§53.15 Diapers and clothing

(a) Soiled linens, including diapers and other infant clothing, shall be freed from fecal matter and then immediately placed in a covered receptacle provided for the purpose. If the linens are laundered on the premises they shall be thoroughly washed and cleaned in a manner acceptable to the Department.

(b) Sufficient and suitable clothing shall be available so that children who soil their clothing may receive a change. All such clothing shall be thoroughly washed after each use.

NOTES: Subsection (a) is new and is similar to S.C. §198 Reg. 4(f).
Subsection (b) is new and is similar to S.C. §198 Reg. 4(h).

§53.17 Supervision, food, rest and play

(a) A child in a family day care home shall not be left at any time without the competent adult supervision which a prudent mother would give to her own child.

(b) The food supplied to children shall be wholesome, of good quality, properly prepared and varied and sufficient in quantity according to a diet approved by the Department. Food shall be served to the children at intervals of no more than four hours. Proper refrigeration and storage of food shall be provided.

(c) The diet or feeding formula provided for a child under one year of age and the feeding schedule for such child shall be as prescribed by a physician. Formulae shall be prepared under sanitary conditions and the bottles, nipples, eating and cooking utensils used shall be properly cleaned and sterilized.

(d) Adequate periods of rest, sleep and indoor and outdoor play appropriate to the ages of the children shall be provided.

NOTES: Subsection (a) is new but is similar to S.C. §197 Reg. 8(c).
Subsection (b) is new. It is similar to sections 45.15(b) and 47.17(a).
Subsection (c) is new and is similar to S.C. §198 Regs. 5(c) and 11(2).
Subsection (d) is new and is similar to section 47.17(b) and (c).

§53.19 Health and medical care

(a) The person who provides family day care shall have on file written authorization from the parents or guardian of each child to obtain necessary emergency medical, surgical and dental care.

(b) When a child is injured or becomes ill under such circumstances that immediate medical care is needed, the necessary emergency medical care shall be obtained, and the parents or guardian of the child shall be promptly notified. The name, home and business addresses and telephone numbers of the parents or guardians and the name, address and telephone number of the physician or hospital to be called in an emergency shall be readily available.

(c) A child who is a case, carrier or contact or a suspected case, carrier or contact of communicable disease shall be isolated or excluded pursuant to Article 11 of this Code.

NOTES: This section is new. Subsection (b) is similar to sections 47.19(b) and 49.15(b).

DECLARATION OF THE RIGHTS OF THE CHILD

The United Nations General Assembly, on November 20, 1959, unanimously adopted and proclaimed a Declaration of the Rights of the Child, setting forth those rights and freedoms which, the international community has agreed, every child, without any exception whatsoever, should enjoy.

Many of the rights and freedoms proclaimed were already mentioned in the Universal Declaration of Human Rights adopted by the General Assembly in 1948. It was, however, thought that the special needs of the child justified a separate declaration. In the preamble to the new Declaration it is specifically stated that the child, by reason of his physical and mental immaturity, needs special safeguards and care, before as well as after birth. The preamble also affirms that mankind owes to the child the best it has to give.

Like the Universal Declaration, the Declaration of the Rights of the Child sets a standard which all should seek to achieve. Parents, individuals, voluntary organizations, local authorities and governments are all called upon to recognize the rights and freedoms set forth and to strive for their observance.

The United Nations first indicated its interest in such a declaration as long ago as 1946, inspired by the Declaration of Geneva adopted, on September 26, 1924, by the Assembly of the League of Nations. A recommendation was made to the Economic and Social Council of the United Nations in 1946 that the Geneva Declaration "should bind the people of the world today as firmly as it did in 1924." Two of the Council's functional commissions— the Social Commission and the Commission on Human Rights—

PRINCIPLE 1

The child shall enjoy all the rights set forth in this Declaration. All children, without any exception whatsoever, shall be entitled to these rights, without distinction or discrimination on account of race. color. sex, language, religion, political or other opinion, national or social origin. property, birth or other status. whether of himself or of his family.

PRINCIPLE 2

The child shall enjoy special protection, and shall be given opportunities and facilities, by law and by other means, to enable him to develop physically, mentally, morally, spiritually and socially in a healthy and normal manner and in conditions of freedom and dignity. In the enactment of laws for this purpose the best interests of the child shall be the paramount consideration.

PRINCIPLE 3

The child shall be entitled from his birth to a name and a nationality.

PRINCIPLE 4

The child shall enjoy the benefits of social security. He shall be entitled to grow and develop in health; to this end special care and protection shall be provided both to him and to his mother, including adequate pre-natal and post-natal care. The child shall have the right to adequate nutrition. housing, recreation and medical services.

PRINCIPLE 5

The child who is physically, mentally or socially handicapped shall be given the special treatment, education and care required by his particular condition.

PRINCIPLE 6

The child, for the full and harmonious development of his personality, needs love and understanding. He shall, wherever possible, grow up in the care and under the responsibility of his parents, and in any case in an atmosphere of affection and of moral and material security; a child of tender years shall not, save in exceptional circumstances, be separated from his mother. Society and the public authorities shall have the duty to extend particular care to children without a family and to those without adequate means of support. Payment of state and other assistance toward the maintenance of children of large families is desirable.

PRINCIPLE 7

The child is entitled to receive education, which shall be free and compulsory. at least in the elementary stages. He shall be given an education which will promote his general culture, and enable him on a basis of equal opportunity to develop his abilities, his individual judgment, and his sense of moral and social responsibility, and to become a useful member of society.

The best interests of the child shall be the guiding principle of those responsible for his education and guidance; that responsibility lies in the first place with his parents.

The child shall have full opportunity for play and recreation, which should be directed to the same purposes as education; society and the public authorities shall endeavor to promote the enjoyment of this right.

PRINCIPLE 8

The child shall in all circumstances be among the first to receive protection and relief.

PRINCIPLE 9

The child shall be protected against all forms of neglect, cruelty and exploitation. He shall not be the subject of traffic, in any form.

The child shall not be admitted to employment before an appropriate minimum age; he shall in no case be caused or permitted to engage in any occupation or employment which would prejudice his health or education, or interfere with his physical, mental or moral development.

PRINCIPLE 10

The child shall be protected from practices which may foster racial, religious and any other form of discrimination. He shall be brought up in a spirit were responsible for the preliminary drafting of the new Declaration. The Social, Humanitarian and Cultural Committee of the General Assembly gave it its final form. Representatives of seventy-eight countries were present when the unanimous vote was taken in the General Assembly.

The full text of the United Nations Declaration of November 20, 1959, is reproduced below. In ten carefully worded principles the Declaration affirms the rights of the child to enjoy special protection and to be given opportunities and facilities to enable him to develop in a healthy and normal manner and in conditions of freedom and dignity; to have a name and a nationality from his birth; to enjoy the benefits of social security, including adequate nutrition, housing, recreation and medical services; to receive special treatment, education and care if he is handicapped; to grow up in an atmosphere of affection and security and, wherever possible, in the care and under the responsibility of his parents; to receive education, to be among the first to receive protection and relief in times of disaster; to be protected against all forms of neglect, cruelty and exploitation; and to be protected from practices which may foster any form of discrimination. Finally, the Declaration emphasizes that the child shall be brought up "in a spirit of understanding, tolerance, friendship among peoples, peace and universal brotherhood."

Declaration of the Rights of the Child

PREAMBLE

Whereas the peoples of the United Nations have, in the Charter, reaffirmed their faith in fundamental human rights, and in the dignity and worth of the human person, and have determined to promote social progress and better standards of life in larger freedom.

Whereas the United Nations has, in the Universal Declaration of Human Rights, proclaimed that everyone is entitled to all the rights and freedoms set forth therein, without distinction of any kind, such as race, color, sex, language, religion, political or other opinion, national or social origin, property, birth or other status.

Whereas the child, by reason of his physical and mental immaturity, needs special safeguards and care, including appropriate legal protection, before as well as after birth.

Whereas the need for such special safeguards has been stated in the Geneva Declaration of the Rights of the Child of 1924, and recognized in the Universal Declaration of Human Rights and in the statutes of specialized agencies and international organizations concerned with the welfare of children.

Whereas mankind owes to the child the best it has to give.

Now therefore,

The General Assembly

Proclaims this Declaration of the

Rights of the Child to the end that he may have a happy childhood and enjoy for his own good and for the good of society the rights and freedoms herein set forth, and calls upon parents, upon men and women as individuals and upon voluntary organizations, local authorities and national governments to recognize these rights and strive for their observance by legislative and other measures progressively taken in accordance with

the following principles:
of understanding, tolerance, friendship among peoples, peace and universal brotherhood and in full consciousness that his energy and talents should be devoted to the service of his fellow men.

Publicity to be given
to the Declaration of the Rights of the Child

The General Assembly,

Considering that the Declaration of the Rights of the Child calls upon parents, upon men and women as individuals, and upon voluntary organizations, local authorities and national governments to recognize the rights set forth therein and strive for their observance.

1. *Recommends* governments of member states, the specialized agencies concerned and the appropriate non-governmental organizations to publicize as widely as possible the text of this Declaration;

2. *Requests* the Secretary-General to have this Declaration widely disseminated and, to that end, to use every means at his disposal to publish and distribute texts in all languages possible.

Published by United Nations Office of Public Information
OPI/43—04697—March 1965–35M
Reprinted in U.N.

OPI/43

From the film "A Child Went Forth"

The Mayor's Medal
for
Outstanding Performance
in the service of
The City of New York
is awarded to

Cornelia Goldsmith

Those contributions toward increasing the breadth and excellence of the City's services to its people merit the highest commendation.

She initiated and directed the first public health program in this country for the supervision of agencies engaged in the group day care of young children.

Her comprehensive, imaginative and dynamic program insures that the children of our city receive the highest level of day care services. Her program has served as a pattern for the nation.

With deepest personal appreciation.

May 29, 1963

Robert F. Wagner
Mayor

GEYER STUDIO, NY

226